A.C. Ainger, H.G. Wintle

Elementary Latin Exercises

Salzwasser

A.C. Ainger, H.G. Wintle

Elementary Latin Exercises

1. Auflage | ISBN: 978-3-84604-826-9

Erscheinungsort: Frankfurt, Deutschland

Erscheinungsjahr: 2020

Salzwasser Verlag GmbH

ELEMENTARY LATIN EXERCISES;

ADAPTED TO THE

ETON LATIN GRAMMAR.

COMPILED, WITH THE SANCTION OF THE HEAD MASTER,

BY A. C. AINGER, M.A.,

TRINITY COLLEGE, CAMBRIDGE;

AND H. G. WINTLE, M.A.,

CHRIST CHURCH, OXFORD;

ASSISTANT MASTERS AT ETON COLLEGE.

LONDON:

JOHN MURRAY, ALBEMARLE STREET.

ETON: R. INGALTON DRAKE.

1885.

LONDON: PRINTED BY WILLIAM CLOWES AND SONS, LIMITED,
STAMFORD STREET AND CHARING CROSS.

CONTENTS.

NOTICE TO BOYS USING THIS BOOK.

1. VOCABULARY. Figures after Nouns show the Declension. Figures after Verbs show the Conjugation. Irr., irregular. For the Construction of Verbs refer to List in Grammar, pp. 162, etc.

Up to Exercise C. words used for tho first time are printed at the head of each Exercise. All words will be found at the end of the book.

2. RULES. In the early Exercises the Sentences are generally examples of the Rules printed at the head of the Exercise, but from the first you will have to refer to, and follow, Rules already learnt.

3. EXERCISES. Words printed in *Italics* are to be looked out in the List of English Prepositions and Conjunctions in the Grammar, pp. 218, etc.

ELEMENTARY LATIN EXERCISES.

EXERCISE I.

VOCABULARY.

bark, verb	lătrō, 1	*quake*, verb	trĕmū, 3
city, subst.	ūrbs (ūrbĭs), 3 f.	*run*, verb	cūrrō, 3
come, verb	vĕnĭō, 4	*shine*, verb	fūlgĕō, 2
dog, subst.	cănĭs (cănĭs), 3 m.	*sing*, verb	cănō, 3
fall, verb	cădō, 3	*sleep*, verb	dōrmĭō, 4
hare, subst.	lĕpŭs (lĕpŏrĭs), 3 m.	*start*, verb	prŏfĭcīscŏr, 3 dep.
king, subst.	rēx (rēgĭs), 3 m.	*summer*, subst.	aēstās (aēstătĭs), 3 f.
nightingale, subst.	phĭlŏmēlă, 1 f.	*sun*, subst.	sōl (sōlĭs), 3 m.

RULE 1.—**The Verb agrees with the Subject in Number and Person.**

RULE 4.—**The Subject of a Finite Verb is usually a Substantive or Pronoun in the Nominative.**

---

1. The nightingale sings. 2. The dogs bark. 3. The hares quake. 4. Thou sleepest. 5. The sun will shine. 6. The king has started. 7. Shine, O Sun. 8. The city has fallen. 9. Summer comes. 10. Thou singest, O nightingale. 11. Bark, you dogs. 12. The hare will run.

    6. *Has started.* Perfect tense.
    7. *Shine.* 2nd sing. pres. imperative.
   11. *Bark.* 2nd pl. pres. imperative.

EXERCISE II.

VOCABULARY.

ache, verb	dŏlĕō, 2	*head*, subst.	căpŭt (-ĭtĭs), 3 n.
always, adv.	sĕmpĕr	*hither*, adv.	hūc
bird, subst.	ăvĭs, 3 f.	*hope*, subst.	spēs (spĕī), 5 f.
boy, subst.	pŭĕr (pŭĕrī), 2 m.	*pigeon*, subst.	cŏlūmbă, 1 f.
bravely, adv.	fŏrtĭtĕr	*remain*, verb	mănĕō, 2
coo, verb	gĕmō, 3	*shout*, verb	clāmō, 1
end, verb	cōnfĭcĭō, 3	*soldier*, subst.	mīlĕs (mīlĭtĭs), 3 m.
eye, subst.	ŏcŭlŭs, 2		
fail, verb	dēfĭcĭō, 3	*who*, pron.	quĭs
fight, verb	pūgnō, 1	*work*, subst.	ŏpŭs (ŏpĕrĭs), 3 n.
fly, verb	vŏlō, 1		

RULE 1.—**The Verb agrees with the Subject in Number and Person.**

RULE 4.—**The Subject of a Finite Verb is usually a Substantive or Pronoun in the Nominative.**

---

1. *Will* the city fall? 2. *Will* not summer come?
3. Who comes hither? 4. Fight bravely, soldiers.
5. The boys shout. 6. Why dost thou coo, O pigeon?
7. Fly, ye birds. 8. The head aches. 9. The eyes
fail. 10. Will the work be ended? 11. Hope always
remains. 12. The work is ended.

1. Verb in future tense. Join "-nĕ" to the word standing first
   in the Latin sentence.
2. Begin the sentence with "nōnnĕ." Verb in future tense.
4. 2nd pl. imperative.
6. *Dost coo.* One word in Latin.
10. See 1.
12. 3rd sing. aor. pass.

EXERCISE III.

VOCABULARY.

assemble, verb	cŏĕō, irr.	*limbs*, subst.	mēmbră, 2 pl.
bee, subst.	ăpĭs (ăpĭs), 3 f.	*live*, verb	vīvō, 3
climb, verb	scāndō, 3	*long*, adv.	dĭū
close, verb	claūdō, 3	*moon*, subst.	lūnă, 1 f.
cold (to be), verb	frīgĕō, 2	*Sisyphus*,	Sĭsўphŭs, 2 m.
depart, verb	dīscēdō, 3	*toil*, verb	lăbōrō, 1
frog, subst.	rānă, 1 f.	*wane*, verb	dēcrēscō, 3
hill, subst.	cōllĭs (cōllĭs), 3 m.	*whence*, adv.	ūndĕ
		whistle, verb	sībĭlō, 1
jump, verb	sălĭō, 4	*wind*, subst.	vēntŭs, 3 m.

RULE 1.—**The Verb agrees with the Subject in Number and Person.**

RULE 4.—**The Subject of a Finite Verb is usually a Substantive or Pronoun in the Nominative.**

---

1. Whence comest thou? 2. The winds whistle. 3. The hill will be climbed. 4. Let the dog sleep. 5. The moon is waning. 6. Long live the king. 7. The eyes are closed. 8. The bees assemble. 9. The frogs jump. 10. Toil, O Sisyphus. 11. Summer will depart. 12. Are the limbs cold?

    4. *Let sleep.* 3rd sing. pres. subj.
    5. *Is waning.* One word in Latin.
    6. *Live* here equals *may live.* 3rd sing. pres. subj.
    7. *Are closed.* One word in Latin.
  12. *Are cold.* One word in Latin. Add "-nĕ" to the word which stands first in the Latin sentence.

EXERCISE IV.

VOCABULARY.

applaud, verb	plaūdō, 3	*kid*, subst.	haēdŭs, 2 m.
burn, v. neut.	ārdĕō, 2	*rejoice*, verb	gaūdĕō, 2
citizen, subst.	cīvĭs (cīvĭs), 3 m.	*revolt*, verb	dēfĭcĭō, 3
coward, subst.	īgnāvŭs, 2	*senator*, subst.	sĕnātŏr (sĕnātōrĭs), 3 m.
dormouse, subst.	glīs (glīrĭs), 3 m.	*spectator*, subst.	spĕctātŏr (spĕctātŏrĭs), 3 m.
frisk, verb	sāltō, 1		
ghost, subst.	sĭmŭlācrum, 2 n.	*talk together*, verb	cōllŏquŏr, 3 dep.
guard, subst.	cŭstōs (cŭstōdĭs), 3 m.	*vanish*, verb	vānēscō, 3
harden, verb	dūrēscō, 3	*wake*, verb	ēxpērgīscŏr, 3 dep.
house, subst.	dŏmŭs, irr. f.		
ice, subst.	glăcĭēs (glăcĭēī), 5 f.	*watch*, verb	vĭgĭlō, 1.

RULE 1.—**The Verb agrees with the Subject in Number and Person.**

RULE 4.—**The Subject of a Finite Verb is usually a Substantive or Pronoun in the Nominative.**

---

1. The house is burning.   2. Run, O boys.   3. The senators talk together.   4. The citizens revolted. 5. The ice hardens.   6. *Will* the cowards fight? 7. The guards watch.   8. *Will* the dormouse wake? 9. The ghost vanishes.   10. The soldiers rejoice. 11. Frisk, O kids.   12. *Will* the spectators applaud?

6. Begin the sentence with "num."
8. See 6, note.
12. Join "-nĕ" to the word which stands first in the Latin sentence.

EXERCISE V.

VOCABULARY.

book, subst.	lĭbĕr, 2 m.	*idle*, adj.	ĭgnăvŭs
brave, adj.	fŏrtĭs	*justice*, subst.	jŭstĭtĭă, 1
busy, adj.	sĕdŭlŭs	*love*, verb	ămō, 1
cold, adj.	frīgĭdŭs	*make*, verb	făcĭō, 3
cow, subst.	văccă, 1	*much*, adj.	mūltŭs
escape, verb	ĕffŭgĭō, 3	*no one*, subst.	nēmō (nūllīŭs), irr.
follow, verb	sĕquŏr, 3 dep.		
give, verb	dō, 1 irreg.	*read*, verb	lĕgō, 3
good, adj.	bŏnŭs	*sweet*, adj.	dūlcĭs
have, verb	hăbĕō, 2	*thy*, poss. pron.	tŭŭs
hear, verb	audĭō, 4	*voice*, subst.	vōx (vōcĭs), 3 f.
honey, subst.	mēl (mēllĭs), 3 n.	*winter*, subst.	hĭēms (hĭĕmĭs), 3 f.
honour, verb	cŏlō, 3		
hot, adj.	călĭdŭs	*wounded*, adj.	saucĭŭs.

RULES 1 AND 4.

RULE 2.—**Adjectives and Participles agree with their Substantives in Gender, Number, and Case.**

RULE 6.—**The Object of a Transitive Verb is in the Accusative.**

---

1. The dog follows the hare. 2. The boys will follow the dog. 3. Will the wounded hare escape the dogs? 4. You hear the nightingale. 5. She has a sweet voice. 6. The cow gives much milk. 7. Do you love a brave soldier? 8. O good king, honour justice. 9. Busy bees make honey. 10. No one loves idle wasps. 11. Read thy book. 12. Cold winter follows hot summer.

3. Begin the sentence with "num."
4. Verb in pl.
7. Join "-nĕ" to the word which stands first in the Latin sentence.
8. *Honour.* 2nd sing. imp.

EXERCISE VI.

Vocabulary.

arms, subst.	ārmă, 2 pl.	*just*, adj.	jūstŭs
besieged, part.	ŏbsĕssŭs	*light*, adj.	lĕvĭs
better, comp. adj.	mĕlĭŏr	*magistrate*, subst.	măgīstrātŭs, 4 m.
cat, subst.	fēlĭs (fĕlĭs), 3 f.	*make*, verb	rĕddŏ, 3
dew, subst.	rōs (rōrĭs), 3 m.	*praise*, verb	laūdŏ, 1
		put on, verb	īndŭŏ, 3
drink, verb	bĭbŏ, 3	*rising*, part.	ŏrĭēns
fortune, subst.	fŏrtūnă, 1 f.	*see*, verb	vĭdĕŏ, 2
general, subst.	dūx (dŭcĭs), 3 m.	*take*,	căpĭŏ, 3
		traveller, subst.	vĭātŏr (vĭātōrĭs), 3 m.
grasshopper, subst.	cĭcădă, 1		
hand, subst.	mănŭs, 4 f.		
hard, adj.	dūrŭs	*water*, subst.	ăquă, 1
hate, verb	ōdī, defect.	*when ?* adv.	quăndŏ ?
hope for, verb	spērŏ, 1		

RULES 1 AND 4.

RULE 2.—**Adjectives and Participles agree with their Substantives in Gender, Number, and Case.**

RULE 6.—**The Object of a Transitive Verb is in the Accusative.**

———

1. I saw the rising sun. 2. Why does not the moon shine always? 3. Put on thy arms, good soldier. 4. Many hands make light work. 5. Cats hate water. 6. The besieged city will be taken. 7. The good general will take the besieged city. 8. Climb the hill, ye travellers. 9. When will the hard work be ended? 10. We hope for better fortune. 11. *Does* the grasshopper drink dew? 12. All good citizens praise just magistrates.

2. *Does shine.* One word in Latin.
9. *Will be ended.* One word in Latin.
11. Begin the sentence with "num."

EXERCISE VII.

VOCABULARY.

bear, subst.	ūrsă, 1 f.	*pail*, subst.	mūlctră, 1
bend, verb	flēctŏ, 3	*peacock*, subst.	păvŏ (păvŏ-
betray, verb	făllŏ, 3		nĭs), 3 m.
chick, subst.	pūllŭs, 2	*puff out*, verb	sūfflŏ, 1
cover, verb	tĕgŏ, 3	*scream*, verb	strīdĕŏ, 2
dry, verb	sīccŏ, 1	*slippery*, adj.	lūbrĭcŭs
egg, subst.	ŏvŭm, 2	*snow*, subst.	nīx (nĭvĭs),
elephant, subst.	ĕlĕphāntŭs, 2		3 f.
fill, verb	īmplĕŏ, 2	*stomach*, subst.	vĕntĕr (vĕn-
foot, subst.	pēs (pĕdĭs),		tris), 3 m.
	3 m.	*ten*, num. adj.	dĕcēm
hatch, verb	ēxclūdŏ, 3		(indecl.)
hen, subst.	gāllīnă, 1	*tree*, subst.	ărbŏr (ăr-
high, adj.	āltŭs		bŏrĭs), 3 f.
how many? adj.	quŏt?(indecl.)	*ugly*, adj.	īnfŏrmĭs
its, poss. pron. refl.	sŭŭs	*up*, adv.	sūrsum
knee, subst.	gĕnū, 4	*your*, poss. pron.	tŭŭs.
lark, subst.	ălaūdă, 1	(referring to	
lay, verb	părĭŏ, 3	one person)	

RULES 1 AND 4.

RULE 2.—**Adjectives and Participles agree with their Substantives in Gender, Number, and Case.**

RULE 6.—**The Object of a Transitive Verb is in the Accusative.**

---

1. Bend your knees, O elephant. 2. Why does the peacock scream? 3. It has ugly feet. 4. The frog puffs out its stomach. 5. The rising sun dries the dew. 6. Will not the milk fill the pail? 7. The snow covers the high hills. 8. Climb the tree, O bear. 9. Up flies the lark. 10. The hen laid ten eggs. 11. How many chicks will be hatched? 12. Slippery ice betrays the feet.

2. *Does scream.* One word in Latin.
3. *It.* Latin "īllĕ."
6. Begin the sentence with "nŏnnĕ."

EXERCISE VIII.

VOCABULARY.

bite, verb	mŏrdĕō, 2	*lake*, subst.	lăcŭs, 4
burnt, part.	ămbūstŭs	*man*, subst.	hŏmŏ (hŏmĭnĭs), 3 m.
calm, adj.	plăcĭdŭs		
child, subst.	pŭĕr (pŭĕrī), 2	*nine*, num. adj.	nŏvem (indecl.)
country, subst.	pătrĭă, 1		
dread, verb	tĭmĕō, 2	*old*, adj.	prīscŭs
eat, verb	ĕdō, 3 irr.	*reflect*, verb	rēddō, 3
exile, subst.	ēxŭl (ēxŭlĭs), 3 m.	*ripen*, verb	cŏquō, 3
		seek, verb	pĕtō, 3
fire, subst.	īgnĭs (īgnĭs), 3 m.	*song*, subst.	cărmĕn (cărmĭnĭs), 3 n.
fish, subst.	pīscĭs (pīscĭs), 3 m.	*strawberry*, subst.	frāgum, 2 n.
		tailor, subst.	sārtŏr (sārtŏrĭs), 3 m.
flourish, verb	flōrĕō, 2		
glory, subst.	dĕcŭs (dĕcŏrĭs), 3 n.	*thief*, subst.	fūr (fūrĭs), 3 m.
happy, adj.	bĕātŭs		
hay, subst.	fēnum, 2	*wakeful*, adj.	vĭgĭl
horse, subst.	ĕquŭs, 2	*what?* adj.	quĭs?
isle, subst.	īnsŭlă, 1	(See p. 33 in Grammar.)	

RULES 1 AND 4.

RULE 2.—**Adjectives and Participles agree with their Substantives in Gender, Number, and Case.**

RULE 6.—**The Object of a Transitive Verb is in the Accusative.**

---

1. Let us all seek glory. 2. The horse eats the hay. 3. The wakeful dog bit the thief. 4. The burnt child dreads a fire. 5. Nine tailors make a man. 6. What cat loves not fish? 7. Will not the sun ripen the strawberries? 8. The calm lake reflects the moon? 9. Who loves idle boys? 10. May our country flourish. 11. Let us sing the old songs. 12. The exiles sought the happy isles.

1. *Let us seek.* One word in Latin. Pres. subj.
7. Begin the sentence with "nŏnnĕ."
10. *May flourish.* One word in Latin.
11. See 1, note.

EXERCISE IX.
VOCABULARY.

Alexander, subst.	Ălĕxăndĕr, 2	*lazy*, adj.	īgnāvŭs
Cæsar, subst.	Caēsăr (Caē-sărĭs), 3 m.	*mother*, subst.	mātĕr (mātrĭs),3 f.
conquer, verb	vīncō, 3	*no*, adj.	nūllŭs
Cornelia, subst.	Cōrnēlĭă, 1 f.	*Persian*, adj.	Pĕrsĭcŭs
cowardly, adj.	īgnāvŭs	*pleasant*, adj.	grātŭs
creature, subst.	ănĭmăl (ănĭ-mālĭs), 3 n.	*prisoner*, subst.	căptīvŭs, 2
		produce, verb	părĭō, 3
Darius, subst.	Dārĭŭs, 2	*race*, subst.	gēns (gēntĭs),3 f.
delight,verb(trans.)	jŭvō, 1		
educate, verb	ēdŭcō, 1	*Roman*, adj.	Rōmānŭs
every, adj.	ōmnĭs	*season*, subst.	tēmpŭs (tēmpŏrĭs), 3 n.
fear, verb	tĭmĕō, 2		
four hundred, num. adj.	quădrīngēntī (-āe, -ă)		
		son, subst.	fīlĭŭs, 2
gift, subst.	dōnum, 2	*sound*, subst.	sŏnŭs, 2
Gracchus, subst.	Grācchŭs, 2	*spring*, subst.	vēr (vērĭs), 3 n.
Greek, subst.	Graēcŭs, 2		
hunt, verb	vēnōr, 1 dep.	*surround*, verb	cīngō, 3
idle (to be), verb	cēssō, 1	*timid*, adj.	tĭmĭdŭs
insect, subst.	bēstĭŏlă, 1	*warm*, adj.	călĭdŭs.

RULES 1, 2, 4, 6.

RULE 3.—**Substantives in Apposition agree in Case.**

RULE 5.—**The Subject of a Verb may be a Verb in the Infinitive Mood.**

---

1. The hare, a most timid creature, fears every sound. 2. To hunt delights the dogs. 3. Cæsar, the Roman general, took four hundred prisoners. 4. The hares, a cowardly race, saw the frogs, a more cowardly race. 5. Cornelia, a very good mother, educated her son Gracchus. 6. O wasps, lazy insects, why do you not make honey? 7. To be idle delights many boys. 8. I love summer, the warm season. 9. Alexander, the Greek king, conquered Darius, the Persian king. 10. Spring produces flowers, pleasant gifts. 11. Surround the besieged city, soldiers. 12. Lazy travellers climb no hills.

   1. *Most timid.* Superlative.
   4. *More cowardly.* Comparative.

EXERCISE X.

VOCABULARY.

army, subst.	ĕxĕrcĭtŭs, 4 m.	*receive*, verb	ĕxcĭpĭŏ, 3
Athens, subst.	Ăthēnāĕ, 1 pl.	*seek*, verb	quaērŏ, 3
beautiful, adj.	pŭlchĕr (pŭl-chră, -um)	*Sicilian*, adj.	Sĭcŭlŭs
		silver, subst.	ărgĕntum, 2
contain, verb	hăbĕŏ, 2	*Syracuse*, subst.	Sȳrăcūsāĕ, 1 pl.
deserve, verb	mĕrĕŏr, 2 dep.		
Gallic, adj.	Gāllĭcŭs	*thousand*, num. adj.	mīllĕ (indecl.)
gold, subst.	aūrum, 2		
hidden, part.	ăbdĭtŭs	*tongue*, subst.	līnguă, 1
jewel, subst.	gĕmmă, 1	*tribe*, subst.	gēns (gēntĭs), 3 f.
Latin, adj.	Lătīnŭs		
leader, subst.	dŭx (dŭcĭs), 3 m.	*twelve*, num. adj.	dŭŏdĕcim (indecl.)
learn, verb	dīscŏ, 3	*victory*, subst.	vīctōrĭă, 1
Marcellus, subst.	Mārcēllŭs, 2	*visitor*, subst.	hŏspĕs (hŏspĭtĭs), 3 m.
Nervii, subst.	Nērvĭī, 2 pl.		
ounce, subst.	ŭncĭă, 1	*wealth*, subst.	ŏpēs (ŏpum), 3 pl. f.
pound, subst.	ăs (ăssĭs), 3 m.		
praise, subst.	laūs (laūdĭs), 3 f.	*win*, verb	rĕpŏrtŏ, 1
		wonderful, adj.	ēgrĕgĭŭs
procession, subst.	pŏmpă, 1	*work*, verb	lăbŏrŏ, 1.

RULES 1, 2, 4, 6.

RULE 3.—**Substantives in Apposition agree in Case.**

RULE 5.—**The Subject of a Verb may be a Verb in the Infinitive Mood.**

---

1. Athens, a beautiful city, receives many visitors.
2. To work deserves praise. 3. We learn the Latin tongue. 4. The Romans hoped-for victory. 5. Will not the victory be won? 6. Follow your leader, boy. 7. Cæsar conquered the Nervii, a Gallic tribe. 8. Hither comes the king. 9. We seek gold, silver, jewels, hidden wealth. 10. A pound contains twelve ounces. 11. Marcellus, the Roman general, took Syracuse, the Sicilian city. 12. I saw a thousand horses, a wonderful procession.

5. Begin the sentence with "nōnnĕ." *Will be won.* One word in Latin.

EXERCISE XI.

VOCABULARY.

actor, subst.	hĭstrĭŏ (hĭstrĭō-nĭs), 3 m.	*hook*, subst.	hāmŭs, 2
become, verb	fīŏ, irr.	*learned*, adj.	dŏctŭs
call, verb	vŏcŏ, 1	*make*, verb	crĕŏ, 1
catch, verb	căpĭŏ, 3	*man*, subst.	vĭr (vĭrī), 2
Cicero, subst.	Cĭcĕrō (Cĭcĕrō-nĭs), 3 m.	*never*, adv.	nūnquām
consul, subst.	cōnsŭl (cōn-sŭlĭs), 3 m.	*orator*, subst.	ōrātŏr (ōrātōrĭs), 3 m.
eloquent, adj.	fācŭndŭs	*paint*, verb	pingō, 3
face, subst.	făcĭēs (făcĭēī), 5 f.	*Pompeius*	Pōmpēĭŭs, 2
flower, subst.	flōs (flōrĭs), 3 m.	*rash*, adj.	tĕmĕrārĭŭs
fortunate, adj.	fēlīx	*Rome*, subst.	Rōmă, 1
		seem, verb	vĭdĕŏr, 2 dep.
		wary, adj.	cautŭs.

RULES 1–6.

RULE 7.—**Link Verbs have the Complement in the same Case as the Subject.**

---

1. Paint your face, O actor. 2. Lazy boys become lazy men. 3. The city will be called Rome. 4. The bees, a busy race, seek the flowers. 5. Alexander was called the Great. 6. To fight seemed rash. 7. Cicero, a most eloquent orator, was made consul. 8. We shall never take the besieged city. 9. O boys, when will you become learned? 10. Hooks catch fish, a wary race. 11. Pompeius, called the Great, was not always fortunate. 12. The Nervii, a Gallic tribe, were conquered.

5. *Was called.* Aor. pass.
7. See 5, note.
12. See 5, note.

EXERCISE XII.

VOCABULARY.

air, subst.	ăēr (ăěrĭs), 3 m.	*law*, subst.	lēx (lēgĭs), 3 f.
anything? subst.	nŭmquĭd?	*moon*, subst.	lūnă, 1
Athenian, subst.	Ăthēnĭēnsĭs	*nest*, subst.	nīdŭs, 2
		new, adj.	nŏvŭs
big, adj.	măgnŭs	*not*, adv.	nōn
Carthaginian, subst.	Pœnŭs, 2	*one*, adj.	ūnŭs
Chinese, subst.	Sērěs (Sērum), 3 pl.	*people*, subst.	gēns (gēntĭs), 3 f.
choose, verb	ēlĭgŏ, 3	*Solon*, subst.	Sŏlōn (Sŏlōnĭs), 3 m.
dangerous, adj.	pěrīcŭlōsŭs		
earth, subst.	těrră, 1		
element, subst.	ělěmēntūm, 2	*star*, subst.	ăstrum, 2
		strange, adj.	mīrŭs
food, subst.	cĭbŭs, 2	*straw*, adj.	strămĭněŭs
hesitate, verb	dŭbĭtŏ, 1	*Tyrian*, adj.	Tўrĭŭs
hundred, num. adj.	cēntum (indecl.)	*universe*, subst.	mūndŭs, 2
		wise, adj.	săpĭēns.

RULES 1–6.

RULE 7.—**Link Verbs have the Complement in the same Case as the Subject.**

---

1. Solon, the wise Athenian, made new laws.
2. The Carthaginians were a Tyrian race. 3. The trees chose a king. 4. Who will be made king?
5. To hesitate is dangerous. 6. Straw houses delight bees. 7. The Chinese, a strange people, eat nests, a strange food. 8. A hundred moons will not make one sun. 9. The sun is big, the stars are bigger. 10. How many elements does the universe contain? 11. Earth, air, fire, water, are not elements. 12. Is anything true?

10. *Does contain.* One word in Latin.

EXERCISE XIII.

VOCABULARY.

burn, verb (trans.)	īncēndō, 3	*hawk*, subst.	ăccĭpĭtĕr (ăc-cĭpĭtrĭs), 3 m.
coop, subst.	căvĕă, 1		
Crœsus, subst.	Crœ̄sŭs, 2		
dove, subst.	cŏlŭmbă, 1	*hold*, verb	tĕnĕō, 2
eel, subst.	ănguīllă, 1	*pursue*, verb	sĕquŏr, 3 dep.
famous, adj.	inclўtŭs	*rich*, adj.	dīvĕs
fisherman, subst.	pīscātōr (pīs-cātōrĭs), 3 m.	*rise*, verb	ŏrĭŏr, 4
		roll, verb	vŏlvŏ, 3
		Romulus, subst.	Rŏmŭlŭs, 2
founder, subst.	cŏndĭtŏr (cŏn-dĭtōrĭs), 3 m.	*Tiber*, subst.	Tībĕrĭs (Tī-bĕrĭs), 3 m.
		Xerxes, subst.	Xērxēs (Xēr-xĭs), 3 m.
greet, verb	sălūtō, 1	*yellow*, adj.	flăvŭs.

RULES 1–6.

RULE 7.—**Link Verbs have the Complement in the same Case as the Subject.**

---

1. Rome honoured Romulus, her founder. 2. The Tiber rolls yellow waters. 3. The hen does not love the coop. 4. The lark greets the rising sun. 5. Will the soldier become a general? 6. Crœsus was very rich. 7. The hawk pursues the doves. 8. Will the dove escape the hawk? 9. Athens was a famous city. 10. Xerxes, the Persian king, burnt Athens. 11. To run is pleasant. 12. Hold the eel, fisherman.

EXERCISE XIV.

VOCABULARY.

ancient, adj.	prīscŭs	*poet*, subst.	pŏētă, 1 m.
bring, verb	fĕrō, irr.	*repose*, subst.	rĕquĭĕs (rĕ- quĭētĭs), 3 f.
brother, subst.	frătĕr (frā- trĭs), 3 m.		
build, verb	āedĭfĭcō, 1	*sail*, subst.	vēlum, 2
Chărўbdĭs, subst.	Chărўbdĭs (Chărўb- dĭs), 3 f.	*Scylla*, subst.	Scўllă, 1
		ship, subst.	nāvĭs (nāvĭs), 3 f.
dreadful, adj.	terrĭbĭlĭs	*spread*, verb	pāndō, 3
fly away, verb	ăvŏlō, 1	*swallow*, verb	sŏrbĕō, 2
hither, adv.	hūc	*temple*, subst.	tĕmplum, 2
Homer, subst.	Hŏmērŭs, 2	*terrible*, adj.	dīrŭs
know-not, verb	nĕscĭō, 4	*Troy*, subst.	Trōjă, 1
melt, verb	lĭquēscō, 3	*whirlpool*, subst.	gŭrgĕs (gŭr- gĭtĭs), 3 m.
monster, subst.	mŏnstrum, 2		
night, subst.	nŏx (nŏctĭs), 3 f.	*white*, adj.	cāndĭdŭs
		wing, subst.	ālă, 1.

RULES 1–6.

RULE 7.—**Link Verbs have the Complement in the same Case as the Subject.**

---

1. Is an eel a fish? 2. The ship spreads sails, white wings. 3. Here comes my brother, the general. 4. Cæsar conquered the Gauls, a brave race. 5. The snow is melting. 6. Homer, the Greek poet, will always be honoured. 7. Away flew the bird. 8. Night brings repose. 9. Will the temple be built? 10. The Greeks took Troy, *the* ancient city. 11. Charybdis, *the* terrible whirlpool, swallows ships. 12. Who knows not Scylla, *the* dreadful monster?

1. Begin the sentence with "pīscĭsnĕ."
3. *Here* means *hither*.
5. *Is melting.* One word in Latin.
10. Translate *the* by "īllĕ" in this sentence.
11. See 10, note.
12. See 10, note.

EXERCISE XV.

VOCABULARY.

able (to be), verb	pŏssum, irr.	*our*, poss. pron. (adj.)	nŏstĕr
battle, subst.	pūgnă, 1	*overthrow*, verb	ĕvērtŏ, 3
cherish, verb	fŏvĕŏ, 2	*preserve*, verb	sērvŏ, 1
daughter, subst.	fīlĭă, 1	*safety*, subst.	sălūs, 3 f.
deed, subst.	făctum, 2	*Sălămis*, subst.	Sălămĭs (Sălă-mīnĭs), 3 f.
dictator, subst.	dīctătŏr (dīctătŏrĭs), 3 m.	*slay*, verb	ŏccīdŏ, 3
fat, adj.	pĭnguĭs	*Torquatus*, subst.	Tŏrquātŭs, 2 m.
freedom, subst.	lībērtās, 3 f.	*try*, verb	cŏnŏr, 1 dep.
Greece, subst.	Graecĭă, 1	*understand*, verb	ĭntĕllĭgŏ, 3
hound, subst.	cătŭlŭs, 2	*wall*, subst.	moenĭă (moe-nĭum), 3 pl.
marry, verb	dūcŏ, 3		

RULES 1–7.

RULE 8.—**A Substantive governed by another Substantive is in the Genitive.**

Some Adjectives and Adverbs govern a Genitive.

RULE 33.—**Many Verbs require another Verb following them in the Infinitive Mood, to complete the sense.**

---

1. The king's son married the soldier's daughter. 2. We love to praise the deeds of brave men. 3. The hare will not be able to escape the hounds. 4. The Gauls burnt the city of Rome. 5. The walls of Rome, that famous city, will be overthrown. 6. The son of the dictator slew the Gaul. 7. He was called Torquatus. 8. We will try to understand our books. 9. The leader of the soldiers was Cæsar, father of the dictator. 10. Try to climb the hill, O fattest of travellers. 11. The battle of Salamis preserved the freedom of Greece. 12. We all cherish the hope of safety.

5. *That.* Latin "illĕ."

EXERCISE XVI.

VOCABULARY.

break, verb	frăngŏ, 3	*Macedonia*, subst.	Măcĕdŏnĭă, 1
can, verb	pŏssum, irr.	*merchant*, subst.	mērcātŏr
count, verb	nŭmĕrŏ, 1		(mērcā-
coward, subst.	īgnāvŭs		tōrĭs), 3 m.
cup, subst.	pŏcŭlum, 2	*money*, subst.	pĕcūnĭă, 1
deceive, verb	făllŏ, 3	*only*, adv.	sŏlum
delude, verb	făllŏ, 3	*Philippus*, subst.	Phĭlīppŭs, 2
desirous, adj.	cŭpĭdŭs	*sea*, subst.	mărĕ
enough, adv.	sătĭs		(mărĭs), 3 n.
enter on, verb	īngrĕdĭŏr, 3 dep.	*sense*, subst.	sēnsŭs, 4
fool, subst.	īnsĭpĭēns (īnsĭ-	*top*, use adj.	sŭmmŭs
	pĭēntĭs), 3 m.	*trick*, subst.	fraūs
force, subst.	vīs (no gen.,		(fraūdis), 3 f.
	dat. vī), 3 f.	*wave*, subst.	flŭctŭs, 4 m.
gain, subst.	lŭcrum, 2	*win*, verb	vīncŏ, 3
journey, subst.	ĭtĕr (ĭtĭnĕrĭs),	*wine*,	vīnum, 2
	3 n.	*wont (to be)*, verb	sŏlĕŏ, 2.
learning, subst.	dŏctrīnă, 1		

RULES 1–7.

RULE 8.—**A Substantive governed by another Substantive is in the Genitive.**

Some Adjectives and Adverbs govern a Genitive.

RULE 33.—**Many Verbs require another Verb following them in the Infinitive Mood, to complete the sense.**

---

1. Have you enough money? 2. A *thousand* brave men *can* conquer many *thousands* of cowards. 3. Who can count the waves of the sea? 4. The force of the wind broke the top of the tree. 5. Philippus became king of Macedonia. 6. The merchant, desirous of gain, entered on a dangerous journey. 7. Many cups of wine delude the senses. 8. Learn, O boy, to love learning. 9. We cannot all be famous men. 10. All can run; one only can win. 11. The tricks of the merchant deceived the traveller. 12. The hope of a fool is wont to be deceived.

1. Begin the sentence with " sătĭsnĕ."

EXERCISE XVII.

VOCABULARY.

avoid, verb	vītŏ, 1	*leg*, subst.	crūs (crūrĭs), 3 n.
bind, verb	lĭgŏ, 1		
body, subst.	cŏrpŭs (cŏr-pŏrĭs), 3 n.	*lightning*, subst.	fŭlgŭr (fŭlgŭrĭs), 3 n.
chain, subst.	vīncŭlum, 2		
champion, subst.	vīndĕx (vīn-dĭcĭs), 3 m.	*silly*, adj.	īnsūlsŭs
		sink, verb	sīdŏ, 3
cold, adj.	gĕlĭdŭs	*sleep*, subst.	sŏmnŭs, 2
crow, subst.	cŏrvŭs, 2	*stand*, verb	stŏ, 1
day, subst.	dĭēs (dĭēī), 5 m.	*strike*, verb	fĕrĭŏ, 4
		support, verb	sūstĭnĕŏ, 2
eager, adj.	cŭpĭdŭs	*thing*, subst.	rēs (rĕī), 5 f.
first, adv.	prīmum	*tooth*, subst.	dēns (dēn-tĭs), 3 m.
freeze, verb (neut.)	gĕlŏr, 1		
God, subst.	Dĕŭs, 2	*wolf*, subst.	lŭpŭs, 2
heron, subst.	ārdĕă, 1 f.	*year*, subst.	ănnŭs, 2.
lamb, subst.	ăgnŭs, 2		

RULES 1–7.

RULE 8.—**A Substantive governed by another Substantive is in the Genitive.**

Some Adjectives and Adverbs govern a Genitive.

RULE 33.—**Many Verbs require another Verb following them in the Infinitive Mood, to complete the sense.**

---

1. The lightning strikes the top of the tree. 2. A cold thing is wont to sink. 3. Why does the top of the water freeze first? 4. The fox was able to deceive the crow, a silly bird. 5. Try, O lamb, to avoid the wolf's teeth. 6. Sleep is called the best gift of God. 7. One leg supported the heron's body. 8. Bring your book *here*, boy. 9. *Here* stand I, champion of freedom. 10. Chains bind the king's limbs. 11. Eager for glory fights the soldier. 12. Many days make one year,

3, *Does freeze.* One word in Latin.

EXERCISE XVIII.
VOCABULARY.

admire, verb	ădmīrŏr, 1	*pluck*, verb	cărpŏ, 3
bitter, adj.	ămārŭs	*prison*, subst.	cărcĕr (cār-
crocus, subst.	crŏcŭs, 2		cĕrĭs), 3 m.
despise, verb	cōntĕmnō, 3	*returning*, part.	rĕdĭēns
eager, adj.	stŭdĭōsŭs		(See p. 73.)
early, adj.	mātūtīnŭs	*Socrates*, subst.	Sŏcrătēs (Sŏ-
Hector, subst.	Hĕctŏr (Hĕc-		crătĭs), 3 m.
	tŏrĭs), 3 m.	*spider*, subst.	ărānĕă, 1
imitate, verb	ĭmĭtŏr, 1 dep.	*stone*, adj.	sāxĕŭs
last, adj.	ūltĭmŭs	*too much*, adv.	nĭmĭum
monkey, subst.	sīmĭă, 1 f.	*tribune*, subst.	trĭbūnŭs, 2
perish, verb	pĕrĕŏ, 4 irr.	*trick*, subst.	dŏlŭs, 2
philosopher, subst.	phĭlŏsŏphŭs,	*truth*, subst.	vērum, 2
	2	*wall*, subst.	mūrŭs, 2
pleasure, subst.	vŏlŭptăs	*watch*, verb	spĕctŏ, 1
	(vŏlŭptă-	*weave*, verb	tĕxŏ, 3
	tĭs), 3 f.	*web*, subst.	tēlă, 1
pledge, subst.	pīgnŭs (pīg-	*worm*, subst.	vērmĭs (vēr-
	nŏrĭs), 3 n.		mĭs), 3 m.

RULES 1–7.

RULE 8.—**A Substantive governed by another Substantive is in the Genitive.**

Some Adjectives and Adverbs govern a Genitive.

RULE 33.—**Many Verbs require another Verb following them in the Infinitive Mood, to complete the sense.**

1. Four hundred soldiers followed the tribune.
2. Stone walls do not always make a prison.   3. Pluck the crocus, pledge of returning spring.   4. Sweet water has become bitter.   5. Hector has perished, Troy's last hope.   6. How many webs *can* the spider weave?   7. The king watched the spider weaving its webs.   8. Eager for truth the philosopher despises pleasure.   9. Does the early bird always catch the worm?   10. Can a soldier have *too much* valour? 11. *Do* not imitate the tricks of a monkey.   12. Who does not admire Socrates, the wisest of Greeks?

2. *Do make.* One word in Latin.

8. *For* is here the sign of the Genitive.

9. Begin the sentence with "num." *Does catch.* One word in Latin.

11. Look out "*do*," 4.

12. *Does admire.* One word in Latin.

EXERCISE XIX.

VOCABULARY.

ashamed (to be), verb	pŭdĕt, 2 imp.	*Nero,* subst.	Nĕrō (Nĕrō-nĭs), 3 m.
centurion, subst.	cĕntŭrĭō (cĕntŭrĭō-nĭs), 3 m.	*order,* subst.	ōrdō (ōrdĭnĭs), 3 m.
change, verb	mūtō, 1	*rashness,* subst.	tĕmĕrĭtās (tĕmĕrĭtā-tĭs), 3 f.
cheesecake, subst.	plăcĕntă, 1		
courage, subst.	vīrtūs (vīrtūtĭs), 3 f.	*reason,* subst.	caūsă, 1
		Remus, subst.	Rĕmŭs, 2
		repent, verb	paēnĭtĕt, imp.
cruelty, subst.	saēvĭtĭă, 1	*rival,* subst.	aēmŭlŭs, 2
evident, adj.	mănĭfĕstŭs	*think,* verb	pŭtō, 1
folly, subst.	stūltĭtĭă, 1	*tried,* adj.	spēctātŭs
forbid, verb	vĕtō, 1	*two,* num. adj.	dŭŏ (-aē, -ŏ)
friend, subst.	ămīcŭs, 2	*unheard of,* adj.	ĭnaūdītŭs
imprudent, adj.	ĭncaūtŭs	*war,* subst.	bĕllum, 2
leap over, verb	trănsĭlĭō, 4	*weep,* verb	flĕŏ, 2.

RULES 1–8, 33.

RULE 9.—**Quality is expressed by the Genitive (or Ablative) with Epithet.**

RULE 10.—**Some Impersonal Verbs take a Genitive besides the Accusative of the Object.**

RULE 20.—**Verbs of "making," "calling," "thinking," take two Accusatives.**

---

1. Are you not ashamed of your folly?   2. All thought Cæsar a man of great courage.   3. Why did Romulus call his city Rome?   4. The reason of the war was not evident.   5. Remus, a most imprudent man, leapt over the walls of Rome.   6. We all repent of our rashness.   7. The order of the seasons cannot be changed.   8. Who does not hate Nero, a man of unheard-of cruelty?   9. Socrates forbade his friends to weep.   10. Two centurions, men of tried courage, were rivals.   11. The philosopher thought the cheesecake sweet.   12. Will not the hen try to save her chicks?

1. Begin the sentence with "Nōnnĕ." *You.* Singular. *Are ashamed.* One word in Latin.

3. *Did call.* One word in Latin.

8. *Does hate.* One word in Latin.

12. Begin the sentence with "Nōnnĕ." *Will try.* One word in Latin.

EXERCISE XX.

VOCABULARY.

attack, verb	ŏppūgnŏ, 1	*industry*, subst.	dīlĭgēntĭă, 1
bishop, subst.	ĕpīscŏpŭs, 2 .	*look at*, verb	īntŭĕŏr, 2 dep.
captive, subst.	căptīvŭs, 2	*own* (with *his*,	
consider, verb	pŭtŏ, 1	*her*, *their*, }	sŭŭs
dare, verb	āudĕŏ, 2	&c.)	
example, subst.	ĕxēmplum, 2	*pity*, verb	mĭsĕrĕt, imp.
father, subst.	pătĕr (pătrĭs),	*play*, subst.	lūdŭs, 2
	3 m.	*poor*, subst.	pāupĕr, 3
full, adj.	plēnŭs	*rat*, subst.	mūs (mūrĭs),
hard, adj.	dūrŭs		3 m.
heart, subst.	cŏr (cŏrdĭs),	*tire*, verb	tāedĕt, 2 imp.
	3 n.	*toil*, subst.	lăbŏr (lăbŏrĭs),
honest, adj.	prŏbŭs		3 m.

RULES 1–8, 33.

RULE 9.—**Quality is expressed by the Genitive (or Ablative) with Epithet.**

RULE 10.—**Some Impersonal Verbs take a Genitive besides the Accusative of the Object.**

RULE 20.—**Verbs of "making," "calling," "thinking," take two Accusatives.**

---

1. When will you be tired of play? 2. The toil of bees is an example of industry. 3. Every captive cherishes the hope of freedom. 4. Who does not love to see the full moon? 5. The cat dared to look at the king. 6. Many thousands of rats attacked the bishop. 7. He, a man of hard heart, did not pity his own citizens. 8. Cæsar considered Cicero an honest man. 9. Have the bees enough honey? 10. Who does not pity the poor? 11. Not all great orators are honest men. 12. He loved to be called the father of his country.

1. *Will be tired.* One word in Latin.
4. *Does love.* One word in Latin.
7. *Did pity.* One word in Latin.
9. Use " -nĕ." In the exercises which follow, this note will not be repeated. You must judge for yourself when to use " -nĕ," " num," or " nŏnnĕ."
10. *Does pity.* One word in Latin. This form of help will not occur in the following exercises.

EXERCISE XXI.

VOCABULARY.

Æschylus, subst.	Aeschўlŭs, 2 m.	*send for*, verb	ărcēssō, 3
charioteer, subst.	aūrīgă, 1 m.	*singular*, adj.	ĕgrĕgĭŭs
greatest, superl. adj.	sŭmmŭs	*sister*, subst.	sŏrŏr (sŏrō-rĭs), 3 f.
Jupiter, subst.	Jŭppĭtĕr (Jŏvĭs), 3 m.	*skill*, subst.	cāllĭdĭtās (cāllĭdĭtā-tĭs), 3 f.
kill, verb	ŏccīdō, 3	*story*, subst.	făbĕllă, 1
life, subst.	vītă, 1	*sun*, subst.	sōl (sōlĭs), 3 m.
marvellous, adj.	mīrŭs		
never, adv.	nŭnquam	*tell*, verb (= to narrate)	nărrō, 1
painter, subst.	pīctŏr (pīc-tōrĭs), 3 m.	*thunderbolt*, subst.	fŭlmĕn (fŭl-mĭnĭs), 3 n.
Phaethon, subst.	Phăĕthōn (Phăĕthōn-tĭs), 3 m.	*travel abroad*, verb	pĕrĕgrīnŏr, 1 dep.
physician, subst.	mĕdĭcŭs	*weapon*, subst.	tēlum, 2
poplar, subst.	pōpŭlŭs, 2 f.	*weariness*, subst.	lāssĭtūdō (lāssĭtūdĭ-nĭs), 3 f.
queen, subst.	rēgīnă, 1		
remedy, subst.	rĕmĕdĭum, 2		
save, verb	sērvō, 1	*wisdom*, subst.	săpĭēntĭă, 1 f.

RULES 1–8, 33.

RULE 9.—**Quality is expressed by the Genitive (or Ablative) with Epithet.**

RULE 10.—**Some Impersonal Verbs take a Genitive besides the Accusative of the Object.**

RULE 20.—**Verbs of " making," " calling," " think-ing," take two Accusatives.**

---

1. Will not Phaethon repent of his rashness? 2. He thought himself a good charioteer. 3. The sisters became poplars. 4. Jupiter calls thunderbolts his weapons. 5. The Athenians killed Socrates, a man of singular wisdom. 6. The sun is a painter of marvellous skill. 7. To travel abroad is a remedy for weariness. 8. Of my country I will never be ashamed. 9. The king sent for a physician of the greatest skill. 10. How many stories could the queen tell? 11. The stories saved the queen's life. 12. Æschylus sang the battle of Salamis.

7. *For.* Rule 8.
12. Rule 8 (Explanation).

EXERCISE XXII.

VOCABULARY.

another thing, subst.	ălĭŭd. (See Grammar, p. 21.)	*Horatius,* subst.	Hŏrātĭŭs, 2
		ignorant, subst.	ĭndŏctŭs
believe, verb	crēdŏ, 3	*leap up,* verb	ĕxsĭlĭŏ, 4
contain, verb	cēlŏ, 1	*name,* subst.	nōmĕn (nŏmĭnĭs), 3 n.
Epicurus, subst.	Ēpĭcūrŭs, 2	*ornament,* subst.	ŏrnāmēntum, 2
fountain, subst.	fōns (fŏntĭs), 3 m.	*oyster,* subst.	ŏstrĕă, 1
		pearl, subst.	bācă, 1
genius, subst.	ĭngĕnĭum, 2	*shell,* subst.	cŏnchă, 1
get, verb	dūcŏ, 3	*spur,* subst.	cālcăr (cālcārĭs), 3 n.
height of, render by adj.	sŭmmŭs		
		Stoic, subst.	Stŏĭcŭs, 2
highest, adj.	praēstāns	*supper,* subst.	cĕnă, 1.

RULES 1–8, 33.

RULE 9.—**Quality is expressed by the Genitive (or Ablative) with Epithet.**

RULE 10.—**Some Impersonal Verbs take a Genitive besides the Accusative of the Object.**

RULE 20.—**Verbs of "making," "calling," "thinking," take two Accusatives.**

---

1. Hope of glory is the soldier's spur. 2. Horatius was ashamed of his sister. 3. Why does the water of the fountain leap up? 4. Many oysters make one supper. 5. Epicurus, a man of the highest genius, is believed to have loved pleasure. 6. He called the height of good the height of pleasure. 7. It is another thing to call the height of pleasure the height of good. 8. Whence do Stoics get their name? 9. Do you not pity the ignorant? 10. Let us seek the top of the house. 11. Not all shells contain pearls, the ornaments of queens. 12. Let not your country be ashamed of you.

6. *Height of good.* In Latin *highest good,* "sŭmmum bŏnum."
12. *Not.* Latin "nē." First word in the sentence. *Ashamed.* Present subj.

EXERCISE XXIII.

VOCABULARY.

affair, subst.	rĕs (rĕī), 5 f.	*mouse*	mūs (mūrĭs), 3 m.
arm, verb	ārmō, 1		
chariot, subst.	cūrrŭs, 4	*neck*, subst.	cŏllum, 2
collar, subst.	tŏrquĭs (tŏr- quĭs), m.&f.	*now-a-days*, adv.	hŏdĭĕ
		poison, subst.	vĕnēnum, 2
comrade, subst.	cŏmĕs (cŏmĭ- tĭs), 3 m.	*pumpkin*, subst.	cŭcŭrbĭtă, 1
		spy, subst.	spĕcŭlātŏr (spĕcŭlātō- rĭs), 3 m.
creature, subst.	ănĭmăl (ănĭ- mālĭs), 3 n.		
devour, verb	vŏrō, 1	*such things*, subst.	tālĭă (tālĭum), 3 pl. n.
foe, subst.	hŏstĭs (hŏstĭs), 3 m.	*sword*, subst.	ēnsĭs (ēnsĭs), 3 m.
Gaul, subst.	Gāllŭs, 2		
happen, verb	āccĭdō, 3	*take away*, verb	aufĕrō, irr.
huge, adj.	īngēns	*whole*, adj.	tōtŭs
innocent, adj.	īnnŏcŭŭs	*wish*, verb	vŏlŏ, irr.
lamb, subst.	āgnŭs, 2	*youth*, subst.	ădŏlēscēns (ădŏlēscēn- tĭs), 3 m.
make (war) upon, verb	īnfĕrō, irr.		

RULES 1–10, 20, 33.

RULE 13.—**Many Verbs, especially Compound Verbs, take a Dative besides the Accusative of the Object.**

RULE 29.—**Agent and Instrument are put in the Ablative: Agent with a Preposition, Instrument without.**

---

1. Cæsar, greatest of Romans, was killed by Romans. 2. Give me the book. 3. Lions are not wont to make war upon lions. 4. The youth was armed by his comrades. 5. He killed his foe, a huge Gaul, with a sword. 6. He took away a collar from the foe's neck. 7. The whole affair was told to the general by a spy. 8. A pumpkin became a chariot: mice became horses. 9. Such things are not wont to happen now-a-days. 10. Why is Socrates thought the most famous of all philosophers? 11. The Athenians killed Socrates by poison. 12. The wolf wished to devour the lamb, an innocent creature.

EXERCISE XXIV.

VOCABULARY.

accustomed (to be), verb	sŏlĕō, 2	*leaf*, subst.	fŏlĭum, 2
afterwards, adv.	pŏstĕā	*maiden*, subst.	vīrgŏ (vīrgĭnĭs), 3 f.
beauty, subst.	pŭlchrĭtūdŏ (pŭlchrĭtūdĭnĭs), 3 f.	*put under*, verb	sŭppŏnŏ, 3
		restore, verb	rĕddŏ, 3
beg, verb	mĕndīcŏ, 1	*river*, subst.	flūmĕn (flūmĭnĭs), 3 n.
bull, subst.	tāurŭs, 2	*roll down*, verb	dĕvŏlvŏ, 3
garland, subst.	cŏrŏnă, 1	*sand*, subst.	ărēnă, 1
golden, adj.	āurĕŭs	*say*, verb	dīcŏ, 3
horn, subst.	cŏrnū, 4 n.	*surpassing*, adj.	ĕxĭmĭŭs
husband, subst.	mărītŭs, 2	*tender*, adj.	tĕnĕr.

RULES 1–10, 20, 33.

RULE 13.—**Many Verbs, especially Compound Verbs, take a Dative besides the Accusative of the Object.**

RULE 29.—**Agent and Instrument are put in the Ablative: Agent with a Preposition, Instrument without.**

---

1. A maiden of surpassing beauty was accustomed to beg. 2. Yet she afterwards called a king her husband. 3. Weave garlands with your tender hands, O maidens. 4. Will the lamb be able to escape the teeth of the wolf? 5. I wish to give a book to the best boy. 6. The book, my gift, will not be read by the boy. 7. I pity the lamb devoured by the wolf. 8. The river Tagus was said to roll down golden sands. 9. The wolf makes war on me with his tooth, the bull with his horn. 10. The eggs have been put under the hen. 11. We shall not be able to make Cicero dictator. 12. Will spring restore leaves to the trees?

EXERCISE XXV.

VOCABULARY.

burn, verb	tŏrrĕō, 2	*light*, subst.	lūx (lūcĭs), 3 f.
cake, subst.	plăcĕntă, 1		
chasm, subst.	bărăthrum, 2	*midst (of)*, subst. (render by adj.)	mĕdĭŭs
crown, subst.	dĭădēmă (dĭădēmă-tĭs), 3 n.	*put on*, verb	īmpōnō, 3
		scold, verb	ōbjūrgō, 1
Curtius, subst.	Cūrtĭŭs, 2	*succour*, verb	sŭccŭrrō, 3
drive away	fŭgō, 1	*too much*, adv.	nĭmĭs
English, subst.	Anglī, 2 pl.	*two*, num. adj.	dŭŏ (dŭāe, dŭŏ)
farmer, subst.	ăgrĭcŏlă, 1		
ignorant, adj.	īgnārŭs	*wage (war) against*, verb	īnfĕrō, irr.
ill, subst.	mălum, 2		
Joanna	Jŏānnă, 1	*wife*, subst.	ūxŏr (ūxōrĭs), 3 f.
knight, subst.	ĕquĕs (ĕquĭ-tĭs), 3 m.		sŭpĕrō, 1
		worst, verb	
leap, verb	īnsĭlĭō, 4	*wretched*, adj.	mĭsĕr.

RULES 1–10, 20, 33.

RULE 13.—**Many Verbs, especially Compound Verbs, take a Dative besides the Accusative of the Object.**

RULE 29.—**Agent and Instrument are put in the Ablative: Agent with a Preposition, Instrument without.**

---

1. The king was scolded by the farmer's wife.
2. The cakes were too much burnt by the fire.
3. Not ignorant of ill, she learns to succour the wretched. 4. Curtius gave his life to his country.
5. An armed knight, he leapt into the midst of the chasm. 6. The sun with his light drives away the stars. 7. Put the crown on the king's head, O maiden.
8. The English were worsted by Joanna, an armed maiden. 9. Against his country Coriolanus waged war. 10. Cornelia was not ashamed of her two sons.
11. She called her boys her jewels. 12. The orator thought himself a poet.

5. See Rule 8.
10. See Rule 10.

EXERCISE XXVI.

VOCABULARY.

blind, adj.	cǣcŭs	*liver*, subst.	jĕcŭr (jĕcŏrĭs *or* jĕcĭnŏrĭs), 3 n.
bone, subst.	ŏs (ŏssĭs), 3 n.		
butterfly, subst.	păpĭlĭŏ (păpĭlĭōnĭs), 3 m.	*Mithridates*, subst.	Mĭthrĭdātēs (Mĭthrĭdātĭs), 3 m.
camp, subst.	cǎstrǎ, 2 pl. n.		
exiled, adj.	ĕxŭl	*oak*, subst.	quĕrcŭs, 4 f.
fosse, subst.	fŏssǎ, 1	*prime*, subst.	jŭvĕnĭs (jŭvĕnĭs), 3 m.
French, adj.	Gǎllĭcŭs		
glutton, subst.	hĕlŭŏ (hĕlŭōnĭs), 3 m.	*prophet*, subst.	vātēs (vātĭs), 3 m.
		reach, verb	ǎttĭngō, 3
harp, subst.	cĭthǎrǎ, 1	*short*, adj.	brĕvĭs
Laius, subst.	Lāĭŭs, 2	*solace*, subst.	sŏlātĭum, 2
laugh at, verb	ĭrrīdĕŏ, 2	*Tiresias*, subst.	Tīrĕsĭǎs (Tīrĕsĭae), 1 m.
		useless, adj.	ĭnūtĭlĭs.

RULES 1–10, 20, 33.

RULE 13.—**Many Verbs, especially Compound Verbs, take a Dative besides the Accusative of the Object.**

RULE 29.—**Agent and Instrument are put in the Ablative: Agent with a Preposition, Instrument without.**

---

1. I wish to have a bird's wings. 2. Short is the butterfly's life. 3. Gluttons devour the livers of geese. 4. They give their food a French name. 5. Why are they not ashamed of their cruelty? 6. It is useless to give Mithridates poison. 7. The exiled prince reached the top of the oak. 8. Laius was killed by his own son. 9. The son, ignorant of his deed, became king. 10. He laughed at Tiresias, the blind prophet. 11. The camp was surrounded by a fosse. 12. The harp of the youth brought solace to the king.

5. See Rule 10.

EXERCISE XXVII.

VOCABULARY.

absent (to be)	ăbsum, irr.	*hurt,* verb	nŏcĕō, 2
Apollo, subst.	Ăpŏllō (Ăpŏllĭnĭs), 3 m.	*merciful,* adj.	clēmēns
		old man, subst.	sĕnēx (sĕnĭs), 3 m.
carry, verb	pŏrtō, 1		
command, verb	praēsum, irr.	*oppose,* verb	ōppōnō, 3 (see note)
diligence, subst.	dīlĭgēntĭă, 1		
donkey, subst.	ăsĭnŭs, 2	*power,* subst.	pŏtēstās, 3
enemy, subst.	hŏstĭs (-ĭs), 3 m.	*prophetic,* adj.	fātĭdĭcŭs
forces, subst.	cōpĭaē, 1 pl. f.	*rejoice,* v. n.	gaūdĕō, 2
grudge, verb	invĭdĕō, 2	*republic,* subst.	rēspūblĭcă (gen. rēĭpūblĭcaē), 5 & 1 f.
Hannibal, subst.	Hănnĭbăl (Hănnĭbălĭs), 3 m.	*spare,* verb	părcō, 3.

RULES 1-10, 13, 20, 29, 33.

RULE 14.—Compounds of "sum," except "pōssum," take a Dative.

RULE 15.—Some Verbs take a Dative, and not an Accusative of the Object, as,

Făvĕō, *I favour.*	Pārĕō, *I obey.*
Ignōscō, *I pardon.*	Plăcĕō, *I please.*
Nŏcĕō, *I hurt.*	Sērvĭō, *I serve.*
Ōbstō, *I resist.*	Sūbvĕnĭō, } *I help.*
Ōccŭrrō, *I meet.*	Sūccŭrrō, }
Părcō, *I spare.*	

---

1. Cæsar, a most merciful man, spared his enemies.
2. I am wont to help my friends, to hate my foes.
3. I pity the fish caught by the fisherman with a hook.
4. I do not grudge the king his power. 5. Cæsar will command the army. 6. The lamb did not hurt the wolf. 7. Can the old man carry his donkey? 8. I rejoice to see the boy's diligence. 9. The Greeks called Apollo a prophetic god. 10. The soldiers of Hannibal reached the top of the mountain. 11. The youth opposed the dictator. 12. Who commands the forces of the republic?

11. *Opposed.* Compare *Cæsar opposed Pompey* (Explanation of Rule 13). "Ōppōnō" = *I place in the way of;* "mē ōppōnō," *I place myself in the way of* = *I oppose.*

EXERCISE XXVIII.

VOCABULARY.

allied, part.	sŏcĭātŭs	*pirate*, subst.	praēdō
axe, subst.	sĕcūrĭs (sĕ-		(praēdō-
	cūrĭs), 3 f.		nĭs), 3 m.
bitten, part.	mŏrsŭs	*please*, verb	plăcĕō, 2
countryman, subst.	} cŏlōnŭs, 2	*present (to be)*, verb	ădsum, irr.
		profit, verb	prōsum, irr.
cut down, verb	dēcīdō, 3	*Saguntum*, subst.	Săgŭntum, 2
fault, subst.	cūlpă, 1	*ungrateful*, adj.	īngrătŭs
forgive, verb	īgnōscō, 3	*very*, adv.	ādmŏdum
master, subst.	măgīstĕr	*viper*, subst.	vīpĕră, 1
	(măgīstrī), 2	*woodman*, subst.	līgnātŏr
noble, adj.	măgnŭs		(līgnātō-
obey, verb	pārĕō, 2		rĭs), 3 m.

RULES 1–10, 13, 20, 29, 33.

RULE 14.—**Compounds of "sum," except "pōs-sum," take a Dative.**

RULE 15.—**Some Verbs take a Dative, and not an Accusative of the Object, as,**

Făvĕō, *I favour.*	Pārĕō, *I obey.*
Īgnōscō, *I pardon.*	Plăcĕō, *I please.*
Nŏcĕō, *I hurt.*	Sĕrvĭō, *I serve.*
Ōbstō, *I resist.*	Sŭbvĕnĭō, } *I help.*
Ōccūrrō, *I meet.*	Sŭccūrrō, }
Pārcō, *I spare.*	

---

1. A man of noble heart loves to forgive faults. 2. He took by force Saguntum, a city allied to the Romans. 3. Hannibal, a very young man, commanded an army. 4. He always wished to make war upon the. Romans. 5. The tree was cut down by the woodman with an axe. 6. Try to please your masters, O boy. 7. Many *thousand* citizens obey one king. 8. All good men wish to profit the state. 9. Do you pity the countryman bitten by the viper? 10. O viper, most ungrateful animal, why do you bite your friend? 11. Do you wish to be present at a battle? 12. Cæsar was made prisoner by the pirates.

EXERCISE XXIX.

VOCABULARY.

add, verb	ăddō, 3	*Lycurgus*, subst.	Lўcŭrgŭs, 2
against his will, adj.	invītŭs	*Marathon*, use adj.	Mărăthōnĭŭs
		master, subst.	dŏmĭnŭs, 2
bad, adj.	mălŭs	*resist*, verb	rĕsīstō, 3
beech-tree, subst.	făgŭs, 2 f.	*servant*, subst.	pŭĕr (pŭĕrī), 2
bell, subst.	tīntīnnăbŭlum, 2	*table*, subst.	mēnsă, 1
dish, subst.	lānx (lāncĭs), 3 f.	*tyrant*, subst.	tўrănnŭs, 2
		useful (to be), verb	prōsum, irr.
frighten, verb	tĕrrĕō, 2	*weak*, adj.	imbĕcīllŭs.

RULES 1–10, 13, 20, 29, 33.

RULE 14.—Compounds of "sum," except "pōssum," take a Dative.

RULE 15.—Some Verbs take a Dative, and not an Accusative of the Object, as,

Făvĕō, *I favour.*
Ignōscō, *I pardon.*
Nŏcĕō, *I hurt.*
Ōbstō, *I resist.*
Ŏccŭrrō, *I meet.*
Părcō, *I spare.*

Părĕō, *I obey.*
Plăcĕō, *I please.*
Sērvĭō, *I serve.*
Sŭbvĕnĭō, } *I help.*
Sŭccŭrrō, }

---

1. Elephants were useful to Pyrrhus.　2. Æschylus was present at the battle of Marathon.　3. Spare the beech-tree, O woodman.　4. Darius opposed Alexander called the Great.　5. Who will add the bell to the cat's neck?　6. The servant put the dish upon the table.　7. The donkey will not obey his master. 8. Why do you try to save him against his will?　9. Do you think Lycurgus a wise man?　10. Weak kings favour bad men.　11. The frogs were frightened by the sound of feet.　12. Let us all resist the tyrant.

EXERCISE XXX.

VOCABULARY.

Agamemnon, subst.	Ăgămĕmnŏn (Ăgămĕmnŏnis), 3 m.	*meet,* verb	ŏccŭrrŏ, 3
apple, subst.	pŏmum, 2	*Paris,* subst.	Părĭs (Părĭdĭs), 3 m.
bank, subst.	rīpă, 1	*ought,* verb	dĕbĕŏ, 2
boat, subst.	lĭntĕr (lĭntrĭs), 3 f.	*Scævola,* subst.	Scǣvŏlă, 1 m.
bring (to shore), verb	ăppĕllŏ, 3	*sheep,* subst.	ŏvĭs (ŏvĭs), 3 f.
Cato, subst.	Cătŏ (Cătŏnĭs), 3 m.	*source,* subst.	fŏns (fŏntĭs), 3 m.
countryman, subst.	cīvĭs (cīvĭs), 3 m.	*supply,* verb	prǣbĕŏ, 2
		thrust in, verb	īmmīttŏ, 3
		Trojan, adj.	Trŏjānŭs
		trust, verb	cŏnfīdŏ, 3
fail, verb	dĕsum, irr.	*Venus,* subst.	Vĕnŭs (Vĕnĕrĭs), 3 f.
ferryman, subst.	pŏrtĭtŏr (pŏrtĭtŏrĭs), 3 m.	*wicked,* adj.	nĕquam (indecl.)
		woman, subst.	mŭlĭĕr (mŭlĭĕrĭs), 3 f.
goddess, subst.	dĕă, 1	*wool,* subst.	lānă, 1
kite, subst.	mīlŭŭs, 2	*yesterday,* adv.	hĕrī.

RULES 1–10, 13, 20, 29, 33.

RULE 14.—**Compounds of "sum," except "pōssum," take a Dative.**

RULE 15.—**Some Verbs take a Dative, and not an Accusative of the Object, as,**

Făvĕŏ, *I favour.*	Ŏccŭrrŏ, *I meet.*	Sĕrvĭŏ, *I serve.*
Ignōsco, *I pardon.*	Pārcŏ, *I spare.*	Sŭbvĕnĭŏ, } *I help.*
Nŏcĕŏ, *I hurt.*	Pārĕŏ, *I obey.*	Sŭccŭrrŏ, }
Ŏbstŏ, *I resist.*	Plăcĕŏ, *I please.*	

---

1. The sheep supplies wool to the tailor. 2. Scævola, a man of great courage, thrust his hand into the fire. 3. The king admired the young man's courage. 4. Paris gave the apple to Venus, most beautiful of goddesses. 5. This deed was the source of the Trojan war. 6. I will never fail my friends. 7. Do not trust the kite, O pigeons. 8. Agamemnon was killed by his wife, a most wicked woman. 9. I met your father yesterday. 10. Cato was ashamed of his countrymen. 11. Bring your boat to the bank, O ferryman. 12. You ought to pardon the faults of your friend.

          2. *Thrust into.* Rule 13.

EXERCISE XXXI

VOCABULARY.

ability, subst.	ĭndŏlĕs (ĭn-dŏlĭs), 3 f.	*rampart,* subst.	văllum, 2
ask for, verb	rŏgō, 1	*remarkable,* adj.	ĕgrĕgĭŭs
coal, subst.	cărbō (cär-bŏnĭs), 3 m.	*return,* verb	rĕdĕō, 4 irr.
		Sertorius, subst.	Sĕrtōrĭŭs, 2
dagger, subst.	pŭgĭō (pŭ-gĭŏnĭs), 3 m.	*silent (to be),* verb,	tăcĕō, 2
girl, subst.	pŭĕllă, 1	*soil,* subst.	sŏlum, 2
home = home-wards, subst.	dŏmum (acc. of dŏmŭs)	*Sparta,* subst.	Spărtă, 1
		state, subst.	cīvĭtās (cīvĭ-tātĭs), 3 f.
mountain, subst.	mŏns (mŏn-tĭs), 3 m.	*stone,* subst.	lăpĭs (lăpĭ-dĭs), 3 m.
nearly, adv.	fĕrĕ	*traitor,* subst.	prŏdĭtŏr (prŏ-dĭtōrĭs), 3 m.
put round, verb	cīrcumdō, 3		
rain, subst.	plŭvĭă, 1	*twenty-seven,*	vīgĭntī sĕptem.

RULES 1–10, 13–15, 20, 29, 33.

RULE 19.—**Verbs of asking, as " rŏgō," " ōrō," " pōscō," and the Verbs " dŏcĕō " (I teach), " cēlō " (I conceal), take two Accusatives.**

RULE 22.—**Motion towards a person or a place is expressed by the Accusative with a Preposition.**

But names of towns, and the words " dŏmum " (homewards), " rūs " (to the country), stand in the Accusative without a Preposition.

RULE 23.—**Length of Time or Space is put in the Accusative.**

---

1. *When* will you return home, O son of Agamemnon? 2. Sparta waged war against Athens *for* twenty-seven years. 3. Cicero, an exile, was absent from Rome nearly two years. 4. The farmer is wont to ask the gods for rain. 5. Sertorius, a man of remarkable ability, was killed by a traitor's dagger. 6. He put round the camp a rampart ten feet high. 7. The philosopher was silent for a whole year. 8. Let us boys try to be useful to the state. 9. *Do* not hurt the butterfly. 10. Will the stone of Sisyphus reach the top of the mountain? 11. Much coal is under the soil of our country. 12. The girl wished to become learned.

11. *Is under.* Use " sŭbsum."

EXERCISE XXXII.

VOCABULARY.

Achilles, subst.	Ăchĭllēs (Ăchĭllĭs), 3 m.	*last*, verb	dūrō, 1
ant, subst.	fŏrmīcă, 1 f.	*make prisoner*	căpĭō, 3
broad, adj.	lātŭs	*mile*, subst.	mīllĕ păssūs (pl. mīlĭă păssŭum)
collect, verb	cŏllĭgō, 3		
corn, subst.	frūmēntum, 2	*Myrmidons*, subst.	Mȳrmĭdŏnĕs (Mȳrmĭdŏnum), 3 pl.
deny, verb	nĕgō, 1		
flower, subst.	rōbŭr (rō-bŏrĭs), 3 m.	*peace*, subst.	păx (pācĭs), 3 f.
followers (his)	sŭī	*pray*, verb	ōrō, 1
foreseeing, adj.	prŏvĭdŭs (with gen.)	*prisoner*, see *make prisoner*	
future, subst.	fŭtūrum, 2	*some*, pron. adj.	quīdam
go, verb	ĕō, 4 irr.	*swallow*, subst.	hĭrūndō (hĭrūndĭ-nĭs), 3 f.
good for (to be)	prōsum, irr.		
health, subst.	vălētūdō (vălētūdĭ-nĭs), 3 f.	*swim*, verb	nătō, 1
heap, subst.	ăcĕrvŭs, 2	*victor*, subst.	vīctŏr (vīc-tōrĭs), 3 m.

RULES 1–10, 13–15, 20, 29, 33.

RULE 19.—**Verbs of asking, as " rŏgō," " ōrō," " pōscō," and the Verbs " dŏcĕō " (I teach), " cēlō " (I conceal), take two Accusatives.**

RULE 22.—**Motion towards a person or a place is expressed by the Accusative with a Preposition.**

But names of towns, and the words " dŏmum " (homewards), " rūs " (to the country), stand in the Accusative without a Preposition.

RULE 23.—**Length of Time or Space is put in the Accusative.**

1. The river is two thousand feet broad. 2. To swim is good for the health. 3. Five hundred soldiers, the flower of the army, were made prisoners by the enemy. 4. O bee, teach the boy diligence. 5. The ant, foreseeing the future, collects a heap of corn. 6. Some philosophers deny this. 7. The king is able to help his friends. 8. Go home, boy; I will go to Rome. 9. How many miles will the swallow fly? 10. Achilles, bravest of the Greeks, called his followers Myrmidons. 11. The war lasted ten years. 12. Shall we pray the victor for peace?

EXERCISE XXXIII.

VOCABULARY.

Africa, subst.	Lǐbўǎ, 1	*Marsyas*, subst.	Mársўǎs (Mārsўāē), 1 m.
bring upon, verb	*infĕrō*, irr.		
displease, verb	*displǐcĕō*, 2	*Nestor*, subst.	Nĕstŏr (Nĕstŏrǐs), 3 m.
envy, verb	īnvǐdĕō, 2		
flay, verb	pĕllem dē̆trāhō (lit. *I strip off the skin*)	*sedition*, subst.	sĕdītǐō (sĕdītǐōnǐs), 3 f.
		Telemachus, subst.	Tĕlĕmăchŭs, 2
Helen, subst.	Hĕlĕnă, 1 f.		
Juno, subst.	Jūnō (Jūnōnǐs), 3 f.	*three*, subst.	trēs, trǐă
		treachery, subst.	fraūs (fraūdǐs), 3 f.
lyre, subst.	cǐthărǎ, 1		

RULES 1–10, 13–15, 20, 29, 33.

RULE 19.—**Verbs of asking, as "rŏgō," "ōrō," "pōscō," and the Verbs "dŏcĕō" (I teach), "cēlō" (I conceal), take two Accusatives.**

RULE 22.—**Motion towards a person or a place is expressed by the Accusative with a Preposition.**

But names of towns, and the words "dŏmum" (homewards), "rūs" (to the country), stand in the Accusative without a Preposition.

RULE 23.—**Length of Time or Space is put in the Accusative.**

---

1. Sedition hurts a state. 2. Telemachus went to Nestor, the wise king. 3. Paris took away Helen from her husband. 4. Was he not ashamed of his treachery? 5. *That* deed brought ruin upon Troy. 6. He led into Africa ten thousand soldiers eager for glory. 7. Marsyas envied Apollo his lyre. 8. Apollo flayed Marsyas. 9. Paris displeased two goddesses. 10. He made Juno, queen of the gods, his enemy. 11. The Roman state obeyed ten men. 12. I will build a wall ten feet high.

EXERCISE XXXIV.

VOCABULARY.

avenge, verb	ulcīscŏr, 3 dep.	*inventor,* subst.	auctŏr (auctōrĭs), 3 m.
conceal from, verb	cēlŏ, 1	*lance,* subst.	cŭspĭs (cŭspĭdĭs), 3 f.
death, subst.	mŏrs (mŏrtĭs), 3 f.	*often, see so often*	
		Olympus, subst.	Ŏlўmpŭs, 2
design, subst.	cōnsĭlĭum, 2	*pardon,* subst.	vĕnĭă, 1
determine, verb	cōnstĭtŭŏ, 3	*Perillus,* subst.	Pĕrīllŭs, 2
die, verb	mŏrĭŏr, 3 dep.	*repeat,* verb	ĭtĕrŏ, 1
eagle, subst.	ăquĭlă, 1 f.	*retire,* verb	cōncēdŏ, 3
Ganymede, subst.	Gănўmēdēs (Gănўmēdĭs), 3 m.	*so often*	tŏtĭēs
		Syria, subst.	Sўrĭă, 1
		vain, see in vain	
in vain, adv.	frūstrā	*youth,* subst.	ădŏlēscēns, 3 m.

RULES 1–10, 13–15, 20, 29, 33.

RULE 19.—**Verbs of asking, as "rŏgō," "ōrō," "pōscō," and the Verbs "dŏcĕō" (I teach), "cēlō" (I conceal), take two Accusatives.**

RULE 22.—**Motion towards a person or a place is expressed by the Accusative with a Preposition.**

But names of towns, and the words "dŏmum" (homewards), "rūs" (to the country), stand in the Accusative without a Preposition.

RULE 23.—**Length of Time or Space is put in the Accusative.**

---

1. Despised by his friends, he retired to the country. 2. To Syria went the young Frenchman. 3. Juno concealed her design from Jupiter. 4. Remus dared to leap over his brother's walls. 5. He was killed by a soldier with a lance. 6. In vain did Perillus pray the tyrant for pardon. 7. The bull brought death to its inventor. 8. Dying he repented of his deed. 9. Jupiter's eagle carried Ganymede to Olympus. 10. The prince determined to avenge his father's death. 11. Who will climb to the top of the mountain ten thousand feet high? 12. Are you not ashamed of your fault so often repeated?

2. *Young Frenchman.* In Latin, "French youth."

EXERCISE XXXV.

VOCABULARY.

accuse, verb	ăccūsŏ, 1	*forget*, verb	ŏblīvīscor, 3 dep.
arise, verb	ĕxŏrĭŏr, 3 dep.	*fresh*, adj.	nŏvŭs
borders, subst.	fīnĕs (fīnĭum), 3 pl. m.	*halt*, verb	sŭbsīstŏ, 3
bring, verb	rĕdūcŏ, 3	*increase*, verb	crēscŏ, 3
Brutus, subst.	Brūtŭs, 2	*injury*, subst.	īnjūrĭă, 1
cross, verb	trănsgrĕdĭŏr, 3 dep.	*Italy*, subst.	Ĭtălĭă, 1
		luck, subst.	fŏrtūnă, 1
disappear, verb	ēvănēscŏ, 3	*overwhelm*, verb	ŏbrŭŏ, 3
ditch, subst.	fŏssă, 1	*remember*, verb	mĕmĭnī, def.
enemy, subst.	ĭnĭmīcŭs, 2	*storm*, subst.	prŏcēllă, 1
		theft, subst.	fŭrtum, 2.

RULES 1–10, 13–15, 19, 20, 22, 23, 29, 33.

RULE 12.—**Verbs of "forgetting" or "remembering," and the Verb "mĭsĕrĕŏr" (I pity), take a Genitive.**

RULE 17.—**Many Adjectives may be followed by the Dative.**

RULE 28.—**A Substantive or a Pronoun combines with a Participle, or an Adjective, or another Substantive, to form the Ablative Absolute.**

---

1. The sun having risen, the stars disappeared. Try to remember this book. 3. Cæsar having been led, a fresh war arose. 4. *Do* not try to leap over a ditch twenty feet broad. 5. The enemy being seen, the general halted. 6. The king of Macedonia will oppose a thousand enemies. 7. *Do* not accuse an enemy of theft. 8. Brutus being consul, the forces of the Gauls crossed the borders of Italy. 9. Who will bring the king home? 10. The storm increasing, the ship was overwhelmed by the waves. 11. Good men love to forget injuries. 12. The name of the city being changed, we shall have better luck.

7. Rule 11.

EXERCISE XXXVI.

VOCABULARY.

approach, verb	ădvĕnĭŏ, 4	*hour*, subst.	hōră, 1
away (to be), verb	ăbsum, irr.	*hunter*, subst.	vĕnātŏr
begin, verb	cōēpī, def.		(vĕnātŏris),
dance, verb	săltŏ, 1		3 m.
end, subst.	fīnĭs (fīnĭs),	*left behind*, part.	rĕlīctŭs
	3 m. & f.	*some*, num. adj.	ălĭquŏt
ground, subst.	hŭmŭs, 2 f.	*struck*, part.	pĕrcŭssŭs,

RULES 1–10, 13–15, 19, 20, 22, 23, 29, 33.

RULE 12.—**Verbs of "forgetting" or "remembering," and the Verb "misĕrĕŏr" (I pity), take a Genitive.**

RULE 17.—**Many Adjectives may be followed by the Dative.**

RULE 28.—**A Substantive or a Pronoun combines with a Participle, or an Adjective, or another Substantive, to form the Ablative Absolute.**

---

1. The hare tried to escape the dogs *for* two hours. 2. The hare being killed, the hunter returned home. 3. He was away from home the whole day. 4. Night approaching, the stars begin to shine. 5. The maiden, left behind, envied her sisters. 6. They danced for some hours: ther they returned home. 7. *When* will the boy be tired of play? 8. The city of Troy was taken by the Greeks. 9. Hector being dead, the Greeks hoped for an end of the war. 10. The victory being won, spare the conquered foes. 11. The whole nation became slaves. 12. Struck by a stone, he fell to the ground.

3. *From home.* "Ā dŏmŏ."
7. *Tired.* Use "taēdĕt."
12. *To.* "In" with Accusative.

EXERCISE XXXVII.

VOCABULARY.

arrow, subst.	săgīttă, 1	*prey*, subst.	prāedă, 1
baffle, verb	fallŏ, 3	*put on*, verb	īmpōnō, 3
cleave, verb	fĭndŏ, 3	*Scīpĭŏ*, subst.	Scīpĭŏ (Scīpĭŏnĭs), 3 m.
earn, verb	mĕrĕŏ, 2		
first, adj.	prīmŭs	*set out*	prŏfĭcīscŏr, 3 dep.
kindness, subst.	bĕnĕfĭcĭum, 2		
Metaurus, subst.	Mĕtaūrŭs, 2	*stag*, subst.	cĕrvŭs, 2
no longer, adv.	nōn jam	*Swiss*, subst.	Hĕlvĕtĭī, 2 pl.
pay, subst.	stīpĕndĭum, 2		

RULES 1–10, 13–15, 19, 20, 22, 23, 29, 33.

RULE 12.—**Verbs of "forgetting" or "remembering," and the Verb "mĭsĕrĕŏr" (I pity), take a Genitive.**

RULE 17.—**Many Adjectives may be followed by the Dative.**

RULE 28.—**A Substantive or a Pronoun combines with a Participle, or an Adjective, or another Substantive, to form the Ablative Absolute.**

------

1. *When* will the Gauls learn to obey Cæsar? 2. The Gauls being conquered, Cæsar set out for Italy. 3. I shall never forget the kindnesses of my friend. 4. His father being general, Scipio served his first campaign. 5. The frogs will remember the king sent by Jupiter. 6. The Swiss, a brave race, were desirous of freedom. 7. The tyrant put the apple on the boy's head. 8. The apple was cleft by the father's arrow. 9. It is pleasant to believe old stories. 10. Learn to remember the battle of Metaurus. 11. His brother being killed, Hannibal no longer hoped *for* victory. 12. Stags, the prey of wolves, try to baffle their foes.

2. *For.* See "*for*," 9, in List of English Prepositions.
4. *Served his first campaign*, in Latin, is "earned his first pay."

EXERCISE XXXVIII.

VOCABULARY.

another, pron.	ăltĕr. (See Grammar, p. 21.)	*exile*, subst.	ĕxĭlĭum, 2
		hold, verb	hăbĕŏ, 2
		infancy, subst.	ĭnfāntĭă, 1
Catilina, subst.	Cătĭlĭnă, 1 m.	*Lentulus*, subst.	Lĕntŭlŭs, 2
confer, verb	cōnfĕrŏ, irr.	*plot*, verb	mōlĭŏr, 4 dep.
conqueror, subst.	vīctŏr (vīctŏrĭs), 3 m.	*put to death*, verb	ĭntĕrfĭcĭŏ, 3
		renown, subst.	lāūs (lāūdĭs), 3 f.
Cyrus, subst.	Cўrŭs, 2		
destruction, subst.	pĕrnĭcĭēs (pĕrnĭcĭēī), 5 f.	*trial*, subst.	jūdĭcĭum, 2.

RULES 1–10, 13–15, 19, 20, 22, 23, 29, 33.

RULE 12.—**Verbs of "forgetting" or "remembering," and the Verb "mĭsĕrĕŏr" (I pity), take a Genitive.**

RULE 17.—**Many Adjectives may be followed by the Dative.**

RULE 28.—**A Substantive or a Pronoun combines with a Participle, or an Adjective, or another Substantive, to form the Ablative Absolute.**

---

1. Are horns useful to a stag?   2. The republic has flourished *for* a hundred years.   3. Who *can* remember his infancy?   4. The hope of glory is pleasant to the soldier.   5. *Do* not envy the renown *of another*. 6. Cicero being made consul saved the republic. 7. Cicero being made consul, Catilina plotted destruction *for* Rome.   8. Lentulus, a Roman citizen, was put to death untried.   9. The death of Lentulus was the cause of Cicero's exile.   10. Rome forgot the benefits conferred on her by Cicero.   11. Who is not ashamed of an ungrateful friend?   12. Conquered by Cyrus, Crœsus became the friend of his conqueror.

8. *Untried.* In Latin, " no trial having been held." Abl. Abs.
9. *Cicero*, in this sentence, should be in the Dative Case rather than the Genitive.

EXERCISE XXXIX.

VOCABULARY.

brush, subst.	cāūdă, 1	*mine*, poss. pron.	mĕŭs
give back, verb	rĕddŏ, 3	*pursue*, verb	sĕquŏr, 3 dep.
lose, verb	pĕrdŏ, 3		

RULES 1–10, 12–15, 17, 19, 20, 22, 23, 28, 29, 33.

RULE 11.—**Verbs of "accusing," "condemning," or "acquitting," take a Genitive besides the Accusative of the Object.**

RULE 24.—**Substantives which qualify the Verb like Adverbs are put in the Ablative.**

RULE 26.—**Several common words take the Ablative, as,**

Verbs—frŭŏr, *I enjoy.*	Adjectives—dīgnŭs, *worthy.*
fŭngŏr, *I perform.*	indīgnŭs, *unworthy.*
pŏtĭŏr, *I get.*	frētŭs, *relying on.*
ūtŏr, *I use.*	Substantives—ŏpŭs, *need.*
vēscŏr, *I eat.*	ūsŭs, *use.*

RULE 39.—**The Relative agrees with the Antecedent in Gender and Number, but its Case is settled by its own Clause.**

---

1. The general, who commands the army, is brave. 2. The fox, who has lost his brush, is sad. 3. We admire the general, who commands the army. 4. We did not see the enemy, whom we pursued. 5. I do not envy the fox, who has lost his brush. 6. Bees make honey, which boys eat. 7. He, whom you saw yesterday, was the general. 8. He, whom you met yesterday, is my friend. 9. Give me back the book, which is mine. 10. Give me back the books which you took away from me. 11. Have you lost the book which I gave you? 12. We ought to love those who hate us.

EXERCISE XL.

VOCABULARY.

diligent, adj.	sēdŭlŭs		*need*, verb	indĭgĕō, 2
help, subst.	auxĭlĭum, 2 n.		*sharp*, adj.	ăcūtŭs
help, verb	jŭvō, 1		*sharpen*, verb	ăcŭō, 3
honour, subst.	laus (laudĭs), 3 f.		*use*, verb	ūtŏr, 3 dep.

RULES 1–10, 12–15, 17, 19, 20, 22, 23, 28, 29, 33.

RULE 11.—**Verbs of "accusing," "condemning," or "acquitting," take a Genitive besides the Accusative of the Object.**

RULE 24.—**Substantives which qualify the Verb like Adverbs are put in the Ablative.**

RULE 26.—**Several common words take the Ablative, as,**

Verbs—frŭŏr, *I enjoy.*	Adjectives—dignŭs, *worthy.*
fŭngŏr, *I perform.*	indignŭs, *unworthy.*
pŏtĭŏr, *I get.*	frētŭs, *relying on.*
ūtŏr, *I use.*	Substantives—ŏpŭs, *need.*
vēscŏr, *I eat.*	ūsŭs, *use.*

RULE 39.—**The Relative agrees with the Antecedent in Gender and Number, but its Case is settled by its own Clause.**

---

1. He, whose tooth aches, cannot sleep. 2. The sword, which I use, is sharp. 3. Brutus, whom Cæsar had spared, became Cæsar's enemy. 4. Cæsar was killed by Brutus, whom he had spared. 5. Here comes a man, whom I ought to love. 6. The general spared the enemy, whom he had conquered. 7. I use the sword, which I have sharpened. 8. We eat the honey, which the bees made. 9. We love *those* who help us. 10. We try to please those whose help we need. 11. Be diligent, ye who seek honour. 12. Save the king, whom his enemies pursue.

EXERCISE XLI.

VOCABULARY.

ancestors, subst.	mājōrēs (mājōrum), 3 pl. m.	*service, to be of* / *service*, verb	prōsum, irr.
appease, verb	plăcō, 1	*steal*, verb	fŭrŏr, 1 dep.
far, adv.	prŏcŭl	*treasure*, subst.	thēsaūrŭs, 2
injure, verb	laēdō, 3	*way*, subst.	vĭă, 1
lead, verb	dūcō, 3	*write*, subst.	scrībō, 3.

RULES 1–10, 12–15, 17, 19, 20, 22, 23, 28, 29, 33.

RULE 11.—**Verbs of "accusing," "condemning," or "acquitting," take a Genitive besides the Accusative of the Object.**

RULE 24.—**Substantives which qualify the Verb like Adverbs are put in the Ablative.**

RULES 26.—**Several common words take the Ablative, as,**

Verbs—frŭŏr, *I enjoy.*	Adjectives—dīgnŭs, *worthy.*	
fŭngŏr, *I perform.*	indīgnŭs, *unworthy.*	
pŏtĭŏr, *I get.*	frētŭs, *relying on.*	
ūtŏr, *I use.*	Substantives—ŏpŭs, *need.*	
vēscŏr, *I eat.*	ūsŭs, *use.*	

RULE 39.—**The Relative agrees with the Antecedent in Gender and Number, but its Case is settled by its own Clause.**

---

1. Try to appease him, whom you have injured
2. We seek the treasure, which the earth conceals. 3. We avoid him, whose book we have stolen.
4. The lamb, which the wolf devoured, was innocent.
5. We hate the wolf, by whom the lamb was killed.
6. We honour those, whose ancestors served the state.
7. Sharpen the sword, which you are *going to* use.
8. Who was the goddess, to whom Paris gave the apple?   9. He was a man whom all men envied.
10. Let us go by the way, which leads to Rome.
11. Remember your sisters, who are far away.
12. Take the book in which I have written your name.

EXERCISE XLII.

VOCABULARY.

bed, subst.	lĕctŭs, 2	*stand by*, verb	ădstŏ, 1
conquer, verb	sŭbĭgŏ, 3	*worthy*, adj.	dīgnŭs
long, adv.	dĭū	*wrong*, verb	laēdŏ, 3.
soft, adj.	mŏllĭs		

RULES 1–10, 12–15, 17, 19, 20, 22, 23, 28, 29, 33.

RULE 11.—**Verbs of "accusing," "condemning," or "acquitting," take a Genitive besides the Accusative of the Object.**

RULE 24.—**Substantives which qualify the Verb like Adverbs are put in the Ablative.**

RULE 26.—**Several common words take the Ablative, as,**

Verbs—frŭŏr, *I enjoy.*
    fŭngŏr, *I perform.*
    pŏtĭŏr, *I get.*
    ūtŏr, *I use.*
    vĕscŏr, *I eat.*

Adjectives—dīgnŭs, *worthy.*
    indīgnŭs, *unworthy.*
    frētŭs, *relying on.*
Substantives—ŏpŭs, *need.*
    ūsŭs, *use.*

RULE 39.—**The Relative agrees with the Antecedent in Gender and Number, but its Case is settled by its own Clause.**

---

1. Give the book to the boy who stands by you.
2. Dead are the bees whose honey we eat.   3. He sleeps long, who uses a soft bed.   4. Let us spare the enemy whose country we have conquered.   5. We will avenge him, whom we could not save.   6. Happy is he who has been made king.   7. I pity the countryman, whom the viper bites.   8. He is worthy of praise, who fights for his country.   9. He was saved by the man, whom he had wronged.   10. He was killed by the soldiers, by whom he had been chosen general.   11. Use the books, which you have.   12. Here comes the man, whose father I always envied.

EXERCISE XLIII.

VOCABULARY.

banish, verb	rĕlēgŏ, 1	*show*, verb	mōnstrŏ, 1
compel, verb	cōgŏ, 3	*slave*, subst.	sĕrvŭs, 2
cut off, verb	ăbscīdŏ, 3	*statue*, subst.	stătŭă, 1
lie, verb	jăcĕŏ, 2	*surpass*, verb	sŭpĕrŏ, 1.
set up, verb	ērĭgŏ, 4		

RULES 1–10, 12–15, 17, 19, 20, 22, 23, 28, 29, 33.

RULE 11.—**Verbs of "accusing," "condemning," or "acquitting," take a Genitive besides the Accusative of the Object.**

RULE 24.—**Substantives which qualify the Verb like Adverbs are put in the Ablative.**

RULE 26.—**Several common words take the Ablative, as,**

Verbs—frŭŏr, *I enjoy.*		Adjectives—dīgnŭs, *worthy.*	
fŭngŏr, *I perform.*		īndīgnŭs, *unworthy.*	
pŏtĭŏr, *I get.*		frētŭs, *relying on.*	
ūtŏr, *I use.*		Substantives—ŏpŭs, *need.*	
vēscŏr, *I eat.*		ūsŭs, *use.*	

RULE 39.—**The Relative agrees with the Antecedent in Gender and Number, but its Case is settled by its own Clause.**

---

1. Here lie we who died *for* our country. 2. Do not envy him by whom you are surpassed. 3. Thou who enviest no one art worthy of praise. 4. He who had been a slave became a king. 5. The boy to whom I gave the book was praised by his father. 6. The bird who would not sing was compelled. 7. The fox whose brush was cut off tried to deceive others. 8. We are citizens whom a tyrant banished. 9. We admire those whose statues we set up. 10. Show me the boy who took your book *from* you. 11. There goes the man whom the Senators made general. 12. We who lie here fought *for* our country.

EXERCISE XLIV.

VOCABULARY.

chastise, verb	căstīgŏ, 1	*Thermopylæ*, subst.	Thĕrmŏ-
hair, subst.	pĭlŭs, 2		pȳlae,
levy, verb	cōnscrībŏ, 3		1 pl.
mercy, subst.	clēmēntĭă, 1	*unworthy*, adj.	indĭgnŭs.

RULES 1–10, 12–15, 17, 19, 20, 22, 23, 28, 29, 33.

RULE 11.—**Verbs of "accusing," "condemning," or "acquitting," take a Genitive besides the Accusative of the Object.**

RULE 24.—**Substantives which qualify the Verb like Adverbs are put in the Ablative.**

RULE 26.—**Several common words take the Ablative, as,**

Verbs—frŭŏr, *I enjoy.*	Adjectives—dīgnŭs, *worthy.*
fŭngŏr, *I perform.*	indĭgnŭs, *unworthy.*
pŏtĭŏr, *I get.*	frētŭs, *relying on.*
ūtŏr, *I use.*	Substantives—ŏpŭs, *need.*
vēscŏr, *I eat.*	ūsŭs, *use.*

RULE 39.—**The Relative agrees with the Antecedent in Gender and Number, but its Case is settled by its own Clause.**

———————

1. He has a tongue which he loves to use. 2. He whose book I am using has gone home. 3. We pity Cæsar, who was killed by his friends. 4. Show yourself just to him whom you envy. 5. Remember those who died at Thermopylæ. 6. Spare those who pray you for mercy. 7. We who chastise you love you. 8. I love those by whom I am praised. 9. Learn to admire those whose deeds you cannot imitate. 10. He whom the soldiers followed was unworthy of praise. 11. He commands the army which he levied. 12. He asked for a hair of the dog which bit him.

12. *Him.* Reflexive pronoun.

EXERCISE XLV.

VOCABULARY.

aid, verb	ădjŭvŏ, 1	*pardon,* verb	ĭgnōscŏ, 3
autumn, subst.	aūtŭmnŭs, 2	*priest,* subst.	săcĕrdōs
cock, subst.	gāllŭs, 2		(săcĕrdōtĭs),
find, verb	ĭnvĕnĭŏ, 4		3 m.
Iacchus, subst.	Iăcchŭs, 2	*province,* subst.	prōvīncĭă, 1
marry, verb (*of a woman*)	nŭbŏ, 3	*ring,* subst.	ānnŭlŭs, 2
morning, in the morning	mānĕ	*tremble,* verb	trĕmō, 3.

RULES 1–15, 17, 19, 20, 22–24, 26, 28, 29, 33, 39.

RULE 21.—**An Accusative or Ablative of the part affected is joined to Verbs, Adjectives, or Participles.**

---

1. Tell me the name of the friend whom you met yesterday. 2. I was aided by him whom I had hurt. 3. Can you love him who envies you? 4. This is the house which Iacchus built. 5. This is the cock which the priest heard in the morning. 6. Here is he whom the maiden married. 7. No one could see him by whom the ring had been found. 8. Cæsar went into Gaul, which was his province. 9. There are many *thousand* men whom I admire. 10. The swallows who depart in autumn will return. 11. We can love those whose faults we pardon. 12. I pitied the boy who was trembling in all his limbs.

12. *In all his limbs.* Use Ablative.

EXERCISE XLVI.

VOCABULARY.

Alps, subst.	Ălpēs (Ālpĭum), 3 pl. f.	*most men*, subst.	plērīquĕ, 2 pl.
		others, pron.	ălīī, 2 pl.
		page, subst.	păgĭnă, 1
blame, verb	cŭlpŏ, 1	*subject*, subst.	cīvĭs (cīvĭs), 3 m.
favour, verb	făvĕŏ, 2		
gather, verb	lĕgŏ, 3	*tear*, verb	lăcĕrŏ, 1.

RULES 1–15, 17, 19, 20, 22–24, 26, 28, 29, 33, 39.

RULE 21.—**An Accusative or Ablative of the part affected is joined to Verbs, Adjectives, or Participles.**

---

1. Ye stars, who shine in heaven, favour me. 2. He who is idle himself makes others idle. 3. No one whom I envied was present. 4. O wolf, spare the lamb who has not wronged you. 5. I am ashamed of the deed which you blame. 6. He told the matter to Cæsar, who praised him. 7. He was slain with the sword which he himself had sharpened. 8. The king whose subjects are happy is worthy of praise. 9. Have you seen the Alps which Hannibal crossed? 10. I pity him whom most men envy. 11. Eat the apples which I have gathered *for* you. 12. Give me the book whose pages you have torn.

EXERCISE XLVII.

VOCABULARY.

cut, verb	sĕcō, 1	*make mistakes*, verb	pĕccō, 1
furrow, subst.	sŭlcŭs, 2	*mistaken (to be)*, verb	ĕrrō, 1
hand, to be at hand, verb	ădsum, irr.	*polished*, adj.	nĭtĭdŭs
illustrious, adj.	īnclўtŭs	*share*, subst.	vŏmĕr (vŏmĕris), 3 m.
imminent (to be)	īmmĭnĕō, 2		
know, verb	scĭŏ, 4		

RULES 1-15, 17, 19-24, 26, 28, 29, 33, 39.

RULE 40.—**The Subject of a Verb in the Infinitive Mood is in the Accusative.**

---

1. I know that the king is at hand. 2. They said that Cæsar had conquered the Gauls. 3. That man was father of an illustrious son. 4. The share, which cuts the furrow, becomes polished. 5. I see the moon is waning. 6. The general thought that the boy was mistaken. 7. I envy that man who never makes mistakes. 8. It is evident that all men favour Cæsar. 9. I hope that you will come. 10. He said that he had come from Rome. 11. We all believe that war is imminent. 12. I know the sun has risen.

6. *Was mistaken.* Present Infinitive. The tense of the Infinitive depends on the tense of the Finite Verb, which was or might have been used in the first instance. Thus here, *the general thought—the boy is mistaken—is* being Present, the Present Infinitive will be used in this sentence.

10. The words used were *I have come from Rome.* Compare note on 6.

EXERCISE XLVIII.

VOCABULARY.

crop, subst.	sĕgĕs (sĕgĕtĭs), 3 f.	*heal*, verb	*mĕdĕŏr*, 2 dep.
		hungry, adj.	ĕsŭrĭēns
disease, subst.	mŏrbŭs, 2	*promise*, verb	*pŏllĭcĕŏr*, 2 dep.

RULES 1–15, 17, 19–24, 26, 28, 29, 33, 39.

RULE 40.—**The Subject of a Verb in the Infinitive Mood is in the Accusative.**

---

1. Remember that war is imminent. 2. That hungry wolf will eat the lamb. 3. We pity that nation whose crops fail. 4. *Do* not tell me that you never saw him. 5. He promised me that he *would* give me the book. 6. He denied that he had promised it. 7. Who does not know that Cæsar was killed by Brutus? 8. The Romans denied that the Gauls burnt Rome. 9. I believe that the house will be burnt. 10. I do not think that I can tell you this. 11. The bear thought that honey was sweet. 12. The physician thought that he could heal the disease.

EXERCISE XLIX.

VOCABULARY.

blunt, verb	rĕtūndŏ, 3	*put up*, verb	ĕxcĭtŏ, 1
divide, verb	dīvĭdŏ, 3	*well (to be)*, verb	vălĕŏ, 2.
messenger, subst.	nūntĭŭs, 3		

RULES 1–15, 17, 19–24, 26, 28, 29, 33, 39,

RULE 40.—**The Subject of a Verb in the Infinitive Mood is in the Accusative.**

---

1. The countryman thought the viper was ungrateful.
2. The messenger told Pompeius that Sertorius had been killed. 3. That book which you are reading was given to me by my father. 4. He said that the water was becoming warm. 5. Do you think that there is any hope of safety? 6. Do you not hope that the Gauls will be conquered? 7. Cæsar tells us that Gaul was divided into three parts. 8. I think that that bird cannot fly. 9. Who told you that I was not well? 10. He said that the king had told him that the war was ended. 11. I tried to use the sword which had been blunted. 12. Follow that stag which the hounds have put up.

EXEROISE L.

VOCABULARY.

certain, adj.	cĕrtŭs	relate, verb	nărrŏ, 1
cheese, subst.	cāsĕŭs, 2	run short, verb	dĕfĭcĭŏ, 3
lose, verb	ămīttŏ, 3	small, adj.	părvŭs, 3

RULES 1–15, 17, 19–24, 26, 28, 29, 33, 39.

RULE 40.—**The Subject of a Verb in the Infinitive Mood is in the Accusative.**

---

1. It is certain that I shall love you always. 2. Tell me the name of the man who said that I was mistaken. 3. O crow, foolish bird, do not believe that fox. 4. The fox will eat the cheese which the crow loses. 5. Brutus denied that he had injured his country. 6. Homer says that Agamemnon commanded the Greeks. 7. That which Homer relates is only a small part of the Trojan war. 8. Who said that he could not hear me? 9. The besieged citizens hoped that the food would not run short. 10. The man whom I asked said that he did not know. 11. All saw that the Romans would be conquered. 12. Who does not rejoice that the hour of play is at hand?

2. *Of the man.* Use "ējŭs," genitive of the demonstrative pronoun "ĭs, ĕă, ĭd." In such expressions as "*he who,*" "*that which,*" &c., "*he,*" "*that,*" &c. (unless emphatic), are regularly translated by "ĭs," "ĭd," &c.

EXERCISE LI.

VOCABULARY.

abroad (*to be*)	pĕrḗgrīnŏr, 1	*open,* verb	ăpĕrĭŏ, 4
Caius, subst.	Cāĭŭs, 2	*play,* verb	lūdŏ, 3
danger, subst.	pĕrīcŭlum, 2	*prefer,* verb	āntĕpōnŏ, 3
game, subst.	lūdŭs, 2	*send,* verb	mīttŏ, 3
just, adv.	mŏdŏ	*take up,* verb	sūscĭpĭŏ, 3
mouth, subst.	ōs (ōrĭs), 3 n.	*triumph,* subst.	trĭūmphŭs, 2
notary, subst.	scrībă, 1 m.	*will,* subst.	tēstămēntum, 2.

RULES 1–15, 17–29, 33, 38–40.

RULE 41.—**The Finite Verb in a Dependent Clause introducing Question, Purpose, or Consequence, is in the Subjunctive Mood.**

RULE 42.—**The Tense of the Finite Verb in a Dependent Clause is settled by the Tense of the Principal Verb in the Clause on which it depends.**

RULE 43.—**Primary Tenses of the Indicative are followed by Primary Tenses of the Subjunctive; Historic Tenses of the Indicative are followed by Historic Tenses of the Subjunctive.**

The word "**that**" in four senses. 1. Demonstrative. 2. Relative. 3. Sign of Accusative and Infinitive. 4. Expressing Purpose or Consequence.

---

1. That man told me that Caius was abroad. 2. He took up arms that he might avenge his father. 3. I have just met the man that I wished to see. 4. Do you know that that man's father is in prison? 5. He sent for a notary that he might make his will. 6. I prefer this book to that. 7. I was so hot that I could not sleep. 8. The crow was so foolish that he opened his mouth. 9. That was a pleasant game which we played yesterday. 10. I think that Cicero has not deserved a triumph. 11. Give me that book that I may read it. 12. He sent his son home that he might not be in danger.

EXERCISE LII.

VOCABULARY.

burnt down (to be), verb	} dēflăgrō, 1	*Lucullus*, subst.	Lūcŭllŭs, 2
buy, verb	ĕmō, 3	*nut*, subst.	nŭx (nŭcĭs), 3 f.
enter, verb	ĭnĕŏ, 4 irr.	*punish*, verb	pŭnĭŏ, 4
entertain, verb	ĕxcĭpĭŏ, 3	*sip*, verb	lībō, 1
fine, adj.	laūtŭs	*tire*, verb	lăssō, 1
house, subst.	aēdēs (aēdĭum), 3 pl. f.	*well*, adv.	bĕnĕ
		wreck, verb	dēmērgō, 3.

RULES 1–15, 17–29, 33, 38–40.

RULE 41.—**The Finite Verb in a Dependent Clause introducing Question, Purpose, or Consequence, is in the Subjunctive Mood.**

RULE 42.—**The Tense of the Finite Verb in a Dependent Clause is settled by the Tense of the Principal Verb in the Clause on which it depends.**

RULE 43.—**Primary Tenses of the Indicative are followed by Primary Tenses of the Subjunctive; Historic Tenses of the Indicative are followed by Historic Tenses of the Subjunctive.**

The word "that" in four senses. 1. Demonstrative. 2. Relative. 3. Sign of Accusative and Infinitive. 4. Expressing Purpose or Consequence.

---

1. That you may sleep well you ought to tire yourself. 2. Bees enter flowers that they may sip honey. 3. That you may become wise be diligent. 4. Cæsar said that he would punish the pirates. 5. The pirates that captured Cæsar, were afterwards put to death. 6. The monkey uses the help of the cat that he may eat the nuts. 7. That house that Lucullus built was burnt down. 8. It is certain that Cæsar is worthy of praise. 9. He bought a fine house that he might entertain the king. 10. All thought that the ship would be wrecked. 11. When will you come that we may talk together? 12. He came that he might tell me that the enemy was at hand.

EXERCISE LIII.

VOCABULARY.

benefit, verb	prōsum, irr.	*often*, adv.	saēpĕ
clothes, subst.	vēstēs (vēstĭum), 3 pl. f.	*palace*, subst.	aūlă, 1
		pretend, verb	sĭmŭlō, 1
		sell, verb	vēndō, 3
dress, subst.	vēstĭs (vēstĭs), 3 f.	*so*, adv.	tam
		stupid, adj.	stŏlĭdŭs
ever (at any time), adv.	ūnquam	*treat*, verb	ūtŏr, 3 dep.
		violet, subst.	vĭŏlă, 1
greatly, adv.	văldē	*wither*, verb	mārcēscō, 3
mad (to be), verb	fŭrō, 3	*wood*, subst.	sĭlvă, 1.

RULES 1–15, 17–29, 33, 38–40.

RULE 41.—**The Finite Verb in a Dependent Clause introducing Question, Purpose, or Consequence, is in the Subjunctive Mood.**

RULE 42.—**The Tense of the Finite Verb in a Dependent Clause is settled by the Tense of the Principal Verb in the Clause on which it depends.**

RULE 43.—**Primary Tenses of the Indicative are followed by Primary Tenses of the Subjunctive; Historic Tenses of the Indicative are followed by Historic Tenses of the Subjunctive.**

The word "that" in four senses. 1. Demonstrative. 2. Relative. 3. Sign of Accusative and Infinitive. 4. Expressing Purpose or Consequence.

---

1. Those violets that you plucked are withering. 2. The maiden that was poor became a queen. 3. Put on that fine dress, O maiden, that you may go to the palace. 4. In that battle Cæsar often thought that he would be conquered. 5. I will sell my clothes that I may buy books. 6. You do not treat that book well whose pages you tear. 7. That they might pluck flowers the maidens went into the wood. 8. Solon pretended that he was mad that he might benefit his countrymen. 9. Who ever thought that Rome would be taken? 10. That which you said yesterday displeased me greatly. 11. He was so stupid that no one could teach him. 12. He wished to depart that he might not fight.

EXERCISE LIV.

Vocabulary.

companion, subst.	cŏmĕs (cŏmĭtĭs), 3 m.	*so,* conj.	ĭtăquĕ
correctly, adv.	rēctē	*suppose,* verb	pŭtŏ, 1
diligently, adv.	dīlĭgēntĕr	*time,* subst.	tēmpŭs (tēmpŏrĭs), 3 n.
force, verb	cŏgŏ, 3		
hide, verb	cēlŏ, 1	*tired,* adj.	fēssŭs
learn by heart, v.	ēdīscŏ, 3	*true,* subst.	vērŭs
poem, subst.	cărmĕn (cărmĭnĭs), 3 n.	*useless,* adj.	ĭnūtĭlĭs
		word, subst.	vērbum, 2.

Rules 1–15, 17–29, 33, 38–40.

Rule 41.—**The Finite Verb in a Dependent Clause introducing Question, Purpose, or Consequence, is in the Subjunctive Mood.**

Rule 42.—**The Tense of the Finite Verb in a Dependent Clause is settled by the Tense of the Principal Verb in the Clause on which it depends.**

Rule 43.—**Primary Tenses of the Indicative are followed by Primary Tenses of the Subjunctive; Historic Tenses of the Indicative are followed by Historic Tenses of the Subjunctive.**

The word "**that**" in four senses. 1. Demonstrative. 2. Relative. 3. Sign of Accusative and Infinitive. 4. Expressing Purpose or Consequence.

---

1. *On* that night that city was taken. 2. Alexander, that famous king, thought that he was like Achilles. 3. We believe that the poems that Homer composed were never written by Homer. 4. We believe that no one could write in the time of Homer. 5. So we suppose that Homer was wont to learn them by heart. 6. The fox that lost his brush tried to persuade his friends that brushes are useless. 7. I have come that I may tell you that I cannot be your companion. 8. The boy promised that he would use his book diligently. 9. So tired were our men that they could not pursue the enemy. 10. He hid himself that he might not be forced to go to the war. 11. I think all that you have said is true. 12. I did not think you could write those Latin words correctly.

EXERCISE LV.

VOCABULARY.

ambuscade, subst.	īnsĭdĭae, 1 pl. f.	*hit*, verb	pĕrcŭtĭŏ, 3
badly, adv.	mălĕ	*obliged*, part.	cŏāctŭs
bring back, verb	rĕdūcŏ, 3	*order*, verb	jŭbĕŏ, 2
Camillus, subst.	Cămīllŭs, 2	*post*, verb	lŏcŏ, 1
do, verb	făcĭŏ, 3 irr.	*Regulus*, subst.	Rēgŭlŭs, 2
each, pron.	quīsquĕ	*rout*, verb	fŭgŏ, 1
feel, verb	sēntĭŏ, 4	*sacred*, adj.	săcĕr
file, subst.	līmă, 1	*step-mother*, subst.	nŏvĕrcă, 1
		throw, verb,	jăcĭŏ, 3.

RULES 1–15, 17–29, 33, 38–40.

RULE 41.—**The Finite Verb in a Dependent Clause introducing Question, Purpose, or Consequence, is in the Subjunctive Mood.**

RULE 42.—**The Tense of the Finite Verb in a Dependent Clause is settled by the Tense of the Principal Verb in the Clause on which it depends.**

RULE 43.—**Primary Tenses of the Indicative are followed by Primary Tenses of the Subjunctive; Historic Tenses of the Indicative are followed by Historic Tenses of the Subjunctive.**

The word "**that**" in four senses. 1. Demonstrative. 2. Relative. 3. Sign of Accusative and Infinitive. 4. Expressing Purpose or Consequence.

To. 1. Preposition. 2. Sign of Infinitive. 3. = "**that**" 4.

---

1. Who ordered the viper to bite the file? 2. The geese that saved Rome were sacred to Juno. 3. Pray the Gauls *not* to attack Rome. 4. Camillus, the Gauls being routed, was called the father of his country. 5. To deceive the enemy, the general posted four hundred men in ambuscade. 6. Cæsar went to Gaul to make war upon the Gauls. 7. He said that the enemy were coming to attack the camp. 8. He who threw a stone at a dog hit his step-mother. 9. He did not think that he had done badly. 10. Regulus was sent to Rome to bring back the captives. 11. He felt himself obliged to return to Carthage. 12. The king being dead, the citizens returned *each* to his own home.

3. See "not," 8.

EXERCISE LVI.

VOCABULARY.

English	Latin	English	Latin
Ægisthus, subst.	Aegīsthŭs, 2	*look down on*, verb	dĕspĭcĭŏ, 3
cross, verb	trănsĕŏ, 4 irr.	*out of doors*, adv.	fŏrās
dine, verb	cēnŏ, 1	*ready*, adj.	părātŭs
finish, verb	cōnfĭcĭŏ, 3	*sea*, subst.	pĕlăgŭs, 2 n.
hero, subst.	vĭr (vĭrī), 2 m.	*to-morrow*, adv.	crās
lie down, verb	dēcŭmbŏ, 3	*town*, subst.	ūrbs (ūrbĭs), 3 f.

RULES 1–15, 17–29, 33, 38–40.

RULE 41.—**The Finite Verb in a Dependent Clause introducing Question, Purpose, or Consequence, is in the Subjunctive Mood.**

RULE 42.—**The Tense of the Finite Verb in a Dependent Clause is settled by the Tense of the Principal Verb in the Clause on which it depends.**

RULE 43.—**Primary Tenses of the Indicative are followed by Primary Tenses of the Subjunctive; Historic Tenses of the Indicative are followed by Historic Tenses of the Subjunctive.**

The word "that" in four senses. 1. Demonstrative. 2. Relative. 3. Sign of Accusative and Infinitive. 4. Expressing Purpose or Consequence.

To. 1. Preposition. 2. Sign of Infinitive. 3. = "that" 4.

---

1. Ægisthus *ought* not to have killed Agamemnon. 2. Many heroes who went to Troy never returned. 3. Come to Rome to-morrow to dine with Cæsar. 4. He promised to give the boy a book. 5. Why do you not try to finish your work, that you may be able to go out of doors? 6. The messenger came to the general to tell him that the enemy were at hand. 7. I am going home to lie down. 8. He went to the top of the hill to look down on the town. 9. I am ready to cross the sea to seek wealth. 10. I said you were going to fall. 11. All wished Marius to become consul. 12. To save the republic we will obey a general we hate.

EXERCISE LVII.

VOCABULARY.

Ajax, subst.	Ājāx (-ăcĭs), 3 m.	*Henricus*, subst.	Hēnrīcŭs, 2
annoy, verb	lăcēssō, 3	*nail*, subst.	clāvŭs, 2
barons, subst.	prīncĭpēs (-cĭpum), 3 pl.	*Plato*, subst.	Plătō (-tŏnĭs), 3 m.
boot, subst.	călīgă, 1	*pool*, subst.	stăgnum, 2
bottom of, render by adj.	īmŭs	*so much*, adv.	ădĕō
		useful, adj.	ūtĭlĭs
endure, verb	pătĭŏr, 3 dep.	*visit*, verb	vīsō, 3.
free, adj.	lībĕr		

RULES 1–15, 17–29, 33, 38–40.

RULE 41.—**The Finite Verb in a Dependent Clause introducing Question, Purpose, or Consequence, is in the Subjunctive Mood.**

RULE 42.—**The Tense of the Finite Verb in a Dependent Clause is settled by the Tense of the Principal Verb in the Clause on which it depends.**

RULE 43.—**Primary Tenses of the Indicative are followed by Primary Tenses of the Subjunctive; Historic Tenses of the Indicative are followed by Historic Tenses of the Subjunctive.**

The word "**that**" in four senses. 1. Demonstrative. 2. Relative. 3. Sign of Accusative and Infinitive. 4. Expressing Purpose or Consequence.

To. 1. Preposition. 2. Sign of Infinitive. 3. = "**that**" 4.

---

1. Try to understand that book that you are reading. 2. Romulus forbade all men to leap over his walls. 3. The lamb denied that he had wished to annoy the wolf. 4. Henricus wished to kill one wife that he might marry another. 5. To make England free, the barons went in arms to the king. 6. To be useful, a sword ought to be sharp. 7. To climb a mountain, add nails to your boots. 8. Plato went to Sicily to visit a tyrant. 9. That bread is useful to all men no one denies. 10. To avoid the hares, the frogs went to the bottom of the pool. 11. Ajax was so much ashamed of his folly that he could not endure life. 12. Let us cross the sea to take Troy.

5. *In arms.* Is expressed in Latin by "ārmātŭs," *armed.*
11. Latin, *It shamed Ajax of his folly so much* ("ădĕō").

EXERCISE LVIII.

Vocabulary.

bride, subst.	nūptă, 1	*outpost*, subst.	stătĭŏ (stătĭŏnĭs), 3 f.
gain, verb	ădĭpīscŏr, 3 dep.		
guide, verb	dūcŏ, 3	*Pluto*, subst.	Plūtŏ (Plūtŏnĭs), 3 m.
ill (to be), verb	āegrŏtŏ, 1		
middle of, render by adj. }	mĕdĭŭs	*wait for*, verb	ĕxspĕctŏ, 1.

Rules 1–15, 17–29, 33, 38–40.

RULE 41.—**The Finite Verb in a Dependent Clause introducing Question, Purpose, or Consequence, is in the Subjunctive Mood.**

RULE 42.—**The Tense of the Finite Verb in a Dependent Clause is settled by the Tense of the Principal Verb in the Clause on which it depends.**

RULE 43.—**Primary Tenses of the Indicative are followed by Primary Tenses of the Subjunctive; Historic Tenses of the Indicative are followed by Historic Tenses of the Subjunctive.**

The word "**that**" in four senses. 1. Demonstrative. 2. Relative. 3. Sign of Accusative and Infinitive. 4. Expressing Purpose or Consequence.

To. 1. Preposition. 2. Sign of Infinitive. 3. = "**that**" 4.

---

1. To avoid Cæsar he went from Rome to Greece. 2. To the middle of the night I will wait for you. 3. Hannibal was so ill, that he became blind of one eye. 4. Are you saying this to deceive me? 5. All can try: it does not follow that all can win. 6. You who envy the good ought to imitate them. 7. Who does not wish to go to Greece to see Athens? 8. Go home to find your sword. 9. He promised to guide him to the outposts. 10. What will not men do to gain glory? 11. Pluto went to Sicily to find a bride. 12. There is the boy to whom I promised to give the book.

    2. *To.* "Ūsquĕ ăd" with Accusative.

    3. *Of* here shows the part affected. See Rule 21. Use the Ablative.

    . *That* may be expressed by Accusative and Infinitive, or by "ŭt" with Subjunctive.

EXERCISE LIX.

VOCABULARY.

advance, verb	prŏgrĕdĭŏr, 3 dep.	*opportunity,* subst.	ŏccāsĭŏ (ŏccāsĭŏnĭs), 3 f.
approve, verb	prŏbŏ, 1		
avail, to avail oneself of	ūtŏr, 3 dep.	*ox,* subst.	bŏs (bŏvĭs), 3 m.
burst, verb	rŭmpŏ, 3	*panic-stricken,* adj.	pĕrtĕrrĭtŭs
crush, verb	ŏpprĭmŏ, 3	*parent,* subst.	părēns (părēntĭs), 3 m. & f.
declare, verb	īndīcŏ, 3		
discharge, verb	fŭngŏr, 3 dep.		
duty, subst.	mūnŭs (mūnĕrĭs), 3 n.	*Rubicon,* subst.	Rŭbĭcŏ (Rŭbĭcōnĭs), 3 m.
embrace, verb	āmplĕctŏr, 3 dep.		
equal, adj.	pār (părĭs)	*sailor,* subst.	nāută, 1 m.
escape, verb	ĕvădŏ, 3	*salute,* verb	sălūtŏ, 1
gird, verb	cīngŏ, 3	*so many,* num. adj.	tŏt
harbour, subst.	pŏrtŭs, 4 m.	*suffer,* verb	pătĭŏr, 3 dep.
hardship, subst.	mălum, 2		
make for, verb	pĕtŏ, 3	*think,* verb	rĕŏr, 2 dep.

RULES 1–43.   Use of Participles.   Deponent Verbs. Ablative Absolute.

---

1. Having crossed the Rubicou, Cæsar declared war against his country.   2. The frogs, *on* hearing the sound of feet, were panic-stricken.   3. I will try to discharge the duty which I owe to my parents.   4. *On* hearing of Cæsar's death Cicero approved the deed. 5. Girt with a sword, he advanced to meet his enemy. 6. Availing himself of the opportunity, he escaped. 7. Without saluting the consul, he retired to his own house.   8. When the storm arose, the sailors made for the harbour.   9. Embracing his father, he promised to return home.   10. Cicero, when made consul, crushed the conspiracy of Catiline.   11. I pity you who have suffered so many hardships.   12. The frog, thinking she could become equal to the ox, burst herself.

1. *Against.*   Included in the verb " īndīcŏ."
2. *On hearing.*   Use " āudĭŏ," 4.
4. *On hearing of.*   Use " cŏgnōscŏ," 3.
7. See " *without,*" 3.
9. *Embracing.*   Use the Past Participle.
12. *Thinking.*   Use the Past Participle.

EXERCISE LX.

Vocabulary.

abandon, verb	ăbjĭcĭŏ, 3	*harvest,* subst.	mĕssĭs (mĕs- sĭs), 3 f.
approach, subst.	ădvĕntŭs, 4 m.	*hear,* verb	cŏgnōscō, 3
bay, subst.	laurŭs, 2 (and 4) f.	*husbandman,* subst.	cŏlōnŭs, 2
climb, verb	ăscēndō, 3	*insult,* subst.	cŏntŭmēlĭă, 1
crown, verb	cŏrōnō, 1	*ivy,* subst.	hĕdĕră, 1
eighteen, num. adj.	dŭŏdēvīgintī (indecl.)	*leave* (i.e. *depart from*), verb	ēxcēdō, 3
enjoy, verb	frŭŏr, 3	*reconnoitre,* verb	ēxplōrō, 1
finish, verb	pĕrăgō, 3	*scout,* subst.	spĕcŭlātŏr (spĕcŭlā- tōrĭs), 3 m.
ground, subst.	lŏcă (lŏcōrum), 2 pl. n.	*snatch up,* verb	ărrĭpĭō, 3
		trunk, subst.	trŭncŭs, 2.

Rules 1–43.   Use of Participles.   Deponent Verbs. Ablative Absolute.

1. *When* the harvest is finished, the husbandman rejoices.   2. *Snatching up* his sword, he said that he would not endure such insults.   3. Seeing this, he abandoned all hope.   4. Hearing of the approach of Cæsar, Pompey left Rome.   5. Having reconnoitred the ground, the scout returned to the camp.   6. The camp being taken, the general *must* be conquered. 7. Having climbed the hill, he said he could not see the enemy.   8. The republic enjoyed peace for eighteen years.   9. Who, when the sun has risen, wishes to sleep?   10. The ivy embracing the trunk hurts the tree.   11. The general, his head crowned with bay, entered the temple.   12. He discharged his duty so well that he was praised by all.

2. *Snatching up* is equivalent to *having snatched up.*   Turn by Abl. Abs.   *Said that he would not* is expressed in Latin by " denied ('nĕgō') that he would."   *Such insults* is best rendered by "insults of that kind" (*of that kind* is "ējūs- mŏdī").   See "*such,*" 3.

3. *Seeing.* } Compare note on "*snatching up*" in the pre-
4. *Hearing.* } ceding sentence.

7. *Said he could not.*   Express by "denied that he could." Compare Sentence 2.

10. *Embracing.*   Use the Past Participle.

EXERCISE LXI.

Vocabulary.

bind, verb	cōnstrīngō, 3	*meditate,* verb	mĕdītŏr, 1 dep.
children, subst.	lībĕrī, 2 pl.		
country (opposed to *town*)	rūs (rūrĭs), 3 n.	*Niŏbē,* subst.	Niŏbē (Niŏbēs), 1 f.
encourage, verb	hōrtŏr, 1 dep.	*persuade,* verb	suādĕō, 2
frost, subst.	gĕlū, 4 (used in abl. only)	*possession of (to get),* see *to get possession of*	
get possession of	pŏtĭŏr, 3 & 4 dep.	*revenge,* subst.	ūltĭō (ūltĭōnĭs), 3 f.
grape, subst.	ūvă, 1	*rock,* subst.	sāxum, 2
lieutenant, subst.	lēgātŭs, 2	*shut up,* part.	īnclūsŭs
		sour, adj.	ăcĕrbŭs.

RULES 1–43.   Use of Participles.   Deponent Verbs. Ablative Absolute.

---

1. Followed by his soldiers the general entered the city.   2. All hope of taking the city must be abandoned.   3. Niobe, having lost her children, became a rock.   4. Encouraging his men, he leapt into the fosse. 5. He said he would persuade Cæsar to spare the Gauls.   6. He got possession of the gold by force. 7. The birds when the ground is frost-bound come to the windows to seek food.   8. The fox said that the grapes which he could not reach were sour.   9. The lieutenant was followed by four hundred men.   10. Shut up in a prison for ten years he meditated revenge. 11. Give me the sword which my father used. 12. Having discharged his duty, he returned to the country to his oxen.

1. Since " sĕquŏr," the Latin for *I follow,* is a Deponent Verb, and has no Past Participle Passive, the sentence must be changed thus—*The general, his soldiers following, entered the city.*   *Following,* being the Present Participle Active, can be rendered by the Present Participle of " sĕquŏr."
2. *Of taking.*   Gerund in " dī."
4. *Encouraging.*   Past Participle.
9. *Was followed.*   The difficulty in Sentence 1 occurs again here. The sentence must be changed into another, meaning the same thing, but employing the verb *to follow* in the Active Voice.

EXERCISE LXII.

VOCABULARY.

burn, verb	ūrō, 3	*March,* render by adj.	Mārtĭŭs.
certain, pron. adj.	quĭdam		
country house, subst.	vīllă, 1	*promise*, subst.	prōmīssum, 2
		relying on, adj.	frētŭs
credit, subst.	fĭdĕs (fĭdĕī), 5 f.	*scarcity*, subst.	paūcĭtās (paūcĭtātĭs), 3 f.
East-wind, subst.	Eūrŭs, 2		
expel, verb	ĕxpĕllō, 3	*show*, verb	praēstō, 1
lay down, verb	pōnō, 3	*trial*, subst.	jŭdĭcĭum, 2.

RULES 1–43.   Use of Participles.   Deponent Verbs. Ablative Absolute.

---

1. Hoping to gain learning, he went to Athens. 2. Such was the scarcity of leaders, that he became a tribune of the soldiers. 3. To help his friends, he set out for Gaul. 4. Having bought a country house, he hoped to enjoy rest. 5. Relying on your promises, I lay down my arms. 6. The fox showed himself unworthy of credit. 7. As the tyrants are expelled, the war is ended. 8. Since my books are burnt, I shall never become a learned man. 9. One of the girls spared her husband. 10. *Certain* Roman citizens were put to death without a trial. 11. With the month of March returns the East wind. 12. Spring is followed by summer: summer by autumn.

1. *Hoping.* Use "quum" with the Imperfect Subjunctive.
2. *Such.* Use "tāntŭs" or "ĭs." See "*such.*"
9. *Of.* See "*of*," 2.
11. *With = together with.* See "*with*," 3.
12. *Is followed.* See Exercise LXI., Sentences 1 and 9.

·EXERCISE LXIII.

Vocabulary.

ambassador, subst.	lēgātŭs, 2	*Rhone,* subst.	Rhŏdănŭs, 2
friendship, subst.	ămīcǐtǐă, 1	*rising,* subst.	ŏrtŭs, 4
keep, verb	sĕrvŏ, 1	*strength,* subst.	vīrĕs (vīrĭum),
move, verb	mŏvĕŏ, 2		3 pl. f.

Rules 1–43.   Especially 32, 34–37.   Also pp. 124–128.

---

1. He led his soldiers eager for fighting across the Rhone.   2. Ambassadors were sent to make peace. 3. Let us climb the hill to see the sunrise.   4. Cæsar is favoured by the soldiers.   5. Having entered the wood he lost his way.   6. We must win the victory. 7. We *must* go into the wood.   8. By helping your friends you will keep their friendship.   9. Let us not abandon the hope of saving our country.   10. Shall not the conquered enemy be spared?   11. I have come to tell you that there is no hope.   12. Use all your strength to move that stone.

    3. *The sunrise.*   Say, " the rising of the sun."
    4. *Is favoured.*   Rule 32.
  10. *Be spared.*   Rule 32.

EXERCISE LXIV.

VOCABULARY.

done (= *con-ferred*), part. }	cŏllātŭs
dry, adj.	sīccŭs
go abroad, verb	pĕrĕgrīnŏr, 1
ladder, subst.	scālāē, 1 pl.
long, adj.	lōngŭs
need, subst.	ŏpŭs, 3 (nom. & acc. only)
philosophy, subst.	phĭlŏsŏphĭă, 1
prudence, subst.	prūdēntĭă, 1
refresh, verb	rĕcrĕō, 1
scale, verb	scāndō, 3
study, verb	stŭdĕō, 2
well, subst.	pŭtĕŭs, 2.

RULES 1–43.   Especially 32, 34–37.   Also pp. 124–128.

---

1. The summer being dry, the wells failed. 2. I lived ten years at Athens to study philosophy. 3. He went abroad to refresh himself. 4. He was so eager for fighting that he forgot prudence. 5. I will never forget the kindnesses done me by my friends. 6. The general sent a spy to reconnoitre the ground. 7. The captive cherished hopes of breaking his chains. 8. He ordered four hundred men to scale the wall. 9. For scaling the wall we need long ladders. 10. This fault will be pardoned. 11. I am eager to see the general. 12. That tree *must* be cut down by the woodman.

    1. Rule 28.
    2. Rule 23.
    9. See "*for*," 5.
    11. *To see.* Gerund in " dī."

EXERCISE LXV.

VOCABULARY.

bound forward	prōsĭlĭŏ, 4	*mind*, subst.	ănĭmŭs, 2
cool, verb	rĕfrīgĕrŏ, 1	*spirit*	ănĭmī, 2 pl.
doe, subst.	cĕrvă, 1	*spring* (*of water*)	fŏns (fŏntĭs), 3 m.
fear, verb	vĕrĕŏr, 2	*strike* (*a camp*)	mŏvĕŏ, 2
influence, verb	mŏvĕŏ, 2	*suddenly*, adv.	sŭbĭtŏ
jump out, verb	prōsĭlĭŏ, 4	*Themistocles*, subst.	Thĕmĭstŏclēs (Thĕmĭstŏclĭs), 3 m.
keep (i.e. *to feed*)	pāscŏ, 3	*withdraw*	ăbdūcŏ, 3
messenger, subst.	nūntĭă, 1		

RULES 1–43. Especially 32, 34–37. Also pp. 124–128.

---

1. Hearing a sound, he jumped out of bed. 2. Fearing the enemy, he withdrew his forces. 3. Put your head under the spring, to cool it. 4. The Athenians were persuaded by Themistocles to fight. 5. Caius, followed by his servant, went home. 6. To influence his soldiers' minds, Sertorius kept a white doe. 7. The soldiers were persuaded that the doe was a messenger of the gods. 8. The doe being lost, the spirits of the men fell. 9. All hope of finding the doe being abandoned, the camp was struck. 10. Suddenly the doe bounded forward to greet her master. 11. Some thought that it was a trick of the general. 12. To cross the river, he built a bridge.

1. *Jumped out of.* Use "ē" with the Ablative after "prōsĭlĭŏ."
2. *Fearing.* Past Participle.

EXERCISE LXVI.

VOCABULARY.

art, subst.	ărs (ärtĭs), 3 f.	*funeral pile,* subst.	rŏgŭs, 2
ascend, verb	ăscĕndŏ, 3		
attendant, subst.	fămŭlŭs, 2	*increase,* verb	āugĕŏ, 2
call upon, verb	īnvŏcŏ, 1	*kindle,* verb	ăccĕndŏ, 3
consult, verb	cōnsŭlŏ, 3	*kingdom,* subst.	rĕgnum, 2
cultivate, verb	cŏlŏ, 3	*oracle,* subst.	ŏrācŭlum, 2
deceit, subst.	frāūs (frāūdĭs), 3 f.	*piety,* subst.	pĭĕtās (pĭĕtātĭs), 3 f.
empire, subst.	īmpĕrĭum, 2	*propitiate,* verb	plācŏ, 1
extinguish, verb	rĕstīnguŏ, 3	*wage,* verb	gĕrŏ, 3.

RULES 1–43. Especially 32, 34–37. Also pp. 124–128.

---

1. Let the laws be obeyed. 2. Crœsus was desirous of increasing his empire. 3. He sent messengers to consult the oracle. 4. He afterwards accused Apollo of deceit. 5. Having lost his kingdom, he ascended the funeral pile. 6. Thrice he called upon Solon, that illustrious philosopher. 7. Cyrus ordered his attendants to extinguish the fire. 8. No water was at hand to extinguish the fire. 9. Crœsus prayed the gods for help. 10. The fire which had been kindled at the king's orders was extinguished by the rain which the gods sent. 11. Let us all cultivate piety, the art of propitiating the gods. 12. War must be waged for ten years.

10. *At the king's orders.* Latin, "the king ordering."

EXERCISE LXVII.

VOCABULARY.

intend, verb	cōgĭtŏ, 1	*when,* conj.	quum.
intention, subst.	cōnsĭlĭum, 2		

RULES 1–43.   Dependent Sentences.

---

1. Tell me what is your name.   2. Persuade him to go.   3. When he saw him he rejoiced.   4. I wish to know whence you come.   5. Will you help me or not?
6. They told me whence they had come.   7. Who will be our general?   8. We ask who will be our general.
9. If you come I shall rejoice.   10. I say this, that you may know my intention.   11. I will tell you what I intend.   12. Go home to say I am coming.

5. *Or not?* (in direct questions) *ānnōn?* See "*or,*" 2.

EXERCISE LXVIII.

VOCABULARY.

knife, subst.   cŭltĕr (cŭltrĭ), 2   *whet-stone*, subst.   cŏs (cŏtĭs), 3 f.

RULES 1–43.   Dependent Sentences.

---

1. Bring a whet-stone to sharpen my knife. 2. Who will be our guide to the top of the hill? 3. I have told you who will be our guide. 4. When will the war be ended? 5. When the war was ended, the soldiers returned home. 6. Will you go or not? 7. Tell me whether you will go or not. 8. Who dined with Cæsar yesterday? 9. Do you know who dined with Cæsar yesterday? 10. Let us pray Jupiter for a king. 11. The frogs repented of having prayed for a king. 12. Tell me who was the king of the frogs.

11. *Of having prayed for.* Say, "that they had prayed for."

EXERCISE LXIX.

VOCABULARY.

at home, see "*at*" in Grammar		*perform*, verb	pĕrăgŏ, 3
elect, verb	crĕŏ, 1	*stop*, verb	mănĕŏ, 2
enquire, verb	quaērŏ, 3	*stretch out*, verb	pŏrrĭgŏ, 3
hard, adj.	dūrŭs	*tell lies*, verb	mēntĭŏr, 4
labour, subst.	lăbŏr, 3 m.	*though*, see Grammar.	

RULES 1–43.   Dependent Sentences.

---

1. *Though* I love you I punish you. 2. Spare your foe, Cæsar, that he may become your friend. 3. Enquire who has been elected consul. 4. I did not know that you were coming. 5. If I had known it I would have stopped at home. 6. He stretched out his hand to take the sword. 7. Hercules, *though* he was Jupiter's son, was forced to be his brother's slave. 8. Hercules *had* to perform hard labours. 9. Tell me how many were the labours of Hercules. 10. If you lo-e your brush, do not tell lies. 11. What good is a brush to me? 12. The fox asked what good his brush was to him.

8. *Had to perform.* See "*have*," 2.
10. *Brush.* "Caūdă."
11. *What good is a brush to me?* Say, "what does a brush profit ('prōsum') me?"
12. *What good his brush was to him.* Say, "what his brush profited ('prōsum') him."

EXERCISE LXX.

VOCABULARY.

Æneas, subst.	Āenĕās (Āenēaē), 1	*grieve*, verb	dŏlĕō, 2
clean, verb	pūrgō, 1	*ground*, subst.	sŏlum, 2
defeat, verb	vīncō, 3	*hoe*, subst.	sărcŭlum, 2
Dido, subst.	Dīdō (Acc. Dīdō), f.	*how large*, pron. adj. }	quāntŭs
forsake, verb	dēsĕrō, 3	*Metellus*, subst.	Mĕtĕllŭs, 2
		pyramid, subst.	pȳrămĭs (pȳrămĭdĭs), 3 f.

RULES 1–43. Dependent Sentences.

---

1. Do you know how large the pyramids are?
2. *Not even* Plato shall persuade me that this is true.
3. I wonder why the soldier is eager to gain glory?
4. I will tell you why Æneas forsook Dido. 5. *If* we conquer, the enemy shall be spared. 6. *If* I were to see you, you would grieve. 7. *If* Metellus had not come, Pompey would have been defeated. 8. Did the Spartans obey the laws of Lycurgus? 9. Who does not know what has happened? 10. Use your hoe if you wish to clean your ground. 11. Tell me how many books you have read. 12. The art of swimming is useful to a sailor.

3. *Eager to gain.* Say, "desirous ('cŭpĭdŭs') of gaining" (Gerund in "dī").

EXERCISE LXXI.

VOCABULARY.

all, see Grammar	*meet*, verb, use	ŏbvĭam
if, see Grammar	*robe*, subst.	tŏgă, 1
how, see Grammar	*senate*, subst.	sĕnātŭs, 4.

---

1. Who can say whence comes the wind?   2. I ought to know *how* to do this.   3. The fox persuaded the crow to sing.   4. *How often* have I told you *how* Cæsar died?   5. O crow, if you had not opened your mouth you would not have lost the cheese.   6. Say *whether* you will come *or not*.   7. Putting on his robe he went to meet the messenger of the Senate.   8. He asked the messenger *if* all was well.   9. I wish to know why you have come.   10. They could not tell how to escape.   11. Why you are here I know not.   12. When he had come, he heard that Cæsar had started.

2. *How.*   Use "quōmŏdŏ."
7. Rule 28.   *Went to meet.*   "Ŏbvĭam īvĭt" with Dative.
8. See "*if*," 6.
10. *They could not tell.*   Express by one word "nĕscĭŏ."   *How to escape.*   Say, "how they could ('pŏssum') escape."

EXERCISE LXXII.

VOCABULARY.

despatch, verb	mīttŏ, 3	*scarcity*, subst.	ĭnŏpĭă, 1
gladly, adv.	lĭbĕntĕr	*soon*, adv.	mŏx
murmur, verb	frĕmŏ, 3	*surrender*, verb	dĕdŏ, 3
prepare, verb	părŏ, 1	*wakeful (to be)*, verb	vĭgĭlŏ, 1.

---

1. If Caius is general, I abandon all hope of conquering the enemy. 2. If Cæsar is *going* to dine with you, I will gladly be present. 3. If they had known that help was at hand, they would not have surrendered the city. 4. Such was the scarcity of food, that the soldiers murmured. 5. *Before* you came, I had despatched my letter. 6. When Hercules had finished his labours, he became a god. 7. When the sun rose, Cæsar saw that the enemy had retired. 8. Unless you are wakeful, the town will be taken. 9. May the messenger soon come to tell me the truth. 10. It is hard to count how many stars are shining. 11. Unless you profit the state, you ought not to live. 12. If you wish for peace, prepare war.

1. *If Caius is general.* Use Abl. Abs., *Caius being general;* and see note at the end of " Conditional Sentences," p. 128.
5. *Before.* See "*before*," 5.

EXERCISE LXXIII.

VOCABULARY.

catch at, verb	cāptŏ, 1	*owl*, subst.	būbō (būbŏnĭs), 3 m.
fly, subst.	mŭscă, 1		
greedy, adj.	ăvīdŭs	*stay*, verb	mănĕŏ, 2.

---

1. The soldiers did not know what they *ought* to do. 2. Tell me what is to be done. 3. The fish was so greedy, that it caught at the fly. 4. Cæsar asked Pompey what he was *going* to do. 5. Do you understand what I say, or not? 6. The senators thought that a general *must* be sent to the army. 7. Did you see him or not? 8. Why does not the owl seek food by day? 9. How many *thousand* soldiers will the general command? 10. I know not how many thousand soldiers the general will command. 11. *Though* you bid me go, I will stay. 12. If you had been silent I would have departed.

8. *By day.* See "*by*," 3.

EXERCISE LXXIV.

VOCABULARY.

again and again	Ĭdentĭdem	*rumour*, subst.	rŭmŏr (rŭmōrĭs), 3 m.
careless, adj.	ĭncāutŭs		
lady, subst.	dŏmĭnă, 1	*strive*, verb	ēnītŏr, 3
overtake, verb	āssĕquŏr, 3 dep.	*succeed*, verb	vīncŏ, 3.

---

1. The knight uses his spurs *to* overtake his enemy.
2. To please his lady he performed duties unworthy of a knight. 3. Though I cannot see you, I hear your voice. 4. If the child had not been burnt, he would have been more careless. 5. I wish to know *whether* I *must* go. 6. I do not understand what I am to do. 7. *While* they were talking together, Cæsar came. 8. *Though* you spoke again and again, I have forgotten your words. 9. *May* I perish if I do not love you. 10. Whence this rumour arose I know not. 11. Strive *till* you succeed. 12. They fought *till* night came.

6. *Am to do = ought to do.* See "*ought.*"
9. *If I do not love you.* Say, "unless I love you."

EXERCISE LXXV.

VOCABULARY.

break up, verb	dīscēdŏ, 3	*how many times*, adv. }	quŏtĭĕs
by, see Grammar		*place at*, verb	āppŏnŏ, 3
complain, verb	quĕrŏr, 3	*procure*, verb	cŏmpărŏ, 1
council, subst.	cŏnsĭlĭum, 2	*resolve*, verb	stătŭŏ, 3
doors	fŏrĕs (fŏrum), 3 f.	*scarce*, adj.	rārŭs
dwell, verb	hăbĭtŏ, 1	*senate-house*, subst. }	cūrĭă, 1
Epaminondas	Ĕpămĭnŏndăs (ae), 1 m.	*sit down*, verb	cŏnsīdŏ, 3
hold, verb	hăbĕŏ, 2	*tablet*, subst.	tăbĕllă, 1.

---

1. How many times have I warned you *not to* fight?
2. *Had you come*, I should have rejoiced. 3. Epaminondas when dying said that peace *must* be made.
4. If you say this, you are mistaken. 5. Bring me my tablets, that I may write a letter. 6. While I am writing, you *must* be silent. 7. Having entered the senate house, he placed guards at the doors. 8. When he sat down the ambassadors withdrew. 9. A council being held, they resolved to fight. 10. Those who dwell by the sea complain that fish are scarce. 11. We must procure food for the great city. 12. If the harvest is good, the farmer rejoices.

3. *When dying.* Future Participle.
7. *He placed guards at the doors.* Rule 13.

EXERCISE LXXVI.

VOCABULARY.

bring, verb	ăffĕrŏ, 3 irr.	*fit for*, adj.	ăptŭs
Cimbri, subst.	Cĭmbrī, 2 pl.	*men*, subst.	fămŭlī, 2 pl.
cloud, subst.	nūbĕs (nūbĭs), 3 f.	*set*, verb	cădŏ, 3
		show, verb	ĭndĭcō, 1
contractor, subst.	rĕdēmptŏr (rĕdēmptŏrĭs), 3 m.	*South-wind*, subst.	} Auster (Austrī), 2
		sport, subst.	lūdŭs, 2.

1. In vain did we ask the king *to* spare our city.
2. When Cæsar *comes*, all will be well. 3. If Marius
had not been made consul, the Cimbri would have
entered Italy. 4. *Do not* cross the Rubicon, Cæsar,
unless you wish to make war on your country. 5. I
hope you will come to tell me everything. 6. If you
are away, I shall not know what to do. 7. The con-
tractor sent his men to build a bridge. 8. When the
cat is away, the mice play. 9. South wind and clouds
show a day fit for hunting. 10. If you wish, I can help
you. 11. *While* the battle was being fought, the sun
set. 12. That which is sport to you brings death to me.

2. *Comes.* Say, " shall come " *or* " shall have come."
4. *To make war on your country.* Rule 13.
6. *Are.* Say, " shall be."
9. *For hunting.* " Ăd " with the Gerund in " dum."

EXERCISE LXXVII.

VOCABULARY.

Ætna, subst.	Aetnă, 1	*learn*, verb	cŏgnŏscŏ, 3
Cincinnatus, subst.	} Cīncīnnătŭs, 2	*nearer*, comp. adj.	} prŏpĭŏr
cold, subst.	frīgŭs (frīgŏrĭs), 3 n.	*plain*, subst.	cămpŭs, 2
		plan, subst.	cōnsĭlĭum, 2
desire, verb	cŭpĭŏ, 3	*plough*, subst.	ărŏ, 1
duck, subst.	ănăs (ănătĭs), 3 f.	*send forth*	ēmīttŏ, 3
		smoke, subst.	fūmŭs, 2
field, subst.	ărvum, 2	*swan*, subst.	cўgnŭs, 2
flame, subst.	flămmă, 1	*then*, conj.	ĭgĭtŭr.

1. *Before* Cæsar died, the republic had fallen. 2. Did those who killed Cæsar repent of their deed? 3. Cincinnatus desires to return home to plough his field. 4. Do you believe that the ugly duck became a swan? 5. *Why* do you not tell me what you are *going* to do? 6. Do you know why Ætna sends forth smoke and flame? 7. It is certain that mountains are nearer to the sun than plains. 8. Why then do we complain of cold on the top of the mountain? 9. The apple, by falling, taught the philosopher many things. 10. Having learnt the plans of the Gauls, Cæsar set out *by* night. 11. I hope that the Gauls will be conquered. 12. I fear *that* the city will be taken.

EXERCISE LXXVIII.

VOCABULARY.

bold, adj.	aūdāx	*lingerer,* subst.	cūnctătŏr (cūnc-tātŏrĭs), 3 m.
delay, verb	cŭnctŏr, 1	*Mercury,* subst.	Mĕrcŭrĭŭs, 2
Eurystheus, subst.	Eurӯstheūs (Eurӯsthĕī), 2 m.	*Phœbus,* subst.	Phœbŭs, 2
Fabius, subst.	Făbĭŭs, 2	*rush upon* (= *make a rush*)	īmpĕtum făcĭŏ
imbibe, verb	bĭbŏ, 3	*store,* verb	cŏndŏ, 3
invent, verb	rĕpĕrĭŏ, 4	*strong,* adj.	rŏbūstŭs.
language, subst.	līnguă, 1		

1. Do you think that summer is more pleasant than winter? 2. Bolder than a lion, he rushed upon his foes. 3. Hercules, by the order of Juno, became the slave of Eurystheus. 4. The slave was *much* stronger than the master. 5. Mercury is said to have invented the lyre which he gave to Phœbus. 6. Phœbus accused Mercury of theft. 7. A Roman stored wine in the top of his house, that it might imbibe smoke? 8. Fabius by delaying profited his country. 9. Can you tell me why Fabius was called the lingerer? 10. *Until* you return, I will read my book. 11. I must go to Gaul to learn the language. 12. It cannot be doubted *that* Cæsar was more fortunate than Pompey.

EXERCISE LXXIX.

VOCABULARY.

ally, subst.	sŏcĭŭs, 2	*gate*, subst.	pŏrtă, 1
as well as, see Grammar		*happen*, verb	ēvĕnĭŏ, 4
conclude	cōnfĭcĭŏ, 3	*prevent*, verb	īmpĕdĭŏ, 4
Fabricius, subst.	Făbrĭcĭŭs, 2	*stronger*, comp. adj.	mājŏr
franchise, subst.	cīvĭtās (cīvĭtātĭs), 3 f.	*summon*, verb	ărcēssŏ, 3.

1. *Had* not the gates been opened by a traitor, the city would not have been taken. 2. Do you remember what cities were taken by Hannibal? 3. Philosophers love play *as well as* work. 4. Cicero's brother served many campaigns under Cæsar in Gaul. 5. Those who read much become more learned. 6. When will you tell me why you summoned me? 7. If you are diligent, you will deserve praise. 8. We believe that a mouse once helped a lion. 9. The hope of glory is stronger than the fear of death. 10. Fabricius showed that he could not be frightened by an elephant. 11. Who knows what will happen to-morrow? 12. If you cannot help me, I know not what to do.

EXERCISE LXXX.

VOCABULARY.

answer, verb	rēspŏndĕō, 2	*Naples*, subst.	Nĕăpŏlĭs (Nĕăpŏlĭs), 3 f.
ask questions	pĕrcŏntŏr, 1	*pass*, verb	ăbĕō, 4
barbarian, subst.	bărbărŭs, 2	*Pericles*, subst.	Pĕrĭclēs (Pĕrĭclĭs), 3 m.
be distant (*from*)	ăbsum, irr.	*prevent*, verb	prŏhĭbĕō, 2
blow, verb	flō, 1	*questioner*, subst.	pĕrcŏntătŏr (pĕrcŏntătŏrĭs), 3 m.
foolish, adj.	stŭltŭs		
form (*a plan*)	ĭnĕō, 4	*scourge*, verb	vĕrbĕrō, 1
Hellespont, subst.	Hĕllēspŏntŭs, 2 m.	*soften*, verb	mŏllĭō, 4
hungry (*to be*), verb	ēsŭrĭō, 4	*tell*, *order*	jŭbĕō, 2
		vinegar, subst.	ăcētum, 2.

1. *While* I was waiting for you, a whole hour passed. 2. If the fish will not leap, we had better go home. 3. When the East wind blows, some say that fish are not hungry. 4. *As* the sun is shining, let us go out to kill birds. 5. Do you remember how many miles Rome is from Naples? 6. It is easier to ask many questions than to answer the questioner. 7. What did Pericles say when he was dying? 8. The barbarians tried to prevent Hannibal from crossing the Alps. 9. Hannibal is said to have formed the plan of softening rocks with vinegar. 10. Xerxes was so foolish that he scourged the sea. 11. Having made a bridge of boats he crossed the Hellespont. 12. He told his slaves to prevent him *from* forgetting the Athenians.

2. *We had better go home.* Say, "it is better ('praēstăt') to go home."

5. *From.* Use "ăb."

.EXERCISE LXXXI.

.VOCABULARY.

April, use adj.	Aprīlĭs	*schoolmaster*, subst.	lūdī (gen.) mǎgīstĕr, 2
beg, verb	ŏrŏ	*surrender*, verb, use	mĕ dĕdŏ, 3
contented, adj.	cŏntĕntŭs	*threaten*, verb	mĭnŏr, 1 dep.
first, see Grammar		*vigorously (more)*, comp. adv.	ūbĕrĭŭs.
heather, subst.	ĕrīcă, 1		
if only, see Grammar			
nothing, subst.	nĭhĭl, indecl.		

---

1. Cæsar asked Casca what he had come *to* beg.
2. I will do all I can to prevent you. 3. Who has not been made a fool on the first of April? 4. If the laws are obeyed, the state flourishes. 5. It cannot be doubted *that* those who killed Cæsar made a mistake. 6. *If only* I become worthy of praise, I shall be contented. 7. *While* the city was burning, Æneas escaped. 8. Let us burn the heather, that it may grow more vigorously. 9. I can remember my books *as well as* you. 10. We pity him who complains that he has nothing *to* do. 11. Tell me what was the name of the tyrant who became a schoolmaster. 12. He threatened the citizens with death, unless they surrendered.

7, 8. Notice the two meanings of the English word *burn*.
12. *Unless they surrendered.* Use Imperfect Subjunctive.

EXERCISE LXXXII.

VOCABULARY.

bronze, adj.	āĕrĕŭs	*pity,* verb	mĭsĕrĕŏr, 2
daily, adv.	īndĭēs	*possess,* verb	hăbĕō, 2
get, verb	pŏtĭŏr, 4	*ready,* adj.	părātŭs
lamp, subst.	lŭcĕrnă, 1	*severely,* adv.	grăvĭtĕr
lift, verb	tŏllŏ, 3 irr.	*thorny,* adj.	spīnōsŭs.

---

1. *Before* the holidays come, I shall have finished this book. 2. The wealth of the man who possessed the lamp increased daily. 3. *When* he had lost the lamp, he became *as* poor *as* he was before. 4. I wish I had a lamp, to increase my wealth. 5. How often men are envied whom we should rather pity ! 6. When he had got his wealth, he did not know how to use it. 7. If I had seen you throwing stones, I should have punished you severely. 8. Some trees are *so* thorny *that* monkeys cannot climb them. 9. I doubt *whether* I have enough strength to lift that stone. 10. Cæsar was killed on the 13th of March. 11. Unless you are ready to fight you *had better* make peace. 12. Let us dig *till* we find a bronze statue.

2, 4. Notice the two meanings of the word *increase.*
4. *I wish that* = *would that.* See " *would,*" 6.
6. *When he had got.* May be rendered by Participle.

EXERCISE LXXXIII.

VOCABULARY.

advice, subst.	cōnsĭlĭum, 2	*mean,* verb	sĭgnĭfĭcŏ, 1
alike, adv., use	ĭdem	*nearly,* adv.	prŏpĕ
destroy, verb	dēlĕŏ, 2	*opinion,* subst.	sĕntĕntĭă, 1
exhausted, part.	cōnfēctŭs	*picture,* subst. (phr.)	tăbŭlă pīctă
famine, subst.	fămēs (fămĭs), 3 f.	*stop (prevent),* verb	prŏhĭbĕō, 2
		stop (cease), verb	dēsĭnŏ, 3
foot (of a mountain)	rādīcēs (rādĭcum), 3 pl. f.	*talent,* subst.	tălēntum, 2
		therefore, see Grammar.	

1. Nearly exhausted with famine, the citizens prayed the victor for peace. 2. He set out for Italy, and came to the foot of the Alps. 3. *If* Hannibal had *not* crossed the Alps, the battle *of* Trebia would not have been fought. 4. After the battle of Cannæ, the advice of Fabius was followed by the Romans. 5. Cato being asked his opinion, said that Carthage must be destroyed. 6. *The* more you ask me for the book, *the* less I am willing to give it you. 7. I would not sell my liberty for ten thousand talents. 8. He said that he had bought the picture for a great price. 9. They praised the general *for* saving the state. 10. The rain stopped me from going out. 11. Before it was time to go out, the rain stopped. 12. Words which sound alike do not *therefore* mean the same.

2. *He set out for Italy and came.* Say, "having set out for Italy, he came."
3. You may say here, "the battle would not have been fought at ('ăpŭd') the river Trebia."

EXERCISE LXXXIV.

VOCABULARY.

curtain, subst.	vēlum, 2	*grass*, subst.	hĕrbă, 1
drop, verb (neut.)	stīllŏ, 1	*reply*, verb	rēspŏndĕŏ, 2
drop, verb (act.)	prōjĭcĭŏ, 3	*run away*, verb	fŭgĭŏ, 3
early, adv.	mātūrē	*shield*, subst.	scūtum, 2
easy, adj.	făcĭlĭs	*withdraw* (*a curtain*)	} rĕdūcŏ, 3.

1. When the sun had set, the dew dropped upon the grass. 2. He dropped his sword and shield and ran away. 3. Why do you not use your wealth in helping the poor? 4. *To* catch the worm the bird *must* rise early. 5. Let us *have* a bridge built *so as to* cross the river. 6. You are not worthy *of* being praised. 7. The ambassadors *having* said why they had come, withdrew. 8. That he might see the picture, he bade the painter withdraw the curtain. 9. The painter replied that the curtain was the picture. 10. It is easier to deceive a bird than a man. 11. By dancing, young man, you have lost your bride. 12. The young man replied that he did not care for losing her.

2. The second *and* in this sentence should be got rid of. See " *and*," 3.
6. *Worthy of being praised.* See " *of*," 5.
10. *Than.* Use " quam."
12. *Said that he did care for losing her.* Say, " denied that it repented him that ('quŏd') he had lost (Pluperfect Subjunctive) her."

EXERCISE LXXXV.

VOCABULARY.

join (battle)	cōmmīttŏ, 3	*sesterce*, subst.	sĕstĕrtĭŭs, 2
older, comp. adj.	nātū mājŏr	*take (advice)*,	sĕquŏr, 3 dep.
put aside	dēpōnō, 3	verb	

1. One cannot say *which of the two* generals is the greater. 2. *At* Rome I met Caius: he told me *that* he had bought a horse *for* two *thousand* sesterces. 3. *Unless* we would betray our country, we *must* resist the enemy. 4. It cannot be denied *that* Rome produced great men. 5. We *ought* not to put aside the book *till* we thoroughly understand it. 6. It is *possible* to travel *much without* seeing much. 7. He said that if he had known it, he would have come to Rome. 8. When will you be persuaded to take my advice? 9. *Without* waiting for the allies, he advanced to join battle with the enemy. 10. Although you are older than I, it does not follow that you are wiser. 11. Buying books will not make you wise unless you read them. 12. I never met a man more worthy *of* being praised by all.

1. *Which of the two.* See "*who*," 2.
3. *Would = are willing.*
8. Rule 32.
10. *That.* "Ŭt" with Subjunctive.
11. *Buying.* Infinitive.

EXERCISE LXXXVI.

VOCABULARY.

afraid (*to be*)	věrĕŏr, 2 dep.	*punishment,* subst.	pōēnă, 1
catch, verb	ĕxcĭpĭŏ, 3		
cautious, adj.	caūtŭs	*quarry,* subst.	lătŭmīaē, 1 pl.
for fear (= *lest*)	nĕ	*take care*	cūrō, 1
listen, verb	aūdĭŏ, 4		(or *căvĕō,* 2)
point out, verb	ĭndĭcŏ, 1	*weather,* subst.	tĕmpĕstăs, 3.

---

1. Take care you tell me the truth. 2. *Do* try to avoid the fault which I have so often pointed out. 3. Take care not to drop that cup, for fear you should break it. 4. *Though* I threatened him with punishment he became more careless. 5. *The* more he spoke, *the* less I listened. 6. *All* the wisest men think that war is the greatest of evils. 7. The lady was afraid *lest* she should fall from the ladder. 8. The young man promised to catch her *if* she fell. 9. *I wish* I knew what will be the weather to-morrow. 10. *At* Syracuse there are quarries which the citizens used *for* prisons. 11. The general was *too* cautious *to be* led into an ambush. 12. Up to the middle of the night, I hoped you were coming.

2. *Do try* = *be sure you try.* See "*făcĭō,*" note.
9. *Will be.* Say, "is about to be." Notice that the statement is indirect.

EXERCISE LXXXVII.

VOCABULARY.

amuse, verb	dēlēctŏ, 1	*human*, adj.	hūmānŭs
basket, subst.	cŏrbĭs (cŏrbĭs), 3 f.	*meat*, subst.	cărŏ (cărnĭs), 3 f.
changeable, adj.	mūtăbĭlĭs	*moderation*, sub.	tĕmpĕrāntĭă, 1
confident, adj. (phr.)	fīdēī plēnŭs	*obstinate*, adj.	ŏbstĭnātŭs
		pity, subst.	mĭsĕrĭcŏrdĭă, 1
decide, verb	stătŭŏ, 1	*race*, subst.	gĕnŭs (gĕnĕrĭs), 3 n.
eat, verb	vēscŏr, 3		
empty, adj.	ĭnānĭs	*retreat*, verb	rĕcēdŏ, 3
flee, verb	fŭgĭŏ, 3	*young*, use	tĕnĕrā aetătĕ
have leisure, verb	văcŏ, 1		(*of tender age*).

---

1. *There* are *some* who doubt *whether* it is right to eat meat. 2. Others deny that wine is useful to the human race. 3. The philosopher thinks that all things are good, *if only* there be moderation. 4. The poet says that women are more changeable than the wind. 5. Some donkeys are *so* obstinate *that* they cannot be taught. 6. We have more leisure to read books which amuse us than those which teach us. 7. I know not *whether* the idle *or* those who teach them are more worthy of pity. 8. The poet said that those whom the gods love die young. 9. *Though* the lake is full of fish, the fisherman's basket comes home empty. 10. He was *so* cowardly *as to* flee. 11. *As* this was so, the general decided that he *must* retreat. 12. *After* the battle, the soldiers were not *as* confident *as* they had been.

1. Use "sŭnt quī" with Subjunctive. See "*some*." *Right* (= *lawful*), " Fās," indecl.
6. *More.* Use "măgĭs" (adverb). *Than.* Use "quam."
11. *As this was so.* See "*as*," 5.

EXERCISE LXXXVIII.

VOCABULARY.

brush, subst. (*of a painter*)	pĕnĭcĭllŭs, 2	*play*, verb	ăgŏ, 3
		preferable, adj.	pŏtĭŏr
fetch water	ăquŏr, 1 dep.	*rest of*, use adj.	rĕlĭquŭs (*remaining*)
fruit, subst.	pŏmă, 2 pl.		
go up (i.e. *climb*)	ăscĕndŏ, 3	*ripen*, verb	mātūrĕscŏ, 3
limit, phr.	mŏdum ădhĭbĕŏ	*sign*, subst.	sīgnum, 2
		spend (*of time*)	dĕgŏ, 3
measure	mētĭŏr, 4 dep.	*stoop*, verb, use	mĕ dēmĭttŏ
noise, subst.	strĕpĭtŭs, 4	*water* (*to fetch water*)	ăquŏr, 1 dep.
old, adj.	vĕtŭstŭs		
part, subst.	pārtēs (pār-tĭum), 3 pl.	*wax*, subst.	cēră, 1
		wheel, subst.	rŏtă, 1.
pick up, verb	tŏllŏ, 3		

---

1. The boy and girl went up the hill *to* fetch water.
2. *If* we do not know the language, we *must* use signs.
3. *Unless* the sun shines, the fruit will not ripen. 4. It is sometimes colder on May 1st than on December 13th.
5. The song of birds is, in my opinion, preferable to the noise of wheels. 6. Having lived at Rome for eighteen years, he spent the rest of his life in the country.
7. That which you do not need is always bought at a high price. 8. The king measured the hours by burning wax. 9. Athenian orators used water *to* limit their speeches. 10. The water, by dropping, showed how much time had passed. 11. In old houses rats often play the part of ghosts. 12. The king stooped *to* pick up the painter's brush.

5. *In my opinion.* Say, "I being judge." *Preferable to.* Say, "more desirable ('pŏtĭŏr') than."

EXERCISE LXXXIX.

VOCABULARY.

beach, subst.	līttŭs (līttŏrĭs), 3 n.	*rise (of the tide)*	ăccēdŏ, 3
bells, subst.	āĕră, 3 pl.	*soap*, subst.	sāpŏ (sāpŏnĭs), 3 m.
brick, subst.	lătĕr (lătĕrĭs), 3 m.	*still*, adv.	nĭhĭlŏmĭnŭs
deem, verb	hăbĕŏ, 2	*straw*, subst.	strāmĕn (strămĭnĭs), 3 n.
dirty, adj.	īmmŭndŭs	*take away*, verb	ădĭmŏ, 3
fail, phr.	mălĕ rĕm gĕrŏ	*tide*, subst.	āestŭs, 4 m.
foreigners, subst.	bărbări, 2 pl.	*turn back*, verb	rĕvĕrtŏr 3 dep.
give away,	lārgĭŏr, 4	*valley*, subst.	văllĭs (văllĭs), 3 f.
leave, verb	ăbĕŏ, 4 irr.		
perfect, subst.	prāefĕctŭs, 2	*walk*, verb	ămbŭlŏ, 1
rightly, adv. use	jūrĕ	*warmth*, subst.	călŏr (călŏrĭs), 3 m.
ring, verb	sŏnŏ, 1		

---

1. Foreigners say *that only* dogs and Englishmen love to walk in the sun. 2. Do you not think that those who walk in the sun are wise? 3. Those who fail *must* try *till* they succeed. 4. It is useless to demand bricks of him to whom you give no straw. 5. *As* the tide is rising, we *must* leave the beach. 6. *Though* the hills are covered with snow, warmth *may* be found in the valley. 7. Some who use soap and water are still dirty. 8. The boy turned back *when* he heard the bells ring. 9. Not all boys who hear bells ring become prefects of the city. 10. He who gives away his wealth is rightly to be deemed rich. 11. Let us value a beautiful mind more highly than a beautiful body. 12. *Though* his crown is taken away he is still a king.

11. *More highly.* Say, "at a greater price." " Plūrĭs," understanding " prĕtĭī." *Than.* Use "quam."

EXERCISE XC.

VOCABULARY.

blood	săngŭĭs (săn-guĭnĭs), 3 m.	*hastiness,* subst.	tĕmĕrĭtās (tĕmĕrĭtātĭs), 3 f.
callers	sălūtāntĕs, 3 pl.		
cuckoo, subst.	cŭcŭlŭs, 2	*needle,* subst.	ăcŭs, 4 f.
defend, verb	tŭĕŏr, 2 dep.	*right,* subst.	făs, n. indecl.
emperor, subst.	īmpĕrātŏr (īm-pĕrātŏrĭs), 3 m.	*safe,* adj.	īncŏlŭmĭs
		sorely, adv.	văldĕ
ground (on the ground)	hŭmī, used as adverb	*stain,* verb	ăspērgŏ, 3
		trunk, subst.	mănŭs, 4 f.
		unweave, verb	rĕtĕxŏ, 3
		worthless, adj.	vīlĭs.

---

1. The hound, *having* slain the wolf, went to meet his master. 2. Seeing the hound stained with blood, the prince thought his son was slain. 3. He drew his sword *and* slew the hound *for* killing his son. 4. Then entering the house, he saw that the boy was safe. 5. On the ground lay a huge wolf whom the hound had slain *while* defending the child. 6. When he understood the state of the case, the prince repented sorely of his hastiness. 7. Do you believe that an elephant can pick up a needle with his trunk? 8. The emperor's fate teaches us how worthless is glory. 9. Few *of* those who read books know what is the labour of writing them. 10. Is it right to *say* that you are *not* at home to avoid callers? 11. I am ashamed of the cuckoo, *for* laying her eggs in another's nest. 12. The queen unwove by night *as* much as she had woven by day.

2. *Seeing.* Say, " when he saw."
3. Get rid of *and. For killing.* See "*for,*" 4, note.
4. *Entering.* Use the Past Participle of a Deponent Verb.
6. *The state of the case.* Say, " how the matter stood." *Stood* is here rendered by " mĕ hăbĕŏ."
11. *For laying.* See "*for,*" 4, note.

EXERCISE XCI.

VOCABULARY.

alive (*to be*)	vīvŏ, 3	*firm*, adj.	fīrmŭs
beam, subst.	trăbs (trăbĭs), 3 f.	*hinder*, verb	prŏhĭbĕō, 2
		larger, comp. adj.	mājŏr
beggar, subst.	mĕndīcŭs, 2	*many times*, phr.	mūltīs părtĭbŭs
condemn to death, phr.	căpĭtĭs dămnō, 1	*oaken*, adj.	quĕrnŭs
Cleon, subst.	Clĕŏn (Clĕŏnĭs), 3 m.	*question* (*it is a question*)	quaerĭtŭr
cottage	căsă, 1 f.	*seven*, num. adj.	sĕptem, indecl.
farthing, subst.	ās (ăssĭs), 3 m.	*show*, verb	ŏstĕndō, 3.

.1. *Such* was the scarcity of wine, *that* all the richest citizens were compelled to drink water. 2. *Though* he was weary of his chains, he was not ashamed of his crime. 3. It is a question whether the owl was born before the egg or the egg before the owl. 4. *Being* asked to depart, he *would* not. 5. Do not hinder me from giving the beggar a farthing. 6. Have we any reason for thinking ourselves wiser than our fathers? 7. Tyrants never hesitate to prefer their own interest to that of the state. 8. *At* Rome there are seven hills, *at* Thebes seven gates. 9. The king's palace is many times larger than the farmer's cottage. 10. Alcibiades, *when* condemned to death in his absence, said he would show his countrymen he was alive. 11. That your house may be firm, use oaken beams. 12. Let us hope that, *since* Cleon is dead, the war will be ended.

6. *Any reason for thinking.* Say, "any reason why ('cūr') we should think."

7. *To prefer their own interest to that of the state.* Say, "to take counsel for themselves rather than ('pŏtĭŭs quam') for the state." Use "cōnsŭlō."

EXERCISE XCII.

VOCABULARY.

ape, subst.	sīmĭă, 1	*mention*, verb	cŏmmĕmŏrŏ, 1
call upon, verb	ŏrŏ, 1	*pay*, verb	sŏlvŏ, 3
chieftain, subst.	dŭx (dŭcĭs), 3 m.	*politics*, subst.	rēspūblĭcă (rēĭpūblĭcāe), 5 & 1 f.
common, adj. (*of a soldier*)	grĕgārĭŭs	*preside over*, verb	prāesum, irr.
confess, verb	cŏnfĭtĕŏr, 2 dep.	*retire*, verb	dīscĕdŏ, 3
enemy, subst.	ĭnĭmīcŭs, 2	*shame*, subst.	pŭdŏr (pŭdōrĭs), 3 m.
forget, verb	ŏblīvīscŏr, 3 dep.	*smith*, subst.	făbĕr (făbrī), 2
		two days, subst.	bĭdŭum, 2
lack, verb	ĕgĕŏ, 2	*weak*, adj.	īnfīrmŭs.

---

1. I promise to pay you two *thousand* sesterces.
2. I will never believe that the human race arose from apes.
3. The dart hits the general *as* well as the common soldier.
4. Themistocles wished to be taught the art of forgetting.
5. Is the art of writing mentioned *in* Homer?
6. Augustus used to call upon Varus *to* restore him his legions.
7. *Not even* shame could prevent the chieftain *from* running away.
8. The smith said *that* he fought for himself, not for the others.
9. The old man confessed that he was *too* weak to preside over the state.
10. His enemies asked why he had not retired from politics.
11. He who has *enough money* never lacks friends.
12. If you were to come to visit me, I should rejoice.

EXERCISE XCIII.

VOCABULARY.

blind, adj.	cāecŭs	*prove,* verb	prŏbŏ, 1
bowl, subst.	crātĕr (crātĕrĭs), 3 m.	*ray,* subst.	rădĭŭs, 2
		silence, subst.	sĭlĕntĭum, 2
finger, subst.	dĭgĭtŭs, 2	*snail,* subst.	cŏchlĕă, 1 f.
keep off, verb	ārcĕŏ, 2	*twenty-two,* see Grammar, p. 92
large, adj.	māgnŭs	*use,* verb	ădhĭbĕŏ, 2
mix, verb	mīscĕŏ, 2	*value,* verb	āestĭmŏ, 1
move, verb	see note	*without my permission,*	īnjūssū mĕŏ.
pig, subst.	pŏrcŭs, 2		

---

1. Blind men learn to read by using their fingers.
2. The pig was *too* fat to move. 3. The philosopher, *having* said that silence was golden, ought to have proved it by not speaking. 4. Diogenes complained that the king kept off the sun's rays from him. 5. If I were not Alexander, I *would* be Diogenes. 6. The Romans used large bowls, in which to mix water and wine. 7. The hope of enjoying repose after labour makes us work diligently. 8. He prayed to Venus *that* the statue he had made might receive life. 9. The snail will have climbed up the wall in twenty-two days. 10. The boy must say *why* he went out without my permission. 11. The general sent two tribunes with *ten men apiece to* reconnoitre the wood. 12. The poet asked what was the value of a name.

    2. *Move.* "Mŏvĕŏ" is always transitive. *Move* is here neuter, and must therefore be rendered by "mē mŏvĕŏ."

    3. *Not speaking.* Express by one word "sĭlĕŏ."

    5. *If I were not.* Say, "unless I were."

    6. *In which to mix.* Say, "in which they might mix."

    12. *What was the value of a name.* Say, "at how great a price a name was to be valued." Use "quāntī" and the Gerundive.

EXERCISE XCIV.

VOCABULARY.

age, subst.	sāecŭlum, 2	*protect*, verb	tŭĕŏr, dep.
birthday, subst. (phr.)	dĭēs nătālĭs	*red*, adj.	rŭbĕr (-bră-brum).
cruel, adj.	crūdēlĭs	*virtue*, subst.	vīrtŭs (vīrtū-tĭs), 3 f.
desirable, adj.	ŏptăbĭlĭs		
keep, verb	cĕlĕbrŏ, 1	*Zeno*, subst.	Zēnō (Zēnō-nĭs), 3 m.
less, comp. adj.	mĭnŏr		

---

1. Many enemies were spared by the English.
2. Harbours, by which ships are protected, *must* be protected themselves.   3. If Marius had been less cruel, he would have been more worthy of being praised.   4. *It cannot be denied that* fools are often favoured by fortune.   5. *Though* pleasure is desirable, it must not be sought *at* the cost of virtue.   6. The Republic keeps its birthday on the 4th of July.   7. The sea cannot be prevented *from* covering the land. 8. Who can tell *whether* Zeno *or* Epicurus is the wiser? 9. There are some who have such eyes that they think grass red.   10. Though the sun has shone *for* many ages, its heat has not become less.   11. The sun is nearer to the earth in winter than in summer.   12. Do you know why summer is hotter than winter?

2. *Must.* Render by Gerundive.   Rule 37.
3. *Of being praised.* See "*of*," 5.
6. *On the 4th July.* See Grammar, pp. 94, 95.

EXERCISE XCV.

VOCABULARY.

bind, verb	dēlĭgō, 1	*go round*, verb	fĕrŏr, irr. dep.
break one's word, phr.	fĭdem fāllō, 3	*heir*, subst.	hērēs (hērēdĭs), 3 m.
burn, verb	cŏmbŭrō, 3	*hesitate*, verb	dŭbĭtō, 1
charm, verb	mūlcĕŏ, 2	*ignorant of (to be)*, verb	ignōrō, 1
circle, subst.	gȳrŭs, 2		
coolness, subst.	frĭgŭs (frĭgŏrĭs), 3 n.	*nightingale*, s.	lūscĭnĭă, 1
disaster, subst.	clādēs (clādĭs), 3 f.	*put in prison*, phr.	ĭn vīncŭlă cŏnjĭcĭō, 3
doubt, verb	dŭbĭtō, 1	*reign*, verb	rēgnō, 1
ear, subst.	aurĭs (aurĭs), 3 f.	*stake*, subst.	pălŭs, 2
fortify, verb	mūnĭō, 4	*sup off*, v., use	vēscŏr (I eat)
garments, sub.	vēstēs (vēstĭum), 3 pl. f.	*tail*, subst.	caudă, 1
		woollen, adj.	lānĕŭs
give, verb	praebĕŏ, 2	*word = promise*, sub.	fĭdēs (fĭdĕī), 3 f.

1. Brutus condemned his own sons to death *for* being traitors to their country. 2. Do not hesitate to ask questions when you are in doubt what to write. 3. *The* more the peacock's tail pleases the eye, *the* less his voice charms the ear. 4. The philosopher was imprisoned *for* saying that the earth went in a circle round the sun. 5. Cæsar, *being ignorant of* the plans of the Gauls, fortified his camp. 6. He did not know the extent of the disaster *till* he returned home. 7. It is agreed *that* woollen garments give coolness in summer and warmth in winter. 8. *If only* I were heir to half your property, I should be a rich man. 9. The youth said that he would rather die than break his word. 10. To show your opponents that they are wrong, do not bind them to stakes and burn them. 11. That you may be made king, show yourself worthy of reigning. 12. Who is not ashamed of the emperor who supped off nightingales' tongues?

2. *To write.* See "to," 7; or say, *what you ought to write.*
5. *Being ignorant of.* Say, "since ('quum') he was ignorant of."
6. *The extent of the disaster.* Say, "how great the disaster was."
8. *Heir to half your property.* See Grammar, p. 95.
10. It is better to get rid of *and.*
12. *Supped*, i.e. *was in the habit of supping.* Therefore use the Imperfect.

EXERCISE XCVI.

VOCABULARY.

admit, verb	cōnfĭtĕŏr, 2 dep.	*liking (to my)*	see note 4
basket, subst.	cănĭstră, 2 pl.	*net*, subst.	rētĕ (rētĭs), 3 n.
Capua, subst.	Căpŭă, 1	*resting on*, part. adj.	fŭltŭs
column, subst.	cŏlŭmnă, 1		
cover, verb	ŏbdūcō, 3	*rule*, verb	ĭmpĕrō, 1
crowd, subst.	tŭrbă, 1	*same*, pron.	īdem, ĕădem, ĭdem
entrance, sub.	ădĭtŭs, 4		
expose, verb	ŏbjĭcĭō, 3	*stone*, adj.	lăpĭdĕŭs
fully armed, part. adj.	ārmātŭs	*to-day*, adv.	hŏdĭĕ
		trident, subst.	trĭdēns (trĭdĕn-tĭs), 3 m.
inferior, comp. adj.	mĭnŏr	*Tusculum*, sub.	Tŭscŭlum, 2
iron, subst.	fĕrrum, 2	*wonder*, verb	mīrŏr, 1 dep.
like, adj.	see note 4		

1. *All* the best orators *would* admit that they are inferior to Cicero. 2. Neither at Tusculum, Capua, Naples, or Syracuse, could I find a house to my liking. 3. Are we wiser than our ancestors in clothing our ships with iron? 4. *Would* that I knew how to write Latin like Cicero. 5. *At* the entrance of the temple were columns resting on stone lions. 6. We must *either* conquer *or* die. 7. He used a trident and net *to* defend himself *against* a man fully armed. 8. It is hard to believe that men were *so* cruel *as to* expose maidens to wild beasts. 9. Bearing the basket on her head, the maiden entered the temple followed by the crowd. 10. There are some kings who reign *without* ruling their subjects. 11. You are not the *same* to-day *as* you were yesterday. 12. Do you wonder that Sisyphus is tired of rolling the stone?

1. *Inferior to.* Latin, *less than.* See " *than.*"
2. Say, " Neither at Tusculum, nor at Capua, nor at Naples, nor at Syracuse." *To my liking.* " Ex sēntēntĭā."
3. *In clothing.* Say, " who clothe; " and put *clothe* in the Subjunctive, because *who* is not used in its simple sense, but is equivalent to *since we.* See " Qui."
4. *Latin.* Say, " in Latin." " Lătīnē " (adverb). *Like.* Say, " after the manner of (' ăd mōrem ')."
12. *Of rolling.* Use the Infinitive " vŏlvĕrĕ," Rule 34.

EXERCISE XCVII.

VOCABULARY.

abdicate, verb	mē *ăbdĭcō*		*Penelope*, subst.	Pēnĕlŏpē,
except, prep.	praetĕr			Pēnĕlŏpēs, *or*
gloomy, adj.	tĕtrĭcŭs			Pēnĕlŏpaē, 1 f.
hour, subst.	hōră, 1		*suitor*, subst.	prŏcŭs, 2
ill, adj.	aegĕr		*undertake*, verb	sŭscĭpĭō, 3
manfully, phr.	prō vĭrīlī pārtĕ		*world*, phr.	ōrbĭs tĕrrārum
Mardonius, sub.	Mărdŏnĭŭs, 2		*younger*, comp. adj.	jŭnĭŏr.

1. They who often say that they are *too* ill to work are not believed. 2. If I had known the hour of your coming, I should have been ready to receive you. 3. I do not know *whether* there is a better fruit than the strawberry in the whole earth. 4. If you will lead the horse to the water, I will do my best to make him drink. 5. How foolish were the suitors to be deceived by Penelope! 6. Mardonius did not think that the Persians would be conquered by the Greeks. 7. Tyrtæus thought that *the* younger a man was, *the* more he *ought* to fight for his country. 8. Those who undertake to dig through the isthmus are *more* bold *than* prudent. 9. The reason of the king's abdication no one except the priest knew. 10. The number of mistakes I have made who can count? 11. All day long I expected a friend, who never intended to come. 12. He is as gloomy as if he did not know the way to laugh.

3. See "*whether*," 3. "Nĕscĭo ăn," however, implies that the doubt need not have been felt, because the fact is as stated. The English implies the contrary; therefore insert a *not* in the second clause.

4. *I will do my best.* Say, "I will try manfully."

5. *To be deceived.* Say, "who were deceived," putting *deceived* in the Subjunctive, because *who = since they*. See also "*to*," 7.

9. Before rendering this sentence into Latin, you must recast it thus, *No one except the priest knew why the king abdicated.* Such recasting is often necessary when a sentence contains such words as *reason, intention, nature, size, number*, and the like.

10. *The number of mistakes I have made.* Recast (as in preceding sentence) thus, *How many mistakes I have made*, or *How often I have made mistakes.*

11. *Intended to come.* Say, "was about to come."

12. *As gloomy as if.* See "*as*," 3. The first *as* should be translated by "nōn mĭnŭs" or "nōn ălĭtĕr."
Did not know the way to. Use nĕscĭŏ.

EXERCISE XCVIII.

VOCABULARY.

demand, verb	pŏstŭlō, 1	*intend*, verb	cōgĭtō, 1
Elizabeth, subst.	Ělīzăbĕthă, 1	*matter*, subst.	rēs (rĕī), 5 f.
escape, subst.	fŭgă, 1	*papyrus*	păpȳrŭs,
Europe, subst.	Eūrōpă, 1		2 m. & f.
forsake, verb	dēsĕrō, 3	*perceive*, verb	sēntĭō, 4
grow up, verb	ădŏlēscō, 3	*quite*, adv.	prōrsŭs.

---

1. *As* the sun was rising, the soldiers perceived what had happened in the night. 2. *Unless* the Gauls come to help us, we *must* abandon all hope of escape. 3. Ancient philosophers were *quite* ignorant of the size of the stars. 4. You shall have more money than you can use, *if only* you *will* obey me. 5. Cæsar's intentions before he crossed the Rubicon were unknown to *all* his bravest officers. 6. Labienus, after the battle of Pharsalia, repented of having forsaken Cæsar. 7. The Spartans deserve praise, *for* never using more words than the matter in hand demanded. 8. Would you rather have been an Athenian when Pericles lived, or an Englishman *in* the reign of Elizabeth? 9. Can you tell me in what part of Europe the papyrus grows? 10. Hercules complained that he *had* to obey Eurystheus. 11. You give me advice, *as if* I did not know what I *ought* to do. 12. I will try to save you *from* growing up an ignorant man.

3. *The size of.* Say, "how great the stars were." See Exercise XCVII., sentence 9, note.
5. *Intentions.* See Exercise XCVII., sentence 9, note. Begin, "None of his bravest officers knew."
6. *Of having forsaken.* Express by Infinitive. Rule 34.
7. *The matter in hand.* "Rēs īpsă."
10. *Had to obey.* See "have."

EXERCISE XCIX.

VOCABULARY.

America, subst.	Ămĕrĭcă	*go*, verb	mē cōnfĕrō (*I betake myself*)
arrival, subst.	ădvĕntŭs, 4		
Columbus, subst.	Colūmbŭs, 2	*hold* (note)	
culprit, subst.	rĕŭs	*Italy*, adj. (*of Italy*)	Ĭtălĭcŭs
differently, adv.	ălĭtĕr		
discover, verb	rĕpĕrĭō, 4	*join* (note)	
end, verb	ēvĕnĭō, 4	*May*, use adj.	Maiŭs
give up, verb	dēdō, 3	*oak*, adj.	quĕrnŭs
		truce, subst.	indŭcĭae, 1 pl.

1. If the cities of Italy had joined Hannibal, the Punic war would have ended differently. 2. *The* more I understand your intentions, the less I am prepared to join you. 3. Columbus cannot understand why the land which he discovered is called America. 4. Tell me why you pluck oak leaves on the 29th of May. 5. The philosopher said that he profited himself by consulting the interests of others. 6. Without waiting for Cæsar's arrival, Cicero set out from Italy and went to Greece. 7. No one doubted that Caius was worthy to hold the highest office in the state. 8. Even if you were heir to Crœsus' whole estate, I should not envy you your wealth. 9. Fearing *that* he could not resist the enemy's forces, he sent messengers *to* ask for a truce. 10. *Some* think that war between England and Sarmatia is like a contest between a whale and an elephant. 11. He threatened *every* tenth boy with punishment, unless the culprit gave himself up. 12. Before the war began, no one could conjecture its probable nature and extent.

1. *Join* is here a Neuter Verb. "jŭngō" is always Transitive; therefor "mē jŭngō" must be used.
2. *Your intentions.* You may either translate this literally or recast it. Exercise XCVII., sentence 9.
10. *Like.* "Sĭmĭlĭs," followed by Dative. *Between* may be considered merely the sign of a Genitive, or translated by "ĭntĕr," in which case a Participle such as *fought* should be inserted before *between.*
11. *Gave.* Pluperfect Subjunctive.
12. *Its probable nature and extent.* Say, "of what sort and how great the war would be." Compare Exercise XCVII., sentence 9.

EXERCISE C.

VOCABULARY.

agree with, verb	ăssĕntĭŏr, 4 dep.	*invade*, verb	ăggrĕdĭŏr, 3 dep.
Germans, subst.	Gĕrmānī, 2 pl. m.	*neighbour*, subst.	fīnĭtĭmŭs, 2.
		result, subst.	ēvĕntŭs, 4 m.
heap, verb	ĭngĕrŏ, 3	*serious*, adj.	grăvĭs.

---

1. *As* to Cæsar, I agree with you in thinking he must be obeyed. 2. The insults which he has heaped on me are *beyond* endurance. 3. He received *so* serious a wound *that* he was *within* a little of dying. 4. I deny that anyone can tell what will be the result of the war. 5. I am *so far from* blaming Cæsar, that I think he has profited the state. 6. We ought to learn to obey the laws *before* we try to change them. 7. If the Gauls had conquered the Germans, I should have grieved. 8. He said that if the Gauls had conquered the Germans, he would have grieved. 9. Mountains, better than rivers, hinder kings from invading their neighbours. 10. *Without* learning the opinion of the dictator, he advanced to attack the enemy. 11. If the citizens had known *at* what price peace was to be bought, they would have fought longer. 12. I am ashamed to say, I do not understand the meaning of your words.

1. See "*as*," 6. The sentence in full would be, *As to Cæsar, I agree with you in thinking "that" he must be obeyed.* The words *in thinking* are unnecessary in English, and should not be translated in Latin.

12. *The meaning of your words.* Say, "what your words mean." *Mean* = vŏlŏ *or* mĭhĭ vŏlŭ. Compare Exercise XCVII., sentence 9.

THE WOLVES AND THE SHEEP.

The wolves sent an embassy to the sheep, to make peace between them. "*Must* war," said they, "always be waged between us? Do you not see *that* the dogs are the cause of our strife, since they are incessantly barking and provoking us? If you send them away, there is no reason why there should not be perpetual friendship and peace between us." The sheep were so silly that they believed these lies, and, the dogs being dismissed, the flock, deprived of their guardians, became the prey of their foes.

An embassy = ambassadors.
To make = who should make.
Since they = who. See " Qui."
Are incessantly barking and provoking us. Latin, " by incessantly barking (Gerund) provoke us." Verb in Present Subjunctive.
If you send them away. Latin, " Whom if you send away (Future Perfect)."
There is no reason why. Latin, " there is not why."
In the last sentence begin, *Since the sheep were so silly,* &c., and omit the word *and.*

---

1. There was no reason why they should fight.
2. The sheep will become the prey of the wolves.
3. The dogs made war on the wolves on behalf of the sheep.
4. Who would be so foolish as to deprive himself of his only guardian ?
5. Do not believe your enemies.

THE OLD HOUND.

A hound, who had once been of the greatest courage and strength, and had served his master well, was at length worn out with the weight of years and toil. Thus it happened that, when he had caught a wild boar by the ear, his teeth failed and the boar escaped. Upon this, the hunter coming up, severely rated him. But the hound replied, "Spare your old servant. It was the strength, not the will, that failed me. Do you rather remember what I was, than blame me for being so feeble now."

Once = formerly.
Of the greatest courage. Rule 9.
Well. Say, "much" = "multum."
Upon this, the hunter coming up. Latin, "Which being done (Ablative Absolute), when the hunter had come up."
It was; omit. *That;* omit.
What = "qualis."
For being = "because I am."

------

1. Do not blame a faithful servant.
2. It happened that there was a wild boar in the wood.
3. The dog happened to let the wild boar escape.
4. Continual toil impairs the strength.
5. Do not forget benefits.

3. This sentence must be changed into another, beginning, *It happened that*, before being turned into Latin.

THE COUNTRYMAN AND THE SNAKE.

A countryman, as he was returning home towards evening on a winter day, found a snake by the wayside, almost dead with cold. Moved by compassion, he took it up and laid it in his bosom, and brought it home to his fireside to revive it. No sooner had the snake been revived by the warmth, than it began to attack the countryman's children. Upon this the countryman, to save his children, snatched up a mattock and killed the snake with a single blow.

As = while. *Towards* = "Sub." See List of Latin Prepositions.
By the wayside = "in via."
Moved by compassion, &c. Latin, "Which, when moved by compassion, he had laid, taken up (Aorist Participle) in his bosom, he brought it," &c.
No sooner, &c., than. Latin, "As soon as ('quum primum') the snake, &c., it began."
Upon this. Latin, "Which being done."
Snatched up a mattock and killed. Latin, "having snatched up a mattock, killed."
Single = "unus."

---

1. The husbandman pitied the viper.
2. Why did the viper show himself ungrateful?
3. *It is better* to let vipers die.
4. Those who save vipers are sometimes forced to kill them afterwards.
5. Do not injure those who have benefited you.

THE HUNTER AND THE LION.

A man, very skilful with the bow, went to the mountains to hunt wild beasts. At his approach, there was the greatest panic and confusion among all of them. The lion alone determined to await the enemy. When the hunter saw him, he cried out, "Stop a moment, I will send a messenger, who has somewhat to say to you." With these words, he shot an arrow and wounded the lion in the side. The lion, smarting with pain, ran into the midst of the wood. But a fox, seeing him run, bade him take courage and face the enemy. "No," said the lion, "you will not persuade me to do so: for, if the messenger is so powerful, what is the strength of him who sends it ?"

Very skilful with the bow. Rule 8.
At his approach. Latin, " Who when he was approaching."
When the hunter saw him. Latin, " Whom when the hunter saw."
A moment. Latin, " parumper." *Stop* = " moror."
Somewhat to say. Latin, "something which he may say," or the Gerundive.
He shot an arrow and wounded. Latin, "having shot an arrow he wounded."
Midst of the wood. Rule 8.
Seeing, &c. Latin, " Whom when a fox saw run."
Take courage = "animum recipere." *Face* = " se objicere."
No ; omit.
What = " quantus."

---

1. In vain did the fox wish to persuade the lion to fight.

2. The lion was followed by the fox.

3. The hunter is *too* strong to be conquered by the lion.

4. Those who boast before they conquer often appear foolish.

5. I sent a messenger to tell the hunter where the fox was lurking.

THE WOLF AND THE CRANE.

While a wolf was devouring a lamb, a bone stuck in his throat. In great pain, he entreated those whom he met to help him, promising at the same time a great reward to him who should do so. At length a crane, moved by his prayers and promises, put her long neck into the wolf's throat and drew out the bone. Having done this, she asked for the reward. But the wolf, showing his teeth, replied, " Ungrateful creature, you can say you put your head into a wolf's mouth, and drew it out thence unhurt, and yet you ask for other reward besides this."

While a wolf was devouring a lamb, a bone, &c. Latin, "To a wolf, while he, &c., a bone," &c.

In great pain. Latin, " Tortured by great pain." *Great* = " summus."

Promising. Latin, either " when he promised" (Imperfect Subjunctive) or " polliceor," Aorist Participle.

Should do so. Render by Pluperfect Subjunctive.

Put her neck, &c., and drew out. Render first clause by Ablative Absolute.

Having done this. Latin, " Which when she had done," or Ablative Absolute.

Showing = " nudo," 1. Render by Ablative Absolute.

Put your head in and drew it out. Latin, " Drew out your put in (Aorist Participle) head."

---

1. If a bone sticks in the wolf's throat again, the crane will not help him.

2. Do not refuse rewards to those who have earned them.

3. The crane can boast that she has put her head into the wolf's mouth with impunity (" impune").

4. She ought not therefore to go without (" careo") her reward.

5. In vain do we ask the ungrateful man whom we have benefited for a reward.

THE FOX AND THE GOAT.

A fox, who had fallen into a well, for a long while struggled in vain to get out. · At length a goat came to the place, and, wishing to drink, asked the fox *whether* the water was sweet and was plentiful. The fox, pretending to be quite at his ease, said, "Come down, friend, the water is *so* sweet that I cannot drink enough, and is *so* plentiful that it cannot be exhausted. Upon this the goat leapt into the well, and the fox, taking advantage of his horns, leapt out. As he stood on the edge he said to the goat, " If you had *as much* sense *as* you have beard, you would not leap without first looking around you."

To get out = " evado." Insert, "thence," "inde."
Wishing. Latin, "since he wished."
At his ease = " tranquillus."
To be exhausted = " deficere."
Upon this the goat leapt and the fox, &c. Latin, " Which (Plural) being heard when the goat had leapt down, the fox, &c."
Take advantage of = " utor."
If you had. Latin, " If there were to you." *Sense* = " prudentia."
Without looking. Latin, "unless you had looked."

---

1. The goat was so foolish as to believe the fox.
2. The well was too deep for the goat to get out of it.
3. The goat repented of having obeyed the deceitful fox.
4. Those who have beards do not always show themselves wise men.
5. The goat had more beard than sense.

THE NURSE AND THE WOLF.

A wolf, *while* roving in search of food, came to a door where a nurse was scolding a child *that* cried. He heard her say, " If you do not leave off crying *at once*, I will throw you to the wolf." So, thinking the old woman *would* do as she had said, the wolf waited in hopes of a good supper. But as it grew dark he heard the nurse coaxing the child, and saying, " If the wolf comes *to* fetch my baby, we will kill him." The wolf thereupon disappointed thought he *had* better go home, saying, " This comes of listening to those who say one thing and mean another."

In search of = " to seek."
Thinking. Latin, "since he thought," or Aorist Participle of
    Deponent Verb.
In hopes of. Latin, "hoping to get."
As = when. *To grow dark* = " advesperasco." Impersonal Verb.
Coax = " blandior."
Disappointed = " spe dejectus," lit. *cast down from his hope.*
Saying. Latin, " when he said."
This comes of listening, &c. Latin, " Thus it happens (' fio ') if
    you believe."
One thing—another = " aliud—aliud." Omit *and.*

---

1. While the child cried the nurse kept scolding it.
2. Do not threaten with vengeance those who do you a slight injury.
3. If a wolf were to attack a child, the nurse would try to kill the wolf.
4. There are some who say one thing and mean another.
5. Dogs used to prevent wolves *from* eating sheep.

THE CROW AND THE PITCHER.

A crow, almost dead with thirst, flew with joy to a pitcher which he saw in the distance. But when he came there, he found *that* there was so little water in it *that, although* he bent his neck, he could not reach it. Thereupon he tried first to break the pitcher, *then* to overturn it, but he had not enough strength to do *either*. At last, *seeing* some pebbles lying near, he dropped them *one by one* into the pitcher, and, when by so doing he had caused the water to rise to the brim, he managed to quench his thirst. It cannot be denied *that* " Necessity is the mother of invention."

Dead = " confectus." *With joy* = " laetus " (Adjective).
In the distance = " procul."
But when he came there. Latin, " Whither when he had come."
So little water = " tantulum aquae."
He had not enough, &c. Latin, " to him there was not enough strength that he should do either." *Either* = " alteruter."
Seeing. Latin, " when he saw." *Lying* = Present Infinitive.
By so doing = " ita."
Cause = " efficio."
Managed. Render by " possum."

---

1. The crow collected so many pebbles that the water rose to the top of the pitcher.
2. Who would have thought that pebbles could be useful *for* quenching thirst ?
3. It cannot be denied that the crow showed himself very wise.
4. If the crow had broken the pitcher, he would have wasted much water.
5. Try till you succeed.

THE KITE AND THE PIGEONS.

The pigeons were *so much* afraid of the kite that they did not dare to go far from their dovecot. *However*, they were so watchful that for a long time they managed to escape their enemy. The kite, being unsuccessful by violence, determined to try craft. "Why does it please you," said he to the pigeons, "to lead such an anxious life? If you will make me your king, I will keep you safe from every enemy." The pigeons, trusting his words, made him their king. But *as soon as* the kite began to reign, he devoured a pigeon daily, saying that this was the royal prerogative. Then one of the pigeons, while expecting death, said, "We suffer justly, for those who submit to a tyrant ought not to wonder at his acting cruelly."

To be afraid of = to fear.
Managed = were able.
Being unsuccessful. Latin, since he did not succeed. *Not* = "nihil." *Succeed* = "proficio."
You will make. Use Future Perfect.
Keep = "præsto." *From* = against.
Trusting = "confisus."
Devoured. Imperfect.
Saying = "since he said." *Prerogative* = "jus."
While expecting = look out *while.*
We suffer justly. The Verb "patior" is usually followed by an Accusative. Say, "we justly ('merito') suffer a sad fate ('sors tristis')."
At his acting. Latin, "that he acts." Accusative and Infinitive.

---

1. Who can wonder at a tyrant showing himself cruel?

2. The pigeons were so foolish as to make the kite their king.

3. There are some who give money to robbers to save their own goods.

4. The pigeons showed themselves *as silly as* the sheep.

5. Do not use violence.

THE MAN AND THE SATYR.

A man and a Satyr, having formed a friendship, sat down to dinner together. The day being wintry, the man put his fingers to his mouth and blew upon them. The Satyr asked him why he did that. The man answered that his hands were cold, and that he did it to warm them. In a little while, when some hot broth was placed before them, the man, raising the dish to his mouth, blew upon it. Again the Satyr asked the meaning of the action. The man replied that he did it to cool his broth, which was too hot to drink. "But I," said the Satyr, "from this moment, renounce your friendship, for I cannot be the friend of one who, from the same mouth, can blow both hot and cold."

Having formed a friendship. Latin, "when they had become friends."

Sit down to dinner = " accumbo." Use the Imperfect.

The day being wintry = "Since the day was wintry."

Put his fingers and blew on them. Latin, "blew on his fingers, put (Aorist Participle) to his mouth." *To put* = "admoveo."

In a little while. " Postea aliquanto."

Place before them = " appono."

The meaning of the action. Latin, "why he did so."

Too hot to drink. Latin, "hotter than which could (Imperfect Subjunctive) be drunk."

Moment = " tempus."

Of one = " of him."

Can blow both hot and cold. Say, "can send forth both heat and cold."

-----

1. How did it happen that heat and cold came from the same man's mouth?

2. Do not suffer broth to become cold.

3. A certain boy was so unwilling to drink broth that he became quite thin and died.

4. Ask the Satyr why he renounced the man's friendship.

5. Who used to be followed by Satyrs?

1. *How did that happen that.* " Unde effectum est ut."

THE WOLF AND THE LAMB.

A wolf, who was drinking from a brook, saw a little way off a lamb. Though he wished to kill and devour it, he did not know how to get an excuse for attacking it. So he asked the lamb why he kept fouling the water. The lamb replied that this was impossible. "The water," said he, "runs from you to me, so that I cannot foul that which you are drinking." "Well then," said the wolf, "twelve months ago you abused me terribly." "How could that be," said the lamb, "since I was not born twelve months ago?" "*Then*," said the wolf, "if it was not you it was your father; *at all events* by all your arguments I will not be prevented *from* eating you." Tyrants cannot be resisted by those whose only defence is justice.

A little way off = "propter."
To kill and devour it. Latin, "to devour it killed" (Aorist Participle Passive).
How to get an excuse for attacking it. Latin, "whence he should seek a cause of attacking it" (Gerund).
Kept fouling. Imperfect Tense of Subjunctive Mood.
That this was impossible. Latin, "that this could not be." *To be* = "fio."
Well then = "Tu vero."
You abused me terribly. Latin, "(you) heaped much abuse on me," or "you assailed ('lacesso') me with much abuse." *Heap* = "ingero."
Could that be. Be = "fio."
Not. Use "Nondum."
Then if it was not you it was your father. Latin, "if not you then your father did this." *Then* = at.
Tyrants, &c. Rule 16.

---

1. *Though* the wolf wished to appear just, he *would* not spare the lamb.

2. If the water had run from the lamb to the wolf, the wolf *might* have found a better excuse for killing the lamb.

3. *Though* he *could* not find an excuse, he did not therefore spare the lamb.

4. Sparrows sometimes do not hesitate to resist a hawk.

5. When I speak of sparrows, why do you remember a certain husbandman and his sons?

    2. *For killing* = "Why he should kill."

THE WIND AND THE SUN.

A dispute *once* arose between the wind and the sun, which was the stronger of the two. At length they agreed that he who first made a traveller take off his cloak should be accounted the stronger. First the wind blew, with all his might, a blast *as* cold and fierce *as* a Thracian storm. But *the* more the wind blew, *the* closer the traveller wrapped his cloak around him, and grasped it with *both* his hands. But when the sun with his beams dispersed the vapour and the cold, the traveller felt the warmth, and *the* brighter the sun shone *the* slower he went, *till* at last, overcome with heat, he took off his cloak and sat down to rest. Who doubts that persuasion *is better* than force?

Which of the two = " uter." *Strong* = " validus."
They agreed that. Latin, " it was agreed (' convenio ') between them that."
First = " prius."
Made a traveller take off. Latin, " brought it to pass (' efficio,' Pluperfect Subjunctive) that," &c.
Should be accounted. Imperfect Subjunctive, " habeor."
With all his might = " summis viribus." *To blow* (Transitive) " emitto."
Wrapped, &c., and grasped. Latin, " grasped his cloak wrapped " (Aorist Participle Passive). *To wrap* = " obduco." Rule 13.
He went = " progredior." Imperfect.
He took off his cloak and sat down. Latin, " having taken off his cloak (Ablative Absolute) he sat down."
To rest = " that he might rest." *To rest* = " quietem capere."
Persuasion—force. Render by Verbs in the Infinitive Mood. Rule 34. *Force* = " vi agere."

---

1. Can you tell me *whether* the sun *or* the wind is the more powerful?

2. Which of the two does the sailor fear?

3. Why does the soldier fear the sun more than the wind?

4. Who would walk in the sun without taking off his cloak?

5. There are some who pretend that they can predict storms.

THE BUNDLE OF STICKS.

A husbandman, who had sons *that* often quarrelled, *after having* tried in vain to reconcile them by words, thought that he could more easily move them by an example. *So* he called his sons, and bade them bring him some sticks. Then, having tied them together with a cord, he told the lads one after another to take up the faggot and break it. When they had all tried to do so in vain, he untied the faggot and gave them the sticks to break *one by one*. *As* they did this *quite* easily, the old man said to them, "Thus you, my sons, *as long as* you remain united among yourselves, are a match for all your enemies; but if you quarrel and part, you are undone."

Who had sons. Latin, " to whom there were sons."
Reconcile. " In gratiam reducere."
He called his sons and bade them. Latin, "he bade his called (Aorist Participle Passive) sons."
Bring him some sticks. Be sure that you understand the English before you turn it into Latin.
Then having tied, &c. Latin, " which being tied together with a cord, he," &c.
Take up the faggot and break it. Latin, " break the faggot taken up."
One after another = " ex ordine."
When they had all tried to do so. Latin, " Which when they had all tried to do."
He untied the faggot and gave. Latin, " the faggot being untied he gave."
To break. Latin, either " that they might break them," or " to be broken " (Gerundive).
Among yourselves. " Vobiscum."
A match for = " equal to."
You are undone = " all is over with you."

---

1. Who can doubt that example is better than precept ?

2. *Can* this fable teach us *anything* about our own life ?

3. When a nation wages war, all the citizens ought to aid those who govern them, and not remember old quarrels.

4. What nation can do without husbandmen ?

5. Those who have ships must also have harbours.

2. *Anything* = " numquid."

THE HERDSMAN AND THE LOST BULL.

A herdsman, who had lost a bull, went roaming through the forest in search of it. Being unable to find it, he began to pray to all the Nymphs of the forest and of the mountain, to Mercury, and to Pan, and vowed that he *would* offer up a lamb to them *if only* he discovered the thief. *At* that very moment, reaching the top of a hill, he saw a lion, who was standing over the carcase of his bull, which he had just slain. *So* now the unhappy man promises to sacrifice all his herd, *if only* he may escape the claws of him who stole the bull. If the gods always granted our prayers, *how many* of us would be ruined by our own requests !

Went roaming = "roamed." *In search of it* = "to seek it."
Being unable. Latin, "since he was unable."
Of the forest and of the mountain. Latin, "who inhabit the forest and the mountain."
He discovered. Pluperfect Subjunctive.
Moment = "tempus." *Reaching.* Latin, "when he reached."
Granted our prayers. Latin, "granted ('præsto') those things which we pray for."
By our own requests. Latin, "by the vows of ourselves."

---

1. Having obtained his wish, he was still unhappy.
2. He repented of having made foolish promises.
3. There are some who make many promises and do not fulfil them.
4. Mercury is said to have been the inventor of the lyre.
5. If some magician promised to give me whatever I wished, I would not be so foolish as to ask for sausages.

2. *To make foolish promises* = to promise foolish things.

THE LION AND THE GOAT.

On a summer day, when all things were parched with heat, a lion and a goat came at the same time *to* a small spring, *to* quench their thirst. They at once began to dispute *which* should drink first, *till* it seemed that each was ready to resist the other even to death. But, ceasing from the strife for a moment, they saw a flock of vultures, which was hovering over them, ready to devour whichever should fall. Seeing this they instantly made up their quarrel, for they thought that it was far better for them to become friends than to furnish food for crows and vultures.

Summer. Adjective.
Which. See " who."
They at once began to dispute. Latin, " forthwith a quarrel arose
    between them."
Each ... the other, "alter ... alter." Latin, " till each seemed
    ready to resist," &c.
Even to death = " usque ad mortem."
Ceasing from their strife for a moment. Latin, "when for a
    moment (' parumper ') they had ceased to fight."
Whichever should fall. Latin, " him who should fall." (Pluper-
    fect Subjunctive.)
Seeing this. Latin, " Which when they saw," or " Which being
    seen."
Made up = " compono."
To become friends. Rule 7.

---

1. Do you believe that a goat desired to resist a lion ?

2. It made small difference to the goat *whether* he *or* the lion drank first.

3. When there is a dispute about an inheritance, it sometimes happens that the heirs become *no* richer.

4. It would have been better for the goat to have gone away, *without* drinking at *all*, than to have fought the lion.

5. Even if he had fought the goat, the lion would not have become food *for* vultures.

2. *It made small difference.* *It makes small difference* = " parum
    interest." Look out " interest." *He* = " ipse."

THE HORSE AND THE ASS.

A man, who owned a horse and an ass, was wont, *while* journeying, to spare the horse, and put all the burden on the ass's back. The ass, *being* ill, besought the horse one day to take part of his load. "For if," said he, "you *would* take part, I should soon be well again; otherwise this burden will kill me." The horse however bade the ass go on, *and not* trouble him with his complaints. Soon the ass, overcome with the weight, dropped down dead, as he had foretold. On this the master coming up, took the load from the ass and put it on the horse's back, and made him carry the ass's carcase in addition. Thus, *for* refusing to take a part, he had to bear the whole load, and his comrade's body besides.

Own. Use "pasco." *Journey* = "iter facio."
To spare the horse, &c. Here a Latin writer would refer to the horse by the pronoun "ille," to the ass by "hic."
Being ill = "since he was ill." *One day.* Say, "by chance," "forte."
If, &c. See Conditional Sentences. *Be well again* = "convalesco."
Otherwise = "sin minus."
Kill = "conficio."
On this = which being done.
Coming up, &c. Latin, "when he had come up, put on the horse's back the load taken from ('detraho') the ass."
Made him carry = forced him to carry.
In addition = "insuper."
Refusing. Use "nolo."
He had to bear, &c. Latin, "the whole load was to be borne (Gerundive) by him." (Rule 37.)
And...besides. "Necnon."

---

1. Why did not the horse pity the ass?
2. The ass *must* have envied the horse.
3. Do not tell him, who asks you for help, not to trouble you with complaints. (Say, "do not forbid, &c., to trouble.")
4. The horse was angry with the ass *for* asking him *for* help.
5. The horse will repent of having refused what the ass asked.

THE EAGLE AND THE JACKDAW.

An eagle made a swoop from a high rock and carried off a lamb. A jackdaw, who happened to be near, thinking he could do the same, bore down with all his might upon a ram, intending to bear him off as a prey. But his claws being entangled in the fleece, he made such a fluttering in his efforts to escape, *that* the shepherd saw the matter and caught him. Having clipped his wings, he carried him home to his children *at* nightfall. " What bird is this that you have brought us, father ? " exclaimed the children. " If you ask him," said the shepherd, " he will tell you he is an eagle, but, if you believe me, I know him to be but a jackdaw."

Made a swoop and carried. Latin, " having made a swoop (Ablative Absolute) carried." *Swoop* = impetus.
Happened to be near. Latin, " by chance was near."
I am near = adsum.
Thinking. Latin, " when he thought," or Aorist Participle Deponent Verb.
Bore down = " se demittere."
Intending to. Latin, " that he might."
He made such a fluttering. Say, " he fluttered so." *Flutter* = " alis plaudere." Literally, *to flap with the wings. So* = " adeo."
In his efforts = while he tried.
Saw the matter and caught. Latin, " the matter being seen," (Ablative Absolute) caught.
Is this that. These words may be omitted in Latin. Say, " what bird have you brought."
He will tell you he is an eagle. Rule 40. Explanations.
But. Latin, " nothing else than," " nihil aliud quam."

----

1. The shepherd entrusted the jackdaw to his children.
2. *Do* not believe a jackdaw rather *than* a shepherd.
3. That foolish lamb believes that the jackdaw is an eagle.
4. The state entrusts you with this duty.
5. The jackdaw believed himself to be an eagle. (Say, " seemed to himself to be.")

THE LION AND THE ASS.

A lion and an ass agreed *to* go out hunting together. *So* when they had come to a cave in which dwelt many wild goats, the lion posted himself at the mouth of the cave, but the ass, going within, kicked and brayed and made a din to frighten them out. When the lion had caught many of them, the ass came out and asked him *if* he had not done good service and frightened the goats finely. "No doubt about it," said the lion. "Believe me, you would have frightened me too if I had not known you were an ass."

A lion and an ass agreed. Latin, "it was agreed between a lion and an ass."
Hunting. Use the Supine in "um."
Going within. Use Past Participle of Deponent Verb.
Kick = "calces remitto." *Bray* = "rudo, rudivi." *Frighten out* = "excito."
When the lion, &c. Latin, "of whom when the lion had caught many."
Came out and asked. Latin, "having come out (Deponent Verb) asked."
If not = "nonne."
Do good service = "multum proficio."
Finely = "pulchre."
No doubt about it = it is not doubtful.
You would have, &c. Refer to Conditional Sentences and Rule 40.

---

1. Let us all go out hunting together.
2. King Midas could not conceal his long ears from the barber.
3. The wild goats were so frightened that they rushed into the lion's mouth.
4. What proverb bids us not to fear those who make a great noise? (Say, "forbids us to fear.")
5. How foolish the goats were *to* be frightened by an ass!

THE HART AND THE VINE.

A hart, pursued by hunters, concealed himself among the foliage of a vine. The hunters passed by *without* discovering him, and when he thought *that* all was safe, he began browsing on the leaves *that* had concealed him. But one of the hunters, hearing the rustling of the leaves, turned round, and, guessing *that* their prey was there, shot an arrow and killed him. *As* he was dying he groaned, " I suffer justly *for* my ingratitude, since I could not forbear injuring the vine, which had protected me in danger."

Pursued by hunters = " whom the hunters were pursuing."

The hunters, &c. Latin, " when the hunters had passed by, &c., he, thinking (Deponent Past Participle) that all (Neuter Plural) was safe, began," &c.

Hearing the rustling. Ablative Absolute.

Turned round and guessing, &c. Latin, " when, having turned round (Deponent Participle) he had guessed."

Shot an arrow and killed. Latin, " having shot an arrow (Ablative Absolute) killed."

Groaned. Latin, " he said with a groan."

Justly. Say, " a just punishment."

Ingratitude. Say, " ungrateful mind."

I could not forbear injuring. Latin, " I could not restrain myself (mihi temperare) *from* injuring."

Since I could not. Latin, " who could not " (Perfect Subjunctive).

Protected. Say, " had been for a protection."

---

1. The hunters passed the stag without seeing him.

2. Was it really ungrateful of the stag to browse on the leaves of the trees which had prevented the hunters from seeing him. (Say, " was the stag really ungrateful who ('qui' with subjunctive) browsed.")

3. To escape death, a stag will rob another of his lair.

4. Do you know what wife was killed with an arrow by her husband, because he thought that she was a wild beast?

5. Who can count how many colours the sun causes to shine in the dew?

THE MICE IN COUNCIL.

Once upon a time the mice, being much harassed by the cat, came together *to* decide how they should rid themselves of this continual annoyance. When many plans had been rejected, *a* young mouse said that a bell should be fastened to the cat's neck, so that they might hear the sound of her coming, and be able to escape. This proposal was received with unanimous applause. But *an* old mouse, who had sat silent *hitherto*, got up and said that he thought the plan most ingenious, and did not doubt it would succeed. "I have only one thing to ask:" said he, "which of us will put the bell on the cat's neck?" It is one thing to propose a plan, another to execute it.

How they should rid themselves of. Latin, "how they ought (Imperfect Subjunctive) to free themselves from."

Annoyance = "incommodum."

Should be fastened to. Latin, "was to be fastened to." (Gerundive.)

They might have, &c., and be able. Latin, "the sound of her coming being heard (Ablative Absolute), they might be able."

Unanimous applause = "summus omnium consensus."

Old = "ætate gravis."

Got up and said. Latin, "when he had risen, said."

That he thought the plan most ingenious. Latin, "that to him indeed ('quidem') the plan seemed very good."

And did not doubt it would succeed. Latin, "nor did he doubt *that* it would turn out well" ("bene evenio." Historic Future Subjunctive).

To ask. Latin, "which I may ask," or "to be asked" (Gerundive).

Will put on = "alligo." Primary Future Subjunctive.

One thing ... another = "aliud ... aliud."

Propose = "suadeo." *Execute* = "exsequor."

---

1. *Would that* I could rid myself of this questioner.

2. Who told the centurion not to order a common soldier to do that which he was afraid to do himself?

3. Did he not *also* enforce his precept by his example?

4. How comes it about that some cats carry bells? (Use "evenit ut.")

5. Cats attack birds *as well as* mice.

2. Say, who forbade.

THE FOX AND THE WOODCUTTER.

A fox, hard pressed by the hounds, begged a wood-cutter to give him some place where he could hide himself. The man opened the door of his own hut, and the fox went in and hid himself in a corner. The hunters soon arrived and asked the woodcutter *if* he had seen the fox. He said "*No*," but at the same time pointed with his finger towards the hut. The hunters, however, not understanding his meaning, went away. When the fox saw them go he came out of his hiding-place, and began to depart in silence. But the woodcutter upbraided him for departing without thanking his friend. "If,' said the fox, "you had been *as* honest with your fingers *as* with your tongue, I should not have gone away without bidding you farewell."

Hard pressed by the hounds. Latin, "whom the hounds were closely following (' insequor ')."

Some place.—omit.

Could. Imperfect Subjunctive, "possum."

The man opened, &c., and the fox, &c. Render, "who when (he) had opened the door of his own hut, the fox entering (Aorist Participle Deponent Verb) hid himself."

Arrived and asked. Latin, "when they had arrived, asked."

Pointed, &c. Render, *indicated the hut with his finger.*

Not understanding his meaning. Latin, "since what he meant they understood not."

When the fox, &c. Latin, "whom when the fox saw going away (Present Infinitive), coming out (Aorist Participle Deponent) of his hiding place he began to depart (Imperfect) in silence (Adjective, Nominative Case)."

For departing, &c. Latin, "because he was departing, nor was thanking his friend." Verbs in Imperfect Subjunctive. *To thank =* "gratias ago" (with Dative), literally, *I offer thanks.*

Honest = "fidelis."

Without bidding you farewell. Latin, "you not being saluted." (Ablative Absolute.)

---

1. The woodcutter hoped that the fox would thank him.

2. If the woodcutter had lived now-a-days, would he have helped the fox ?

3. Why do those who love to kill foxes prevent others from killing them ?

4. If there were no hunters there would be no foxes.

5. Do foxes therefore love those who hunt them ?

THE SHEPHERD AND THE WOLF.

A shepherd, who fed his flock not far from a village, used in jest to run to the neighbours praying them to help him because the wolf was attacking his sheep. Several times the neighbours who came to help him were only laughed at for their pains. At last one day the wolf came in reality. Then the shepherd, *no longer* in jest, began to cry out to his neighbours for help. But they, thinking that he was trying to deceive them as before, gave no heed to his cries. And so it befell that the wolf devoured the sheep. Thus the shepherd learnt, too late, that liars are not believed even when they tell the truth.

In jest = " per jocum."
Praying them. Latin, " whom he prayed."
Was attacking. Render by Imperfect Subjunctive.
Who came to help him. In Latin, " I come to help you " may be
    rendered "venio tibi auxilio," lit. *I come for a help to you.*
Were laughed at for their pains. Latin, " were for a laughing-
    stock to him." (" Ludibrium," Dative.)
One day the wolf came. Render, " it happened that the wolf
    came."
In reality = " revera."
To cry out for = " oro." Rule 19.
Thinking. Latin, " since they thought," or render by Aorist
    Participle of Deponent Verb.
To give no heed to = " negligo," 3. *His cries.* Say, " him crying."
(Befell) that. *That* is translated by " ut " with Subjunctive.
Liars, &c. Rule 16.

---

1. Do not tell lies even in jest. (*I tell lies* = *I lie.* " Mentior.")

2. There are some who give no heed to their teachers.

3. Why did not the shepherd himself go to meet the wolf? (*Go to meet.* " Obviam eo," with Dative.)

4. Those who weep although they are not hurt, are not believed when they really suffer pain.

5. How much better is it to suffer pain without complaining !

THE LION AND THE MOUSE.

As a lion was sleeping, it happened that a mouse ran across his face. The lion awaking caught the mouse, and was about to devour it, but moved by its entreaties not to punish one who did not mean to offend, he spared its life. Not long after, it happened that the lion, *while* roaming the woods in search of prey, fell into the hunter's toils. Finding himself entangled and unable to escape, he roared so loud that the whole forest echoed. The mouse recognising the voice of him who had spared *him*, ran to the place, and having nibbled through with his teeth the knot which bound the lion, enabled him to get free.

As = while.

The lion, &c. Latin, " when the lion awaking (Past Participle) was about to devour the caught (Aorist Passive Participle) mouse." Omit *but*.

Not to punish. Latin, " that he should not punish." *That not =* " ne."

One = " him."

Who did not mean to offend. " Latin, who had offended (' pecco,' Pluperfect Subjunctive) unintentionally (' imprudens,' Adjective)."

Not long after. " Postea aliquanto."

In search of. Latin, " that he might seek ; " or render the clause, " while he sought prey through the woods."

Finding himself, &c. Latin, " who, when he found that he entangled (Aorist Participle Passive) could not escape."

So loud = " tantum."

Recognising the voice. Latin, " when he recognised ; " or Ablative Absolute, " the voice being recognised."

Having nibbled through. Latin, " when by gnawing (' rodendo ') he had loosed (' solvo,' Pluperfect Subjunctive)."

Which bound the lion. Say, " by which the lion was bound."

Enabled him to get free. Latin, " made for him the power of escaping." (Gerund.)

---

1. The mouse begged the lion not to kill him.

2. Who would have thought that it was the interest of the lion to spare the mouse ?

3. What caused the lion to spare the mouse ?

4. He cannot have thought the mouse would be of service to him. (See note.)

5. Nets catch lions as well as fish.

4. Say, " *could not be* (' fieri ') that (' ut ') he thought."

MERCURY AND THE WOODMAN.

I.

A woodman, who was felling a tree on the bank of a river, by accident let his axe drop into the stream. Thereupon being in great distress, he sat down and wept. But Mercury, whose river it was, taking compassion on him, approached and asked him the cause of his sorrow. Hearing the state of the case, he dived to the bottom of the river, and bringing up a golden axe, asked the woodman *if* that were the axe he had lost. *On* his denying it, Mercury dived a second time and brought up a silver axe. Again the man denied that it was his. *So* diving a third time he showed the woodman the *very* axe which he had lost. " That is mine," said he, delighted to have recovered his own ; and so pleased was Mercury with his honesty that he at once made him a present of the others.

Being in great distress.. Latin, " since he was overwhelmed (' premo ') by great grief."

Taking compassion on. Past Participle of " miseror," 1.

Approached and asked. Latin, " when he had approached, asked."

The cause. Latin, " what was the cause."

Hearing the state of the case. Latin, " when he had heard (' cognosco ') how the matter was (' se habere ')."

Bringing up. Ablative Absolute, or " quum " with Subjunctive.

The axe he had lost = " the axe which he had lost."

Dived a second time and brought up. Latin, " when he had dived, &c., brought up."

Diving a third time. Latin, " when he had dived," &c.

Delighted to have recovered. Latin, " joyful because he had recovered "; or, " joyful his own being recovered." (Ablative Absolute.)

And so pleased was Mercury with his honesty. Latin, " whose honesty pleased Mercury so much."

The others. Use " reliquus."

---

1. Woodman, spare yonder beech-tree.

2. Since this is the case, I must forgive you.

3. *Would that* I could find a golden axe by diving.

4. The woodman was presented by Mercury with two axes.

5. I would rather find a silver axe than an egg made of chalk.

MERCURY AND THE WOODMAN.
II.

When the woodman had returned to his comrades and told them what had happened, one of them determined to try *whether* he might not have the same good fortune. So going to the same place, *as if* for the purpose of cutting wood, he let his axe drop into the river intentionally; then sitting down on the bank he pretended to be overwhelmed with grief. Mercury approached *as* before, and hearing from him that he was weeping because he had lost his axe, dived once more into the stream, and, bringing up a golden axe, asked him *if* that were the axe he had lost. The man swore that it was his own, and was about to grasp it, when Mercury, *to* punish his impudence and lying, not only refused to give it him, but *did not even* restore him his own axe again.

> *Had returned and told.* Latin, " having returned (Deponent Participle) had told."
>
> *What* = " those things which."
>
> *Whether he might not have.* Latin, " whether it were lawful (' licet,' Imperfect Subjunctive) for him to enjoy (' utor ')." Omit *good.*
>
> *Going.* Latin, " when he had gone."
>
> *To the same place* = " eodem."
>
> *For the purpose of cutting* = " to cut." *To cut wood* = " lignari."
>
> *Hearing.* Latin, " when he had heard."
>
> *He had lost.* Pluperfect Subjunctive (in both places).
>
> *Once more.* Say " again."
>
> Begin the last sentence, *when the man swore, &c., Mercury &c.*

1. Mercury determined to punish the woodman who pretended that he had dropped his axe into the river by accident.

2. Do not rashly throw away that which you have, in the hope of getting something better. (Say, " because you hope.")

3. Mind you do not attempt to deceive Mercury, who himself deceived even the god who is worshipped at Delphi.

4. How do you know that Mercury invented the lyre? (*How* = " unde.")

5. Who would believe that a thief would dare to ask a god to help him ?

STORY OF THE TROJAN WAR.

I.

Paris, the son of Priam, King of Troy, was a youth of extraordinary beauty who kept sheep in Mount Ida. *There* came to him three goddesses, Juno, Minerva, and Venus, asking him *to* decide a dispute *for* them. *For* Discord had thrown into the midst of the gods an apple *of* gold, on which were inscribed these words: "Let this be given to the fairest." But who was the fairest? *Since* they could not decide this amongst themselves, they appointed Paris judge. But *before* he spoke, *each for herself* tried to bribe him. Juno promised him a kingdom if he gave her the apple, Minerva wisdom, Venus the loveliest woman on earth to be his wife. Despising power and wisdom he chose the gift which Venus promised, and gave her the prize. Then he forsook the nymph Œnone, who had been betrothed to him, and crossed the sea in search of his promised bride.

Juno, Minerva, and Venus. Latin, "Juno and Minerva and Venus."

Into the midst of the gods. Render by Adjective "medius," in the same way as, *the top of the mountain.* Rule 8. Explanation.

Apple of gold. Latin, "golden apple."

Fairest. Feminine.

If he gave. Verb in Pluperfect Subjunctive.

On earth. Say, "of all."

To be his wife. Latin, "who should be his wife."

Despising power and wisdom. Latin, "power and wisdom being despised."

Then he forsook the nymph Œnone, &c., and crossed, &c. Render, "Then the nymph Œnone, being forsaken, &c., he crossed," &c.

In search of = " to seek."

STORY OF THE TROJAN WAR.
II.

Paris, *on* arriving at Sparta, was hospitably entertained *by* Menelaus, King of Sparta. But he showed himself *very* ungrateful, for in the absence of Menelaus he carried off *his* wife Helen, the fairest of all women, and sailed to Troy. Nor did he only carry off Helen, but also loaded his ship with silver and gold, of which he robbed the Spartan king. The result was *that* all Greece took up arms, *to* avenge the wrongs done to Menelaus. Agamemnon, brother of Menelaus and King of Mycenæ, commanded the host. He summoned all the other kings in Greece *to* follow him. *Some* came willingly, *others* unwillingly. *For* ten years arms were being forged, ships were being built, and all things necessary *for* a great war were being prepared. Let us now enquire who were the chieftains who went *with* Agamemnon *to* besiege Troy.

On arriving. Latin, "when he arrived."
Hospitably. Latin, "with hospitality."
In the absence of Menelaus. Latin, "Menelaus being absent."
    (Ablative Absolute.)
Robbed = "spoliavit." Look out the construction.
The result was that. Latin, "whence it happened that," "unde evenit ut," &c.
The wrongs done to Menelaus. Latin, "the wrongs of Menelaus."
Who were. Verb in Perfect Subjunctive.
All things necessary. Say, "all things which were necessary."
Who were the chieftains who went? Say, "what chieftains went?"

STORY OF THE TROJAN WAR.
III.

Of all the chieftains, whom Agamemnon summoned, the most famous was Achilles. He was the son of Peleus and of Thetis, the most beautiful of the Nereids, the nymphs who inhabit the sea. There is no doubt *that* he was the handsomest and bravest of all the Greeks. He was educated by Chiron, the Centaur, and was taught all the arts which a hero ought to learn. He could play *on* the lyre *as well as* use his weapons; and *such* was his swiftness of foot *that none* could outstrip him. When Agamemnon summoned him, he *had* to chose *whether* he *would* gain the greatest glory as a warrior, *or would* live a long life. For his mother had foretold that he *would* either die before his time *at* Troy *after* gaining greater glory than *anyone* before, or, if he stayed at home, *would* never win renown. Achilles did not hesitate to choose fame, though it was to be bought *at the price* of death. He came to Aulis, whence the fleet was to start, followed by his faithful friend Patroclus.

Was taught all the arts. Rule 19.
He had to choose. Latin, "it was to be chosen (Gerundive) by him."
Whether he would gain. See "*would*," 4. Verb in Imperfect Subjunctive.
As a warrior. Latin, either "a warrior," omitting "*as*" or "in war."
That he would die. See "*would*," 1.
After gaining. Render by Past Participle of "adipiscor." (Deponent.)
Than anyone before. Say, "than there had been to anyone before."
If he stayed. Verb in Imperfect Subjunctive.
To be bought. Gerundive.
Was to start. Latin, "was about to start." (Future Participle.)
Followed by, &c. Remember that "sequor" is a Deponent Verb.

STORY OF THE TROJAN WAR.
IV.

Although Achilles was the bravest and handsomest of the Greeks, there were *some* who were his equals in council. Such a one we believe was Ulysses, King of Ithaca. He ruled a small and barren island, *yet none the less on* that account he had obtained renown *far and wide for* his wisdom and cunning. *At first* he did not wish to go *to* Troy, and *that* he might not be obliged to do so he pretended to be mad. But *one* Palamedes detected the trick. *As* the king was ploughing, Palamedes took *his* infant son Telemachus, and placed him in the field in front of his father's oxen. If Ulysses had been really mad, he would have gone on *without* noticing the baby, but he turned the plough aside, and so was forced to confess *that* he was feigning madness. *So* he went to Troy, and distinguished himself in battle *as well as* in council, nor was *anyone* more useful to Agamemnon.

Such a one = " talis."
On that account. Latin, " *on account of* that thing."
Pretended to be mad. Latin, " pretended that he was mad."
As the king, &c. As = " while."
Took his infant son Telemachus and placed him, &c. Latin, " placed his infant son Telemachus taken," &c. Remember that *his* refers to Ulysses.
In front of = " before."
If, &c. See Conditional Sentences.
He went to Troy and, &c. Latin, " having set out (Past Participle Deponent) to Troy, he," &c.

STORY OF THE TROJAN WAR.

V.

In naming Achilles and Ulysses, we have made mention of the Greek leaders whom *everyone* would rank first. But there were others also who deserve to be praised. Among these was Nestor, King of Pylos, who, *though* now a *very* old man, armed himself and left his home, *that* he might give good advice to the kings, *even if* he were not able to fight himself. From his mouth, says the poet, flowed speech sweeter than honey. Ajax, too, was there *with* his brother Teucer from the island of Salamis, famous many ages after *for* the great sea-fight between the Greeks and Persians. Ajax was the strongest of all the Greeks, and the best fighter *save* only Achilles. But a miserable fate awaited him after the taking of Troy, for, being driven mad by Minerva, he behaved in such a way *that, on* coming to his senses, he *could* not endure the eyes of men, but with his own hand made an end of his life. There was also Diomedes the Argive, a brave warrior who even fought with gods, since he wounded Venus, and made Mars cry out *for* pain. Idomeneus, too, came *from* Crete, followed by seventy ships and many soldiers.

In naming, &c.   Render by Ablative Absolute : " Achilles and Ulysses being named."
Deserve to be praised.   Latin, " are worthy of praise."
Of Pylos.   Adjective, " Pylius."
Armed himself and left, &c. Latin, " having being armed, left," &c.
Famous.   " Made famous," or " which was made famous."
Many ages after.   Latin, " later by many ages."
The taking of Troy.   Latin, " Troy taken."
Driven = " made."
He behaved in such a way.   Latin, " he so bore himself."   *I bear myself* = " me gero."
On coming to his senses. Latin, " when again he had become sane."
Since here = " inasmuch " as.   " Siquidem," followed by Indicative Mood.
Made Mars cry out.   Latin, " brought it to pass ('efficio') that Mars cried out."
Followed.   Remember that " sequor " is a Deponent Verb.

STORY OF THE TROJAN WAR.

VI.

There was on the coast of Bœotia a harbour which was called Aulis. Thither came all the ships of the Greeks *that* from *thence* they might cross the Ægean Sea. There are said to have been *about* twelve hundred vessels, which carried *about* a hundred *thousand* men. But *for a long time* adverse winds prevented the fleet *from* starting. *At last* the seer Calchas, *on being* consulted, told the Greeks that King Agamemnon himself was in fault, because he had offended Diana by killing a fawn which she dearly loved. *Until* the goddess should be propitiated, Calchas said *that* the winds *would* be adverse, and that she *must* be propitiated by the sacrifice of Iphigenia, the king's own daughter. Ambition overpowered fatherly love, and Iphigenia was led to the altar. *Some* say *that* she was sacrificed; *others that* Diana, pitying the maiden, put a fawn in her place, and carried her off to the Chersonese *to* be her priestess.

Twelve hundred vessels. Latin, "ships one thousand two hundred."

Because he had offended. Latin, " who had offended " (Pluperfect Subjunctive).

By killing a fawn. Render by Ablative Absolute.

Dearly = " very much," " admodum."

Should be propitiated. Pluperfect Subjunctive Passive.

The king's own daughter. Latin, " the daughter of the king himself."

Put a fawn in her place, and, &c. Latin, " a fawn having been put in her ('ejus') place, carried her off," &c.

STORY OF THE TROJAN WAR.
VII.

Having enumerated some of the allies of Agamemnon, *let* us now see *what* warriors Troy had *to* oppose to them. In the first place Priam, King of Troy, had many valiant sons, the bravest of whom was Hector. *Everyone* pities Hector when he falls *by* the hand of Achilles, for we feel that a brave man has perished, and *with* him the hopes of his fatherland. Not indeed equal to Hector, but *still* a good warrior, was Æneas, son of the goddess Vènus and Anchises. Æneas has been sung of by Virgil, *the* great Roman poet, in a poem which we hope you will all read some day. *At* Troy he showed himself a brave chieftain, and we are told that he was specially dear to the immortal gods, who knew that the Fates had ordained that Rome *should* be founded by the posterity of Æneas. Sarpedon also came to the aid of the Trojans, a Lycian king who was said to be the son of Jupiter himself. But the Trojans were no match for the Greeks in the field, and they were soon shut up within the walls. *Still* they did not think *of* surrendering the city.

Having enumerated. Latin, "since we have enumerated," or render by Ablative Absolute.

What = "qualis." *Troy.* Say, "the Trojans."

To oppose. Latin, "whom they should oppose."

Priam had. Latin, "to Priam there were."

Many valiant sons. Say, "many and valiant sons."

Not indeed equal to Hector. Latin, "to Hector indeed ('quidem') not equal."

Æneas has been sung of by Virgil. Latin, "Virgil has sung Æneas."

Some day. "Aliquando."

We are told. Latin, "we learn."

Sarpedon also came to the aid, &c. *I come to your aid*, Latin, "I come for an aid to you."

No match for = "impar." *Field* = "acies."

They did not think. Latin, "they thought ('cogito') nothing."

Of surrendering the city. Latin, "about the city to be surrendered (Gerundive)."

STORY OF THE TROJAN WAR.
VIII.

The Trojan war lasted *for* ten years. But Homer, in the Iliad, does not relate nearly all the war. Nine years have passed *before* the time *at* which his poem begins, and he does not tell us *all that* happens in the tenth. It *must* have been very hard to feed *so great* an army *for so many* years; and *although* the Greeks had not taken Troy, they had sacked all the neighbouring towns, and ravaged the country in search of food and plunder. Among the maidens whom the Greeks had taken was Chryseis, daughter of Chryses, priest of Phœbus. She had been given to Agamemnon when the booty was divided. But her father, *out of* grief *for* the loss of his daughter, prayed to Phœbus, who sent a plague upon the Greek host, which killed cattle and men alike. Calchas, the seer, told them why the god had sent the plague. Upon this the Greeks, and especially Achilles, cried out that Agamemnon *must* restore the old man's daughter. The king, very wroth, said he *would* restore her, but *would* take in her place Briseis, a fair maiden, who had been given to Achilles. Hence arose a dire quarrel.

Does not relate nearly all the war. Latin, " relates only a small part of the war."
And he does not = " nor does he."
It must have been = " it could not help being." See "must."
Country. Use " Ager Trojanus."
In search of. Latin, " while they seek," or " that they might find."
For the loss of his daughter. Latin, " for his lost daughter." See "*for*," 10.
Which killed, &c. Say, " by which both cattle and men were killed."
Upon this = " then."

STORY OF THE TROJAN WAR.

IX.

Achilles swore that he *would* not fight any more on behalf of the Greeks, because they had not tried to prevent Agamemnon *from* taking away Briseis. Out of the depths of the sea came his mother Thetis *to* console her son. She bids him abide in his tent. She says she will pray to Jupiter to grant victory to the Trojans, that the Greeks may regret the absence of Achilles. At once she sets out to the abodes of the gods, and clasping the knees of the Thunderer prays him to avenge her son. "If the Fates," says she, "foretold that he is to die early, they also promised that he *should* win immortal renown. But now King Agamemnon has insulted him openly *before* all the host." Jupiter replies that the Trojans shall prevail *until* the wrath of Achilles is appeased. He sends a dream to Agamemnon, by which he bids him attack the city on the morrow. Deceived by the dream, Agamemnon marshals his troops and prepares to fight.

Any more = " ulterius."
On behalf of = " for."
Because they had not tried. Latin, " who had not tried (Pluperfect Subjunctive)."
To grant = " that he should grant," " ut," with Subjunctive after a Verb of asking.
The absence of Achilles. Latin, " the absent Achilles."
Clasping. Render by Past Participle of Deponent Verb.
Is to die. Render by Impersonal Gerundive, " that it is to be died by him."
Shall prevail. Say, " be superior."
Morrow = " dies crastinus."
Marshals his troops and prepares. Latin, " his troops being marshalled (Ablative Absolute) prepares."

STORY OF THE TROJAN WAR.

X.

The battle was fought with courage and firmness on
both sides, but, *according to* the will of Jupiter the
Trojans prevailed. *Only* the approach of night saved
the Greeks' ships *from* being set on fire by Hector.
The Greeks are cooped up within their entrenchments
while the Trojans bivouac on the open plain, hoping
that on the following day they will utterly destroy
their foes, *unless* indeed they escape during the night.
Agamemnon calls a council *to* determine what is to be
done. *At first*, he proposes that they shall at *once*
embark and return home. But afterwards, at the
advice of Nestor, he chooses three chieftains to go *as*
ambassadors to Achilles, and try to appease his wrath.
They are bidden to offer Briseis, and many treasures
besides, *if only* Achilles will be persuaded to enter the
battle. Ajax and Ulysses are two of the envoys. The
third is Phœnix, an old man whom Achilles loved and
honoured *like* a father. Achilles receives them courteously, and listens to their words, but finally refuses to
take the gifts or to fight against Hector.

The battle, &c. Latin, " it was fought courageously and firmly."
Open plain = " campus."
Escape. Perfect Subjunctive Active.
To determine = " that he may determine."
He proposes = " suadet."
That they shall embark and return. Latin, " that having em-
 barked they should return." *Having embarked* = " their ships
 having been entered (' conscendo ')." (Ablative Absolute.)
At the advice of Nestor. Latin, " Nestor (being) adviser." (Ab-
 lative Absolute.)
To go = " who should go."
As ambassadors. See " as," 6.
If only Achilles will be persuaded. Latin, " provided that
 (' dummodo ') it be persuaded to Achilles."
Refuses to take &c. Latin, " denies that he will take ... or
 will fight."

STORY OF THE TROJAN WAR.

XI.

At sunrise the battle was renewed. Either side prevails, according to the will of the gods. Neptune aids the Greeks, Apollo the Trojans. Juno by a crafty device lulls Jupiter to sleep, and prevents him *from* seeing the battle. At length he awakes and sees the Trojans routed. Indignant at the fraud he threatens his spouse with terrible punishment, sends Iris *to* bid Neptune leave the field, and Apollo *to* revive Hector, whom Ajax has stricken *down* with a huge stone. Hector, forgetting his wound and full ·of confidence, assails the Greek ramparts, bursts open the gates, and *almost* sets fire to the ships. Then *at last* Achilles is moved. He *will* not fight himself, but sends his friend Patroclus, clad in *his* arms and followed by *his* men. Patroclus repels the victorious Trojans, but incautiously pursues them too far, and is slain *by* Hector, who strips from *his* limbs the arms of Achilles. *How great* is the sorrow of Achilles *for* his lost friend, no tongue can tell. *In vain* his mother tries to console him. He only lives *that* he may take vengeance on Hector, *though* the Fates have decreed that he himself *must* die when he has slain his foe.

Either side = " uterque." Nominative Plural. *Prevail* = " vinco."
Crafty device = "dolus."
Lulls Jupiter to sleep and prevents him. Latin, "prevents Jupiter lulled to sleep."
He awakes and sees. Latin, " being awakened he sees."
To leave the field = " acie exire."
Assails, bursts, and sets fire. Latin, " assails, &c., and the gates being burst open (Ablative Absolute) almost sets fire," &c.
He will not fight, but sends, &c. Latin, " since he will not fight, he sends," &c.
And followed by his men. Latin, " his (men) following." Omit *and.*
Incautiously pursues and is slain. Latin, "incautiously pursuing (Aorist Participle Deponent) is slain."
Of Achilles. Use the Dative Case.
Lives. Say, " wishes to live."

STORY OF THE TROJAN WAR.

XII.

At the request of Thetis, Vulcan forges new armour *for* her son, *instead of* that which Hector has stripped from Patroclus's body. Clad in this armour, his heart filled with rage, Achilles rushes to the fight. He spares none whom he meets; he fears nothing for himself, *if only* he *may* encounter his foe. The river Scamander is choked with corpses; the god Scamander himself *in* wrath gathers his waves and *almost* overwhelms the Greek chieftain *with* a sudden flood. Saved by the aid of Juno, Achilles drives before him the flying Trojans, *until* they rush headlong into the city gates. *Only* Hector remains outside. The day *on* which he *is* to fall is come; the gods forsake him. Vainly he attempts to escape by flight; vainly he faces the foe. Having received a mortal wound, *while* dying, he entreats Achilles *to* restore his corpse to his parents, *and not* leave it to be torn by dogs and vultures. Not *even* this *will* the conqueror grant. He ties the corpse to his chariot, and drives it triumphantly round the walls of Troy. From the walls his wife and mother see how Hector's limbs are dragged through the dust.

At the request of Thetis. Ablative Absolute.
Gathers his waves and overwhelms. Latin, "gathering his waves (Ablative Absolute) overwhelms."
Rush = "feror."
And not = "nor."
He ties and drives, &c. Latin, "the dead body being tied he drives."

STORY OF THE TROJAN WAR.
XIII.

Patroclus lies upon his bier, and in the dust *before*
the bier is flung the corpse of Hector. Achilles
celebrates with all pomp the obsequies of his friend,
slays Trojan captives *at* the funeral pile, and assembles
all the Greeks *to* hold games in honour of the dead
hero. Meanwhile in Troy there is sorrow and mourn-
ing. *At length* the aged Priam, warned *by* a heavenly
messenger, determines to go to the camp of the Greeks
and entreat Achilles *to* restore the body of his son.
He carries with him precious gifts for his ransom, and
under the guidance of Mercury he escapes the Greek
outposts and safely reaches the Thessalian chieftain's
tent. *At first* Achilles refuses, but *at length* he is
moved *to* comply with the bereaved father's request.
Nay, Priam *even* sits at meat *with* him who had slain
his son, and they weep together *as* each bethinks him
of his home. Then Priam returns to Troy bearing
with him the body of Hector, and having obtained
a truce for twelve days, he buries him with all the
honour which the Trojans owed to *one* who had fought
for them so bravely and so long.

Patroclus lies, &c., and. Latin, " while Patroclus lies, &c. (omitting *and*)."

Celebrates = " facio."

With all pomp. For *all*, say, " the greatest," " summus." Omit
and in this sentence.

Hold = " celebro."

The aged Priam. Render *the* by " ille."

To go and entreat, &c. Latin, " having gone (Past Participle
Deponent) to entreat," &c.

For his ransom. Say, " with which he may ransom him."

Under the guidance of Mercury. Latin, " Mercury (being)
leader." (Ablative Absolute.)

He escapes and reaches. Latin, " when he has escaped, &c., he
reaches."

To comply with, &c. Phrase, " I comply with your request " =
" morem tibi gero."

Nay, even = " quin etiam."

Bethinks him of = " remembers."

Having obtained. Say, " when he had obtained (' impetro ')."

For twelve days. Genitive Case.

STORY OF THE TROJAN WAR.
XIV.

Here ends that part of the Trojan war which Homer relates *for* us in the Iliad. . From other books we learn that the war lasted *for* some months longer, *during* which other allies came to aid the Trojans, among whom were Penthesilea, the warrior maiden, and Memnon, son of Aurora. But *both* of them were slain by Achilles, who himself *at last* fell, struck *by* an arrow which Paris shot. Then, as we learn in *certain* authors, the Greeks *at the* advice of Ulysses, whose mind Minerva guided, built the famous wooden horse, which was big enough to hold *all the* bravest heroes, and pretended to abandon the siege and sail home. The Trojans with their own hands dragged the fatal horse into the city, and then betook themselves to joy and revelry, thinking *that* their enemies had departed. But at midnight the Greek chieftains sallied forth from their wooden hiding-place, and opened the gates to their comrades and got possession of Troy. Priam was slain before the altar of his own home; the men were put to the sword, the women made slaves, and laden with booty the Greeks returned home.

Ends = " finem habeo."
That the war lasted. Say, " that it was fought."
Built and pretended. Latin, " having built (Ablative Absolute) pretended."
The famous = " ille."
To abandon, and sail. Latin, " having abandoned (Ablative Absolute) to sail."
Big enough to hold = " so big that it held." *So big* = " tantus." *Hold* = " contineo."
Dragged and betook, &c. Latin, " when they had dragged, betook," &c.
Thinking. Past Participle of Deponent Verb.
But at midnight, &c. Latin, " having sallied forth (Past Participle of Deponent Verb) when they had opened the gates, got possession of Troy." Omit *and* in both clauses.
Were put to the sword. Say, " were killed with the sword."

ALEXANDER THE GREAT.

I.

Alexander, whom we call the Great, was the son of Philip, King of Macedonia, and *his* wife Olympias. He was born *at* Pella on the 6th of July, B.C. 356. *On* the same day that he was born the temple of Diana *at* Ephesus, the most famous building in the world, was set on fire by Erostratus, and totally destroyed. All the Magi, who were then at Ephesus, said that by the fire a *much* greater calamity was portended. They ran about the streets, beating themselves, and crying that the day had brought forth the great scourge and destroyer of Asia. Philip had *just* taken the city of Potidæa, when three messengers on the same day came to him. The first told him that *his* general, Parmenio, had conquered the Illyrians, the second that *his* horse had won the prize at the Olympic games, the third that *his* wife had given birth to a child. The king was overjoyed, and the soothsayers increased his joy by telling him that a son born in the midst of victories could not *help* hereafter proving invincible.

B.C. 356. In English we read this, "before Christ three hundred and fifty-six." In Latin, "in the year before Christ born three-hundredth, fiftieth, sixth."

That he was born. *That* here = " on which."

In the world = " omnium."

Scourge and destroyer = " pestis et pernicies."

Was overjoyed = " summo gaudio affectus est." Literally, "was affected by the greatest joy."

And the soothsayers, &c. Latin, "which (joy) the soothsayers increased when they told him."

Proving. "I prove myself" = "me praesto."

ALEXANDER THE GREAT.
II.

While Alexander was *still* a boy, in the absence of his father Philip, ambassadors from Persia arrived, and Alexander, receiving them in his father's stead, charmed them greatly, *both* by his courtesy and his good sense. He did not put childish questions, but asked them the distance between cities, what roads led through the provinces of Asia, *what* was the character of their king, and how he behaved *towards* his enemies. The ambassadors were struck with admiration, and valued the shrewdness of Philip at nothing *in* comparison with the lofty genius of his son. Moreover, whenever the news was brought that Philip had taken some strongly fortified town, or won a great victory, the young man, *instead of* rejoicing, used to say to his companions, "My father will go on conquering *till* there be nothing left for you and me to do. *The* more glory he wins, *the* less is left for us." But he did not seek every kind of honour. Being asked *whether* he *would* contend at the Olympic games (for he was very swift of foot), he answered that he would do so if he had kings for his antagonists.

In the absence of, &c. Render by Ablative Absolute.
Ambassadors from Persia. Latin, "ambassadors sent from Persia," or "setting out (Past Participle Deponent) from Persia."
And Alexander receiving them. Latin, "whom when Alexander received."
In his father's stead = "*instead of* his father."
Good sense. Use "prudentia."
Put childish questions = "puerilia percontari."
The distance between cities. Latin, "how much cities were distant one from another." *One from another* = "inter se."
Valued . . . at nothing. Use "nihili facere."
The news was brought. Say, "it was announced."
Strongly fortified = "munitissimus."
Will go on conquering = "vincere perget."
For you and me to do. Latin, "which I and you may do," or "to be done (Gerundive) by me and you."
More glory. Latin, "more of glory."
Contend. Say, "try for a prize."
Swift of foot = "cursu celer."
Antagonist = "aemulus."

ALEXANDER THE GREAT.

III.

When Philonicus, *a* Thessalian, offered the horse Bucephalus to Philip *at* the price of thirteen talents, the king, with his son and many others, went into the field to see him. The horse appeared to be unbroken, and *instead of* allowing himself to be mounted attacked the grooms fiercely. Philip, angry that such an animal should be offered to him, bade them take him away. But Alexander said, " *What* a horse they are losing for want of skill to manage him." He then offered to mount him on condition that, if he could not manage him, he should pay the thirteen talents. On this all the company laughed, but Alexander ran to the horse and seizing the bridle turned him towards the sun. For he had noticed that the horse was *much* disturbed by the motion of his own shadow. Then he patted him with his hand, and encouraged and soothed him with his voice, and so succeeded in mounting him. When, after a little, he began to urge him with voice and spurs, *all* thought that he would be killed. But he returned safe, and was greeted with loud acclamations, while his father wept *for* joy that he had so noble a son.

Offered. Use Imperfect of " vendo."
That is expressed by " quod," with Imperfect Subjunctive.
To take him away. Say, " that he should be led away."
For want of skill to manage him. Latin, " because they lack the skill with which they may manage him."
Offered to mount him. Latin, " said that he would mount him."
All the company. Latin, " all who were present."
Seizing the bridle. Ablative Absolute.
Succeeded in mounting him. Latin, " managed (' efficio ') that he should mount him."
That he had, &c. Say, " to whom there was " (Imperfect Subjunctive).

ALEXANDER THE GREAT.
IV.

Philip perceived that the genius of his son was too great to be trained except by the best masters. He, therefore, summoned Aristotle, the most famous philosopher of that age, and asked him *to* become his son's preceptor. *For* undertaking this duty he gave him a reward *not only* unusual but honourable. For, having formerly destroyed the city of Stagira, where the philosopher was born, he now rebuilt it, and settled there the former inhabitants who had *either* fled *or* had been made slaves. Aristotle taught Alexander philosophy, but the prince's natural thirst for knowledge made him read other books *as well*. He specially loved Homer, whose works he always kept with him. They say indeed that he used to place a copy of the Iliad under his pillow along with his sword. Afterwards he used to keep this copy in a casket which he found among the spoils of Darius. "Darius," said he, "used to keep his perfumes in this casket, but I, who have no time to anoint myself, will employ it for a better use." *On* the death of Philip, Alexander became King of Macedonia, in the twentieth year of his age.

Too great to be trained. Latin, "greater than that which could be trained."

He therefore summoned and asked Aristotle. Latin, "he asked Aristotle summoned (Past Participle)."

For undertaking this duty. Latin, either "on account of this duty undertaken," or "because he undertook this duty."

Having destroyed. Latin, "since he had destroyed."

Made him read. Latin, "brought it to pass ('efficio') that he read."

Kept. Use "habeo."

Who have no time to anoint myself. Latin, "to whom leisure is wanting in which I may anoint myself."

On the death of Philip. Render by Ablative Absolute, or by "quum" with Subjunctive.

ALEXANDER THE GREAT.

V.

When Alexander became king, he found his kingdom
torn by seditions. *Having* quelled these tumults, he
determined to carry out in the first place his purpose
of subjugating Greece. Hearing that the Thebans had
revolted, and that the Athenians were *about* to do so,
he marched *at once* with his army through the famous
pass of Thermopylæ, and attacked Thebes. *Having*
taken the city, he sold thirty *thousand* of the inhabitants for slaves. He only spared the priests and those
who were bound to the Macedonians by the ties of
hospitality. He also gave orders that the house of
Pindar, the celebrated poet, should not be destroyed,
thereby showing that even in the midst of war he did
not forget the liberal arts. *As to* the Athenians he
forgave them, *although* they did not hesitate to show
their sorrow *for* the destruction of Thebes, and received
those Thebans who had escaped. There is reason to
think that he repented of his cruelty towards the
Thebans, and therefore showed himself more merciful
towards other cities which he captured.

Torn = " turbatus."
In the first place = " primum."
Hearing, &c. Latin, " when he heard."
The famous pass of Thermopylæ. Latin, " that famous pass
    which is called Thermopylæ."
He marched and attacked. Latin, " having marched (Deponent
    Participle) he attacked."
For slaves. Say, " into slavery."
Ties of hospitality = " hospitum."
Gave orders that the house should not be destroyed. Latin, " for-
    bade the house to be destroyed."
Thereby showing. Say, " and thereby (' itaque ') showed."
Show. Use " prodo."
The destruction of Thebes. Say, " Thebes destroyed."
There is reason to think. Latin, " there is why we may think."
Of his cruelty towards the Thebans. Say, " that (' quod ') he
    had treated (Pluperfect Subjunctive) the Thebans so cruelly."

ALEXANDER THE GREAT.
VI.

An assembly being held at the Isthmus of Corinth, the Greeks resolved to send their forces *to* fight under Alexander against the Persians. Many philosophers came *to* congratulate the king on this occasion, and he hoped that Diogenes of Sinope, who then dwelt at Corinth, *would* be among them. Finding, however, that he made little account of Alexander, and preferred the enjoyment of his leisure in the suburbs, the king went to see him, accompanied by his courtiers. Diogenes happened to be lying in the sun, and at the approach of so many people he raised himself up and gazed upon Alexander. The king addressed him courteously, and asked him *if* he could do anything for him. "Withdraw a little out of the sunshine," said Diogenes. Alexander was so much surprised at finding himself so little valued, that, *while* his courtiers were ridiculing the philosopher, he said, "If I were not Alexander, I should wish to be Diogenes."

Of Corinth; omit.

Under Alexander. Latin, "Alexander being leader." (Ablative Absolute.)

And he hoped that Diogenes would be among them. Latin, "among whom he hoped that Diogenes would be."

Of Sinope. "Sinopensis."

Finding. Latin, "when he found."

Made little account of Alexander. Latin, "valued ('facio') Alexander at little price."

The enjoyment of his leisure. Latin, "to enjoy his leisure."

Diogenes happened to be lying = "it happened ('accido') that Diogenes was lying."

At the approach of so many people. Latin, "so many people ('vir') approaching." (Ablative Absolute.)

Gazed upon. Imperfect.

Addressed and asked. Latin, "addressing (Past Participle Deponent) asked."

If he could do anything for him. Latin, "if anything ('numquid') he could do ('praesto') for him."

At finding himself. Say, "that he was."

So little valued = "tantuli aestimari." Literally, "to be valued at so small (a price)."

If I were not Alexander, I should wish to be Diogenes. See Conditional Sentences.

ALEXANDER THE GREAT.
VII.

Wishing to consult the oracle *about* the event of the war, he went to Delphi. *On* the day on which he happened to arrive, no one was allowed to consult the oracle, because that day was unlucky. At first he sent messengers to the priestess, and entreated her to perform her office. Finding that she refused he went himself, and dragged her by force into the temple. Then, *as if* she were conquered by violence, she said, "My son, thou art invincible." Alexander, hearing this, said that he wanted no other answer, *since* he had the very oracle he desired. *As to* the number of his forces, he is said to have commanded thirty *thousand* foot and five *thousand* horse. When he was *about* to set out, he distributed all his possessions among his friends, giving *one* an estate, *another* a village. When his friend Perdiccas asked him what he reserved for himself, he answered that he reserved his hopes. Perdiccas said that they who shared his labours *would* also share his hope, and refused the estate which the king offered him.

Wishing. Latin, "when he wished."
He happened to arrive. Latin, "it happened ('accido') that he arrived."
No one was allowed. Latin, "it was allowed to no one."
Sent messengers and entreated. Latin, "entreated through messengers." Omit *sent*.
Hearing this. Latin, "which being heard." (Ablative Absolute.) First in the sentence.
That he wanted no other answer. Latin, "that there was need to him of no other answer."
Giving an estate. Latin, "an estate being given." (Ablative Absolute.)
When his friend Perdiccas asked him. Latin, "to his friend Perdiccas asking."
Refused. Say, "was unwilling to accept."

ALEXANDER THE GREAT.

VIII.

Having crossed the Hellespont, *as soon as* he landed he visited Ilium, where he offered sacrifice to Minerva, and poured libations. He also anointed Achilles' tomb *with* oil, and ran round it *with* his friends, and *afterwards* put a garland upon it, saying that he thought Achilles very fortunate, because, while alive, he *had* a faithful friend, and after death an excellent herald *to* celebrate his praises. *As* he went about the city to look at the buildings, he was asked *whether* he wished to see Paris's lyre. "I set but little value," said he, "on the lyre of Paris, but it would give me pleasure to see the harp of Achilles, to which he sung the glorious actions of the brave." Meanwhile Darius had collected a great army and posted his forces on the banks of the river Granicus. Alexander *had* to cross the river *to* attack the enemy. When his officers seemed unwilling to attempt the passage, the king said, "It will be a disgrace if, after crossing the Hellespont, we are afraid of the Granicus," and *at once* plunged into the stream.

Offered sacrifice = " sacrifico."
He anointed and ran. Latin, " when he had anointed he ran," &c.
That he thought Achilles. Latin, " that Achilles seemed (Present Infinitive) to him."
Because he had. Latin, " to whom there was " (Imperfect Subjunctive).
While alive. Omit " while."
Went. Use " ambulo."
To look at. Use the Supine.
I set but little value on the lyre. Latin, " I value ('facio') the lyre *at* little (Genitive of price)."
It would give me pleasure to see. Latin, " I would gladly see."
To which. Use the Ablative.
The brave. Plural.
Had collected and posted. Latin, " having collected (Ablative Absolute) had posted."
Post = " colloco."
A disgrace. Dative Case. See Rule.
We are afraid of = we fear. See Conditional Sentences.

ALEXANDER THE GREAT.

IX.

Alexander soon routed the Persians *at* the Granicus, but he found the Greek mercenaries foes more worthy of him. They retired to an eminence, and were ready to surrender *on* condition that their lives should be spared. Alexander, more impetuous *than* prudent, *instead of* giving them quarter advanced to attack them. More of his soldiers were killed or wounded here than in *any* other part of the battle, for he *had* to fight with experienced soldiers, whose courage was increased by despair. Of the barbarians there fell in this battle twenty *thousand* foot and two *thousand* five hundred horse, whereas Alexander *had* only thirty-four men killed, nine of whom were foot soldiers. Immediately after this battle the city of Sardis surrendered, and all the other neighbouring towns followed its example, *except* Halicarnassus and Miletus, which Alexander took by storm. *Thence* he marched to Tarsus in Cilicia. On the way he took Gordium, formerly the city of Midas the king, and there he is said to have untied the Gordian knot. It was believed that he who untied the knot *would* be sovereign of the world.

They retired and were ready. Latin, " when they had retired they were ready."

Giving quarter. Say, " sparing."

Alexander had. Latin, " to Alexander there were."

And all the towns followed its example. Latin, " whose example all the towns followed."

To Tarsus in Cilicia. Latin, " to Tarsus, a city of Cilicia," or " situated in Cilicia."

On the way = " in it were."

He took Gordium, and is said. Latin, " having taken Gordium (Ablative Absolute) he is said."

Formerly the city of Midas the king. Say, " where formerly King Midas dwelt."

He who untied the knot. Verb in Pluperfect Subjunctive.

ALEXANDER THE GREAT.

X.

While Alexander was staying in Cilicia, he fell seriously ill. Some say that fatigue was the cause, others that he had bathed imprudently in the river Cydnus, whose waters are very cold. When the other doctors were hesitating, one Philip, an Acarnanian, offered to cure the king, *if only* he would drink a potion. *While* the medicine was being prepared, a letter was brought to the king from Parmenio, in which he advised him to beware of Philip. He said that Darius had persuaded Philip, by a bribe, to kill him by poison. Alexander, *as soon as* he had read the letter, put it under his pillow *without* showing it to any of his friends. Soon Philip entered the chamber, bearing the medicine. The king received it *without* showing any signs of suspicion, and, at the same time, put the letter into Philip's hands. *While* the one read the other drank. The medicine was *of such a kind* that for *some time* Alexander lay senseless *without* showing any sign of life. But within three days he was so far recovered that he was able to shew himself to his faithful troops.

He fell seriously ill. Latin, "he fell ('incido') into a serious ('gravis') illness."
Offered to cure. Latin, "said that he would cure."
Put the letter into Philip's hands. Latin, "gave the letter to Philip into his hands."
So far = "adeo." *To recover* = "convalescere.'

ALEXANDER THE GREAT.

XI.

As soon as Alexander was well, he set out against Darius, and fought him near Issus. *Though* Darius had greatly the advantage in numbers, he was utterly defeated, and narrowly escaped by flight with the loss of a hundred and ten thousand men. Alexander took his chariot and his bow, and returning with them found his men plundering the Persian camp. The tent of Darius they had reserved for their master, in which he found many attendants, rich furniture, and great quantities of gold and silver. *As* he was dining, word was brought him that among the prisoners were the mother and wife of Darius, who, *on* seeing his chariot and bow, began to lament and weep, supposing that he was dead. Alexander sent a friend *to* tell them that Darius was not dead, and that they had nothing to fear. *Though* they were his captives, he showed them the utmost courtesy, so that they were as safe as if they had been in some holy temple, not in the midst of an enemy's camp.

He set out and fought. Latin, "having set out he fought."
Fought him. Latin, "fought with *or* against him."
Had the advantage. Latin, "was superior."
Numbers. Say, "number of soldiers."
With the loss of. Render by Ablative Absolute.
Alexander took, &c. Latin, "when Alexander, having taken his chariot and his bow, returned, he found," &c.
His men plundering. Latin, "his (men) who were plundering."
Rich = "lautus."
Quantities = "vis."
Word was brought him. Latin, "it was reported to him."
Supposing. Past Participle Deponent, or "since they supposed."
And that they had nothing to fear. Latin, "nor was there anything to be feared (Gerundive) by them."
Showed them the utmost courtesy. Say, "used the utmost courtesy towards them."
As safe as if they had been. Latin, "not less safe than if," &c.

ALEXANDER THE GREAT.

XII.

After the battle of Issus, Alexander marched into Phœnicia, and laid siege to the city of Tyre. *After* besieging the city for seven months, he took it by storm. Thence he marched into Syria, and having taken Gaza, advanced further into Egypt. While he was in Egypt, two things in particular are recorded about him; *first*, that he founded the famous city at the mouth of the Nile, which is called after him Alexandria; *secondly*, that he visited the oracle of Jupiter Ammon. To reach this, he *had* to march through the Libyan desert. The march was dangerous, *both* on account of the scarcity of water, *and* also because of the dust which, when stirred by the wind, often rolled in such dense clouds that it overwhelmed whole armies. But it is said that rain fell so often that it *not only* completely laid the dust, *but also* removed all fear of suffering from thirst. Moreover, *whenever* the marks of the road were effaced, a flock of crows is said to have appeared and shown the way. What the priest of Jupiter said to Alexander is uncertain, but some believe that he told the king that he was the son of Jove.

The battle of Issus. " *The city of Tyre.*" See Rule 8.
While he was in Egypt. Translate "was" by "commoror." Literally, "delayed."
After him.. Latin, " from his name."
Rolled. Latin, " rolled itself, *or* was rolled."
It is said. Latin, " they say."
To lay (the dust) = " sedo."
Fear of suffering by thirst. Latin, "fear lest they should be oppressed by thirst." *To be oppressed* = "laborare."

ALEXANDER THE GREAT.

XIII.

After his return from Egypt, Alexander, *having* subdued all nations on this side of the Euphrates, again marched against Darius, who, as they say, was at the head of a million of men. Again he utterly defeated him near Arbela, and *so great* was the victory that the Persian empire was entirely destroyed, and Alexander became king of all Asia. Darius escaped, but was *afterwards* slain by Bessus, one of his own friends, whom Alexander, when he fell into his hands, punished with death *for* this treachery. But *after* he had become King of Persia and all the East, the character of Alexander began to change. He adopted the Persian dress, a thing which greatly displeased his veterans. He no longer trusted his friends. He was so ungrateful that he put to death Parmenio, an old man who had been his companion in all his wars, and his most able general, because his son Philotas had formed a conspiracy against his life. Not long afterwards, when maddened *with* wine and rage, he killed Clitus, one of his dearest friends, *with* his own hand. But he repented this so much that he could hardly be prevented *from* killing himself.

After his return. Say, "after he returned."
On this side of = " citra " (Accusative).
Was at the head of = " prosum."
Punished. Say, " visited " (afficio).
Began to change. Put both Verbs in the Passive Voice in Latin.
A thing which = "id quod."
Able = "belli peritus." Literally, " skilled in war."
His son Philotas, i.e. Parmenio's son.
His life, i.e. Alexander's life.
When maddened. Omit "when." Use "incendo," " to inflame."

ALEXANDER THE GREAT.
XIV.

Though he was now sovereign of a wider kingdom *than any one* before him, Alexander was not content, for he would. not have been content even if he had subdued the whole world. He led his Macedonians as as *far* as India, subduing kings and taking cities. Of these kings the most famous was Porus, whom he fought on the banks. of the river Hydaspes. This battle had the same result as all which had preceded it. When Porus was taken prisoner Alexander asked him how he desired to be treated? He answered, "As befits a king." "And have you nothing *else* to ask?" said the conqueror. "Nothing," said Porus, "in this everything is included." Alexander not only restored to him his own dominions, but added very extensive territories to them. Thence he wished to advance still further, but *at length* the veterans refused to follow him. Worn out with campaigning, and tired of the war, they halted on the banks of the river Hyphasis, and Alexander, *notwithstanding* his entreaties and prayers, was obliged to lead them back. He reached Susa at the beginning of the year 325 B.C.

Subduing and taking. Render by "quum" with Subjunctive.
The same result as = " the same result which."
Which had preceded it. Say, "which had been fought" ('committo') before."
To ask. Latin, " which you may ask."
Everything = " all things."
Refused to follow. Latin, " denied that they would follow."
Tired of the war = " tired with the war."
Notwithstanding his entreaties and prayers = " though he entreated and prayed them."
At the beginning of the year = " ineunte anno." (For the way to express the Date, see the first note on p. 140.)

ALEXANDER THE GREAT.
XV.

There are not many things left for us to tell about Alexander after his return from India. He took measures to set in order the vast kingdom which he had subdued; he himself married a Persian wife, and encouraged his followers to do the same. About this time died Hephæstion, by far his dearest friend, and the grief of Alexander exceeded all bounds. In the following spring he entered Babylon, *though* the Chaldean soothsayers warned him that evil *would* come of it if he did so. *During* that year he planned more wars. He intended first to subdue Arabia, and then to make himself master of Italy, Carthage and the West. Who can tell what he would have done if he had lived? But he was attacked by a fever, and died after an illness of eleven days on the 30th of June, B.C. 323, at the age of thirty-two, after a reign of twelve years and eight months. He taught mankind the same lesson which they had first learnt at the battles of Marathon and Salamis. Asiatic tribes, whatever be their advantage in numbers, can never resist the discipline and valour of European soldiers.

Many things. Neuter Plural.
Are left = " remain."
For us to tell = " which we may tell."
After his return = " after he had returned."
To take measures = " id agere ut."
Come = " evenio."
If he did so. Pluperfect Subjunctive.
Intend = " in animo habeo."
What he would have done = " quid facturus fuerit."
Attack = " corripio."
After an illness = " after he was ill."
B.C. 323. See p. 140.
At the age of 32. Latin, " having been born 32 years."
After a reign. Latin, " when he had reigned."
The same lesson. Say, " the same (thing)."
Whatever, &c. Latin, " though they are much superior in numbers."

VOCABULARY.

A.

abandon (to), v.	abjĭcĭo, 3 ; ŏmitto, 3.
abdicate (to), v.	abdĭco, 1.
abide (to), v.	mănĕo, 2.
ability, sub.	indŏles -is, 3 f.
able, adj.	pĕrītus.
able (to be), v.	possum, irr.
abode, sub.	sēdes -is, 3 f.
abroad (to be), v.	pĕrĕgrīnor, 1 dep.
absent (to be), v.	absum, irr.
absent, adj.	absens.
abuse, sub.	convīcĭum -ii, 2 n.
Acarnanian, sub.	Ăcarnān -ānĭs, 3 m.
accident (by), adv.	cāsū, fortĕ.
acclamation, sub.	plausŭs, 4 m.
accompanied, part.	stīpātŭs.
accuse (to), v.	accūso, 1.
ache (to), v.	dŏlĕo, 2.
Achilles, sub.	Ăchilles -is, 3 m.
across, prep.	trans.
act (to), v.	ăgo, 3.
action, sub.	făcĭnŭs -ŏrĭs, 3 n.
actor, sub.	histrio -ōnĭs, 3 m.
add (to), v.	addo, 3.
address (to), v.	allŏquor, 3 dep.
admiration, sub.	admīrātĭo -ōnĭs, 3 f.
admire (to), v.	admīror, 1 dep.
admit (to), v.	confĭteor, 2 dep.
adopt (to), v.	ūtor, 3 dep.
advance (to), v.	prōgrĕdior, 3 dep.
adverse, adj.	adversŭs.
advice, sub.	consĭlium, 2 n.
advise (to), v.	mŏnĕo, 2.
adviser, sub.	auctŏr -ōris, 3 m.

Ægisthus,	Aegisthŭs, 2 m.
Æneas,	Aenĕās -ae, 1 m.
Æschylus,	Aeschўlŭs, 2 m.
Ætna,	Aetna, 1 f.
affair, sub.	rēs, rĕi, 5 f.
afraid (to be), v.	vĕrĕor, 2 dep.
Africa, sub.	Lĭbўa, 1 f.
afterwards, adv.	postĕā.
again, adv.	rursŭs.
Agamemnon, sub.	Ăgămemnōn, ŏnis, 3 m.
age, sub.	saecŭlum, 2 n. aetās -ātĭs, 3 f.
aged, adj.	sĕnex.
ago, adv.	ăbhinc.
agree, v.	adsentĭor, 4 dep.
agreed (it is), v.	convĕnit, imp.
aid, sub.	auxĭlĭum, 2 n.
aid (to), v.	adjŭvo, 1.
air, sub.	āēr -ĕris, 3 m.
Ajax, sub.	Ăjax -ācis, 3 m.
Alexander, sub.	Ălexander -dri, 2 m.
Alexandria, sub.	Ălexandrēa, 1 f.
alike, adv.	ĭdem (lit. "the same").
alive (to be), v.	vīvo, 3.
all, adj.	omnĭs.
allied, part.	sŏcĭātus.
allow (to), v.	pătĭor, 3 dep.
allowed (it is), v.	lĭcĕt, imp.
ally, sub.	sŏcĭus, 2 m.
almost, adv.	paenĕ.
Alps, sub.	Alpes -ium, 3 pl. m.
also, adv.	ĕtiam.
altar, sub.	āra, 1 f.
although, conj.	quamvīs, etsī, quamquam.

always, adv.	sempĕr.
ambassador, sub.	lēgātŭs, 2 m.
ambition, sub.	glōrĭa, 1 f.
ambuscade, sub. *ambush,*	} insĭdiae, 1 pl. f.
Ammon, sub.	Ammōn -ōnĭs, 3 m.
among, prep.	intĕr.
amuse (to), v.	dēlecto, 1.
ancestor, sub.	ăvus, 2 m.
Anchises, sub.	Anchīses -ae, 1 m.
ancient, adj.	antīquŭs.
angry, adj.	īrātŭs.
angry (to be), v.	īrascŏr, 3 dep.
animal, sub.	ănĭmăl -ālĭs, 3 n.
announce (to), v.	nuntĭo, 1.
annoy (to), v.	lăcesso, 3.
annoyance, sub.	incommŏdum, 2 n.
anoint, v.	ungo, 3.
another, adj.	ălius, altĕr.
answer (to), v.	respondĕo, 2.
ant, sub.	formīca, 1 f.
anxious, adj.	sollĭcĭtus.
any, adj.	quīvīs, ullus.
anyone,	quīvīs.
ape, sub.	sīmia, 1 f.
Apollo, sub.	Ăpollō -ĭnĭs, 3 m.
appear (to), v.	vĭdĕor, 2 ; appāreo, 2.
appease (to), v.	plăco, 1.
applaud (to), v.	plaudo, 3.
apple, sub.	pōmum, 2 n.
appoint (to), v.	crĕo, 1 ; făcĭo, 3.
approach, sub.	adventus -ūs, 4.
approach (to), v.	vĕnĭo, 4 ; accēdo, 3.
approve (to), v.	prŏbo, 1.
April, sub.	Ăprīlĭs -ĭs, 3 m.
Arabia, sub.	Ărăbia, 1 f.
Arbela, sub.	Arbēla, 1 f.
Argive, adj.	Argīvus.
argument, sub.	rătĭo -ōnĭs, 3 f.
arise (to), v.	exĭŏrĭor, 3 dep. ; ŏrĭor, 3 dep.
arm (to), v.	armo, 1.
armour, sub. *arms (of a soldier), sub.*	} arma, 2 pl. n.
army, sub.	exercĭtus -ūs, 4 m.
arrive (to), v.	advĕnĭo, 4.
arrival, sub.	adventus -ūs, 4 m.
arrow, sub.	săgitta, 1 f.
art, sub.	ars, artĭs, 3 f.
ascend (to), v.	ascendo, 3.
ashamed (to be), v.	pŭdĕt, imp.
Asia, sub.	Ăsĭa, 1 f.
Asiatic, adj.	Ăsĭătĭcus.
ask (to), v.	rŏgo, 1.
ask for (to), v.	posco, 3.
ass, sub.	ăsĭnus, 2 m.
assail (to), v.	aggrĕdĭor, 3 dep.
assemble (to), v. neut.	cŏĕo, irr.
assemble (to), v. act.	convŏco, 1.
assembly, sub.	conventus -ūs, 4 m.
at all, adv.	omnīnō.
Athenian, s.	Ăthēnĭensis, 3 m.
Athens, sub.	Ăthēnae -ārum, 1 f. pl.
attack (to), v.	oppugno, 1 ; aggrĕdĭor, 3 dep.; impugno, 1.
attempt (to), v.	tento, 1.
attendant, sub.	fămŭlŭs, 2 m.
Aulis, sub.	Aulis -ĭdĭs, 3 f.
Aurora, sub.	Aurōra, 1 f.
author, sub.	scriptor -ōrĭs, 3 m.
autumn, sub.	autumnus, 2 m.
avail (to avail oneself of), v.	ūtor, 3 dep.
avenge (to), v.	ulciscor, 3 dep.
avoid (to), v.	vito, 1.
await (to), v.	expecto, 1 ; mănĕo, 2.
awake (to), v.	expergiscor, 3 dep.
away (to be), v.	absum, irr.
axe, sub.	sĕcūris -ĭs, 3 f.

B.

baby, sub.	infans -antis, 3 m.
Babylon, sub.	Băbўlōn -ōnĭs, 3 f.
back, sub.	tergum, 2 n.
bad, adj.	mălus, imprŏbus.
badly, adv.	mălĕ.
baffle (to), v.	fallo, 3.
banish (to), v.	rĕlēgo, 1.
bank, sub.	rīpa, 1 f.
barbarian, sub.	barbărus, 2 m.
barber, sub.	tonsŏr -ōrĭs, 3 m.
bark (to), v.	lătro, 1.
baron, sub.	princeps -ĭpis, 3 m.
barren, adj.	stĕrĭlis.

basket, sub.	corbis -ĭs, 3 f.: cănistra, 2 pl.
bathe (to), v.	lăvor, 1.
battle, sub.	pugna, 1 f.; proelĭum, 2 n.
bay, sub.	laurus, 2 f.
beach, sub.	lītŭs -ŏris, 3 n.
beam, sub. (of light)	rădĭus, 2 m.
beam, sub. (of wood)	trabs, trăbĭs, 3 f.
bear, sub.	ursa, 1 f.
bear (to), v.	fĕro, irr.
bear off (to), v.	aufĕro, irr.
beard, sub.	barba, 1 f.
beat (to), v.	tundo, 3.
beautiful, adj.	pulchĕr -chră -chrum.
beauty, sub.	pulchrĭtūdō -ĭnĭs, 3 f.
become (to), v.	fīo, irr.
bed, sub.	lectus, 2 m.
bee, sub.	ăpĭs, ĭs, 3 f.
beech-tree, sub.	fāgus, 2 f.
befall (to), v.	ēvĕnĭo, 4 ; accĭdo, 3.
befit, v.	dĕcĕt, imp.
before, adv.	antĕ, prĭŭs.
beg (to), v.	ōro, 1.
beg (to), v.	mendīco, 1.
beggar, sub.	mendīcus, 2 m.
begin (to), v.	coepi, defect.; incĭpĭo, 3.
behave(to), v. Phr.	mē gĕro, 3.
believe (to), v.	crēdo, 3.
bell, sub.	tintinnābŭlum, 2 n.; āēs, āēris, 3 n.
bend (to), v.	flecto, 3.
benefit (to), v.	prōsum, irr.
benefit, sub.	bĕnĕfĭcium, 2 n.
bereaved, adj.	orbātus.
beseech (to), v.	ōro, 1.
besides, prep.	praetĕr.
besiege (to), v.	obsĭdĕo, 2.
besieged, part.	obsessus.
betake (to), v.	confĕro, irr.
betray (to), v.	prōdo, 3.
betrothed, adj.	desponsus.
better (to be), v.	praesto, 1.
better (to be), v.	praestat, imp.
better, adj.	mĕlĭor.
beware of (to), v.	căvĕo, 2.
bid (to), v.	jŭbĕo, 2.
bier, sub.	fĕrĕtrum, 2 n.

big, adj.	magnus.
bind (to), v.	lĭgo, 1; delĭgo, 1; vincĭo, 4.
bird, sub.	ăvĭs -is, 3 f.; vŏlŭcrĭs -ĭs, 3 f.
birthday, sub. Phr.	dĭes nātālis.
bishop, sub.	ĕpiscŏpus, 2 m.
bite (to), v.	mordĕo, 2.
bitter, adj.	ămārus.
bivouac (to), v.	excŭbo, 1.
blame (to), v.	culpo, 1.
blind, adj.	caecus.
blood, sub.	crŭŏr -ōrĭs, 3 m.
blow, sub.	ictus -ūs, 4 m.
blow (to), v.	flo, 1.
blow upon (to),	afflo, 1.
blunt (to), v.	rĕtundo, 3.
boast (to), v.	glōrĭor, 1.
boat, sub.	lintĕr -trĭs, 3 f.
body, sub.	corpŭs -ŏris, 3 n.
Bœotia, sub.	Boeōtia, 1.
bold, adj.	audax.
bone, sub.	ŏs ossis, 3 n.
book, sub.	lĭber, 2 m.
boot, sub.	călĭga, 1 f.
booty, sub.	praeda, 1 f.
border, sub.	fīnis -ĭs, 3 m. or f.
born (to be), v.	nātus sum.
bosom, sub.	grĕmĭum.
bottom, sub. rendered by adj.	īmus.
bound, sub.	mŏdus, 2 m.
bound forward (to), v.	prōsĭlĭo, 4.
bow, sub.	arcŭs -ūs, 4 m.
bowl, sub.	crātēr -ērĭs, 3 m.
boy, sub.	pŭer, 2 m.
branch, sub.	rāmus, 2 m.
brave, adj.	fortis.
bravely, adv.	fortĭtĕr.
break (to), v.	frango, 3.
break (to break one's word), v.	fĭdem fallo, 3.
bribe, sub.	mūnus -ĕrĭs, 3 n.
bribe (to), v.	corrumpo, 3.
brick, sub.	lătĕr -ĕrĭs, 3 m.
bride, sub.	nupta, 1 f.
bridge, sub.	pons, pontĭs, 3 m.
bridle, sub.	hăbēnae, 1 pl. f.
bright, adj.	clārus.
brim, sub.	ōrae, 1 pl. f.
bring (to), v.	fĕro, irr.; affĕro, irr.

bring back (to), v. rĕdūco, 3.
bring forth (to), v. părĭo, 3.
bring up (to), v. effĕro, irr.
bring upon (to), v. infĕro, irr.
Briseis, sub. Brīsēĭs -ĭdis, 3 f.
broad, adj. lātus.
bronze, adj. ăēnĕus.
brook, sub. rīvus, 2 m.
broth, sub. jūs, jūrĭs, 3 n.
brother, sub. frātĕr -trĭs, 3 m.
browse (to), v. vescor, dep.
brush (of a fox), sub. cauda, 1 f.
brush (of a paint-er), sub. pēnĭcillus, 2 m.
Brutus, sub. Brūtus, 2 m.
Bucephalus, sub. Būcĕphălus, 2 m.
build (to), v. ăēdĭfĭco, 1.
building, sub. ăēdĭfĭcĭum, 2 n.
bull, sub. taurus, 2 m.
burden, sub. ŏnŭs -ĕrĭs, 3 n.
burn, v. act. incendo, 3 ; ūro, 3.
burn, v. neut. ardĕo, 2.
burnt, part. ambustus.
burnt down (to be), v. dēflăgro, 1.
burst (to), v. rumpo, 3.
burst open (to), v. perfringo, 3.
bury (to), v. sĕpĕlio, 4.
busy, adj. sēdŭlus.
butterfly, sub. pāpĭlĭo -ōnĭs, 3 m.
buy (to), v. ĕmo, 3.

C.

Caesar, sub. Caesăr -ăris, 3 m.
Caius, sub. Cāĭus, 2 m.
cake, sub. plăcenta, 1 f.
calamity, sub. călămĭtās, 3 f.
Calchas, sub. Calchās -antis, 3 m.
call (to), v. vŏco, 1.
call (to summon), v. arcesso, 3.
call upon, v. invŏco, 1.
call upon, v. ōro, 1.
caller, sub. sălūtans, 3 m.
calm, adj. plăcĭdus.
Camillus, sub. Cămillus.
camp, sub. castra, 2 pl.
campaign, sub. stĭpendium, 2 n. (lit. " pay.")
campaigning, sub. mīlĭtĭa, 1 f.

captive, sub. captīvus, 2 m.
Capua, sub. Căpŭă -ae, 1 f.
careless, adj. sēcūrus, incautus.
carry (to), v. porto, 1.
carry off (to), v. aufĕro, irr. ; ăvĕho, 3.
carry out (to), v. exsĕquor, 3 dep.
Carthage, sub. Carthāgo -ĭnĭs, 3 f.
Carthaginian, sub. Poenus, 2 m.
casket, sub. capsa, 1 f.
cat, sub. fēlis -ĭs, 3 f.
catch, v. căpio, 3 ; excĭpio, 3.
catch at (to), v. capto, 1.
Catilina, sub. Cătĭlina, 1 m.
Cato, sub. Cătō -ōnĭs, 3 m.
cattle, sub. pĕcŭdes, 3 pl. f.
cause, sub. causa, 1 f.
cause (to), v. effĭcĭo, 3.
cautious, adj. cautus.
cave, sub. spēlunca, 1 f.
cease (to), v. dēsĭno, 3.
celebrate (to), v. cĕlĕbro, 1.
celebrated, adj. cĕlĕber.
Centaur, sub. Centaurus, 2 m.
centurion, sub. centŭriō -ōnis, 3 m.
certain, adj. certus, quīdam.
chain, sub. vincŭlum, 2 n.
Chaldean, adj. Chaldaeus.
chalk, sub. crēta -ae, 1 f.
chamber, sub. conclāve -ĭs, 3 n.
champion, sub. vindex -ĭcis, 3 m.
change (to), v. mūto, 1.
changeable, adj. mūtābĭlis.
character, sub. mōrēs, 3 pl. m.
chariot, sub. currus -ūs, 4 m.
charioteer, sub. aurīga, 1 m.
charm (to), v. capto, 1.
Charybdis, sub. Chărybdis -ĭs, 3 f.
chasm, sub. bărăthrum, 2 n.
chastise (to), v. castīgo, 1.
cheese, sub. cāsĕus, 2 m.
cheesecake, sub. plăcenta, 1 f.
cherish (to), v. fŏvĕo, 2.
Chersonese, sub. Chersŏnēsus, 2.
chick, sub. pullus, 2 m.
chieftain, sub. dux, dŭcis, 3 m.
child, sub. pŭĕr, pŭĕrī, 2 m.
children, sub. lībĕri, 2 pl. m.
Chinese, sub. Sērĕs, 3 pl. m.
Chiron, sub. Chīrōn -ōnĭs, 3 m.

choke (to), v.	implĕo, 2.
choose (to), v.	ēlĭgo, 3.
Cicero, sub.	Cĭcĕrō -ōnĭs, 3 m.
Cilicia, sub.	Cĭlĭcĭa, 1 f.
Cimbri, sub.	Cimbri -ōrum, 2 pl. m.
Cincinnatus, sub.	Cincinnātus, 2 m.
citizen, sub.	cīvĭs -ĭs, 3 m.
city, sub.	urbs -bĭs, 3 f.
clad, part.	indūtus.
clasp (to), v.	amplector, 3 dep.
claw, sub.	unguis -is, 3 m.
clean (to), v.	purgo, 1.
cleave (to), v.	findo, 3.
Cleon, sub.	Clĕōn -ōnĭs, 3 m.
climb (to), v.	scando, 3; ascendo, 3.
clip (to), v.	dēcīdo, 3.
cloak, sub.	lăcerna, 1 f.
close (to), v.	claudo, 3.
close, adj.	arctus.
clothes, sub.	vestes -ĭum, 3 pl. f.
cloud, sub.	nūbēs -ĭs, 3 f.
coal, sub.	carbō -ōnĭs, 3 m.
coast, sub.	lītŭs -ŏris, 3 n.
coax (to), v.	blandior, 4 dep.
cock, sub.	gallus, 2 m.
cold, sub.	frĭgŭs -ŏris, 3 n.
cold (to be), v.	frīgĕo, 2.
cold, adj.	frīgĭdus; gĕlĭdus.
collar, sub.	torquĭs -ĭs, 3 m. or f.
collect (to), v.	collĭgo, 3.
colour, sub.	cŏlŏr -ōrĭs, 3 m.
column, sub.	cŏlumna, 1 f.
come (to), v.	vĕnĭo, 4.
come down (to), v.	descendo, 3.
come out (to), v.	ēgrĕdĭor, 3 dep.
come together (to), v.	convĕnio, 4.
come up (to), v.	accēdo, 3.
coming, sub.	adventus -ūs, 4 m.
command (to), v.	praesum, irr.
commit (to), v.	committo, 3.
common (of a soldier), adj.	grĕgārĭus.
companion, sub.	cŏmĕs -ĭtĭs, 3 m.
compassion, sub.	mĭsĕrĭcordĭa, 1 f.
compel (to), v.	cōgo, 3.
complain (to), v.	quĕrŏr, 3 dep.
complaint, sub.	quĕrēla, 1 f.
comrade, sub.	sŏcĭus, 2 m.; cŏmĕs -ĭtĭs, 3 m.; aequālĭs -ĭs, 3 m.
conceal (to), v.	cēlo, 1.
condemned (to death), Phr.	căpĭtĭs dāmnātŭs.
condition, sub.	lex, lēgĭs, 3 f.
confer (to), v.	confĕro, irr.
confess (to), v.	fătĕor, 2 dep.
confidence, sub.	fīdūcĭa, 1 f.
confident, adj. Phr.	fĭdĕī plēnus.
confusion, sub.	tŭmultus -ūs, 4 m.
congratulate (to), v.	grātŭlor, 1 dep.
conquer (to), v.	vinco, 3; sŭbĭgo, 3.
conqueror, sub.	victŏr -ōrĭs, 3 m.
consider (to), v.	pŭto, 1.
conspiracy, sub.	conjūrātĭo, 3 f.
console (to), v.	sōlŏr, 1 dep.
consul, sub.	consŭl -ŭlĭs, 3 m.
consult (to), v.	consŭlo, 3.
contain (to), v.	hăbĕo, 2.
content, adj.	contentus.
contented, adj.	contentus.
continual, adj.	perpĕtuus.
contractor, sub.	rĕdemptŏr -ōrĭs, 3 m.
coo (to), v.	gĕmo, 3.
cool (to), v.	rĕfrīgĕro, 1.
coolness, sub.	frīgŭs -ŏris, 3 n.
coop, sub.	căvĕă, 1 f.
coop up (to), v.	inclūdo, 3; obsĭdĕo, 2.
copy, sub.	exemplăr -āris, 3 n.
cord, sub.	fūnĭs -ĭs, 3 m.
corn, sub.	frūmentum, 2 n.
Cornelia, sub.	Cornēlĭa -ae, 1 f.
corner, sub.	angŭlus, 2 m.
correctly, adv.	rectē.
corpse, sub.	cădāvĕr -ĕrĭs, 3 n.
cost, sub.	prĕtium, 2 n.
cottage, sub.	căsa, 1 f.
council, sub.	concĭlĭum, 2 n.
count (to), v.	nŭmĕro, 1.
country, sub.	pătrĭa, 1 f.
country (as opposed to town), sub.	rūs, rūrĭs, 3 n.
country house, sub.	villa, 1 f.
countryman, (peasant), sub.	cŏlōnus, 2. rustĭcus, 2.
countryman (fellow citizen), s.	cīvĭs -ĭs, 3 m.

courage, *sub.* — vīrtūs -ūtǐs, 3 f.

courageously, *adv.* — fōrtǐtĕr.

courtesy, *s.* — cōmǐtās -ātǐs, 3 f.

courteously, *adv.* — cōmǐtĕr; bĕnignē.

courtier, *sub.* — aulǐcus, 2 m.

cover (to), *v.* — tĕgo, 3.

cow, *sub.* — vacca, 1 f.

coward, *sub.* — ignāvus, 2 m.

cowardly, *adj.* — ignāvus.

craft, *sub.* — dŏlus, 2 m.

crane, *sub.* — grūs, grŭǐs, 3 f.

creature, *sub.* — ănǐmăl -ālǐs, 3 n.

credit, *sub.* — fǐdēs -ĕī, 5 f.

Crete, *sub.* — Crēta, 1 f.

crocus, *sub.* — crŏcus, 2 m.

crowd, *sub.* — turba, 1 f.

Crœsus, *sub.* — Croesus, 2 m.

crop, *sub.* — sĕgĕs -ĕtis, 3 f.

cross (to), *v.* — transgrĕdǐor, 3 dep.; transĕo, irr.

crow, *sub.* — corvus, 2 m.

crown, *sub.* — dǐădēma -ătis, 3 n.

crown (to), *v.* — cingo, 3 ; cŏrōno, 1.

cruel, *adj.* — crūdēlis.

cruelly, *adv.* — crūdēlǐtĕr.

cruelty, *sub.* — saēvǐtǐa, 1 f.

crush (to), *v.* — opprǐmo, 3.

cry (of a baby), to, *v.* — vāgǐo, 4.

cry (to), *v.* — } clāmo, 1.
cry out (to), *v.* — }

cuckoo, *sub.* — cŭcūlus, 2 m.

culprit, *sub.* — rĕŭs, 2 m.

cultivate (to), *v.* — cŏlo, 3.

cunning, *sub.* — astūtia, 1 f.

cup, *sub.* — pōcŭlum, 2 n.

cure (to), *v.* — sāno, 1.

curtain, *sub.* — vēlum, 2 n.

Curtius, *sub.* — Curtǐus, 2 m.

cut (to), *v.* — sĕco, 1.

cut down (to), *v.* — dēcīdo, 3.

cut off (to), *v.* — abscīdo, 3.

Cydnus, *sub.* — Cȳdnus, 3 m.

Cyrus, *sub.* — Cȳrus, 2 m.

D.

dagger, *sub.* — pūgǐo -ōnǐs, 3 m.

daily, *adv.* — indǐēs, quotīdǐē.

dance (to), *v.* — salto, 1.

danger, *sub.* — pĕrīcŭlum, 2 n.

dangerous, *adj.* — pĕrīcŭlōsus.

dare (to), *v.* — audeo, irr.

Darius, *sub.* — Dărīus -i, 2 m.

daughter, *sub.* — fīlǐa, 1 f.

day, *sub.* — dǐēs -ĕi, 5 m. or f.

dead, *part.* — mortŭus; confectus.

dear, *adj.* — cārus.

death, *sub.* — mors, mortis, 3 f.

deceit, *sub.* — fraus, fraudis, 3 f.

deceive (to), *v.* — fallo, 3; dēcǐpǐo, 3.

decide (to), *v.* — { dēcerno, 3. stătŭo, 3. dǐrǐmo, 3.

declare war (to), *v.* — indīco, 3.

decree (to), *v.* — dēcerno, 3; stătŭo, 3.

deed, *sub.* — factum, 2 n.

deem (to), *v.* — hăbĕo, 2.

deep, *adj.* — altus.

defeat (to), *v.* — vinco, 3; dēvinco, 3.

defend (to), *v.* — tŭĕor, 2 dep.

defence, *sub.* — praesǐdium, 2 n.

delay (to), *v.* — cunctŏr, 1.

delight (to), *v.* — jŭvo, 1.

Delphi, *sub.* — Delphī, 2 pl.

delude (to), *v.* — fallo, 3, dēcǐpǐo, 3.

demand (to), *v.* — posco, 3.

dense, *adj.* — densus.

deny (to), *v.* — nĕgo, 1.

depart (to), *v.* — discēdo, 3 ; ăbĕo, irr.

deprive (to), *v.* — prīvo, 1.

deprived of, *part.* — orbātus.

depth, *sub.* (render by *adj.*) — īmus.

desert, *sub.* — dēserta, 2 pl.

deserve (to), *v.* — mĕrĕor, 2.

design, *sub.* — consǐlǐum, 2 n.

desirable, *adj.* — optābǐlis ; expĕtendus.

desire (to), — cŭpǐo, 3; vŏlo, irr.

desirous, *adj.* — cŭpǐdus.

despair, *sub.* — despērātǐo, 3 f.

despatch (to), *v.* — mitto, 3.

despise (to), *v.* — sperno, 3 ; contemno, 3.

destroy (to), *v.* — dēlĕo, 2 ; perdo, 3 ; ēverto, 3.

destruction, *sub.* — pernǐcǐēs, -ĕi, 5 f.

detect (to), v.	pătĕfăcĭo, 3.
determine (to), v.	constĭtuo, 3 ; stătuo, 3.
devour (to), v.	vŏro, 1.
dew, sub.	rōs, rōrĭs, 3 m.
Diana, sub.	Dĭāna, 1 f.
dictator, sub.	dictātor -ōris, 3 m.
Dido, sub.	Dīdō -ōnis, 3 f.
die (to), v.	mŏrĭor, 3 dep.
difference (to make a), v.	intersum, irr.
differently, adv.	ălĭtĕr.
diligence, sub.	dīlĭgentĭa, 1 f.
diligent, adj.	sēdŭlus.
diligently, adv.	dīlĭgentĕr.
din, sub.	strĕpĭtus -ūs, 4 m.
dine (to), v.	cēno, 1.
Diogenes, sub.	Dĭŏgĕnes -ĭs, 3.
Diomedes, sub.	Dĭŏmēdēs -ĭs, 3.
dire, adj.	dīrus ; grăvĭs.
dirty, adj.	immundus.
disappear (to), v.	ēvānesco, 3.
disaster, sub.	clādēs -ĭs, 3 f.
discharge (to), v.	fungor, 3 dep.
discipline, sub.	discĭplīna, 1 f.
Discordia, sub.	Discordia, 1 f.
discover (to), v.	invēnĭo, 4.
disease, sub.	morbus, 2 m.
disgrace, sub.	dēdĕcŭs -ŏrĭs, 3 n.
dish, sub.	lanx, lancis, 3 f.
disperse (to), v.	dissĭpo, 1.
displease (to), v.	displĭcĕo, 2.
dispute, sub.	contrōversĭa, 1 f.
dispute (to), v.	rixor, 1 dep.
distant (to be), v.	disto, 1.
distinguish (to), v.	illustro, 1.
distribute (to), v.	dīvĭdo, 3.
disturb (to), v.	turbo, 1.
ditch, sub.	fossa, 1 f.
dive (to), v. Phr.	mē mergo, 3.
divide (to), v.	dīvĭdo, 3.
do (to), v.	făcĭo, 3 ; ăgo, 3.
doctor, sub.	mĕdĭcus, 2 m.
doe, sub.	cerva, 1 f.
dog, sub.	cănis -ĭs, 3 m.
dominion, sub.	regnum, 2 n.
donkey, sub.	ăsĭnus, 2 m.
door, sub.	fŏres -um, 3 pl. f.
dormouse, sub.	glīs, glīrĭs, 3 m.
doubt (rendered by adj. doubtful),	dŭbĭus.
doubt (to), v.	dŭbĭto, 1.
dove, sub.	cŏlumba, 1 f.

dovecote, sub.	cŏlumbārĭum, 2 n.
drag (to), v.	trăho, 3.
draw out (to), v.	extrăho, 3.
dread (to), v.	tĭmĕo, 2.
dreadful, adj.	terrĭbĭlis.
dream, sub.	somnĭum, 2 n.
dress, sub.	vestĭs -ĭs, 3 f.
drink (to), v.	bĭbo, 3.
drive (to), v.	ăgo, 3.
drive away (to), v.	fŭgo, 1.
drop (to), v. neu.	stillo, 1.
= fall,	concĭdo, 3.
drop (to), v. act.	prōjĭcio, 3 ; dēmītto, 3.
dry (to), v.	sicco, 1.
dry, adj.	siccus.
duck, sub.	ănăs, ănătis, 3 f.
dust, sub.	pulvĭs -ĕrĭs, 3 m.
duty, sub.	mūnŭs -ĕrĭs, 3 n.
dwell, v.	hăbĭto, 1.
dying,	mŏrĭbundus.

E.

each, pron.	quisquĕ.
eager, adj.	cŭpĭdus, stŭdĭōsus.
eagle, sub.	ăquĭla, 1 f.
ear, sub.	aurĭs -ĭs, 3 f.
early, adj.	mātūtīnus.
early, adv.	mātūrē.
earn (to), v.	mĕrĕo, 2.
earth, sub.	terra, 1 f.
east, sub.	Ŏrĭens -tĭs, 3 m.
east wind, sub.	Eurus, 2 m.
easy, adj.	făcĭlis.
eat (to), v.	ĕdo, 3 ; vescor, 3 dep.
echo (to), v.	rĕsŏno, 1.
edge, sub.	margō -ĭnĭs, 3 m. and f.
educate (to), v.	ēdŭco, 1.
eel, sub.	anguilla, 1 f.
efface (to), v.	dēleo, 2.
egg, sub.	ōvum, 2 n.
eighteen, num. indec.	dŭŏdēvīginti.
elect (to), v.	crĕŏ, 1.
element, sub.	ĕlĕmentum, 2 n.
elephant, sub.	ĕlĕphantus, 2 m.
eleven, num. indec.	undĕcim.

eloquent, adj.	făcundus; dĭsertus.
embrace, v.	amplector, 3 dep.
eminence, sub.	tŭmŭlus, 2 m.
emperor, sub.	impĕrātor -ōris, 3 m.
empire, sub.	impĕrĭum, 2 n.
employ (to), v.	ădhĭbĕo, 2.
empty, adj.	ĭnānis.
encounter (to), v.	invĕnio, 4.
encourage (to), v.	hortor, 1.
end, sub.	fīnĭs -ĭs, 3 m. & f.
end (to), v.	confĭcĭo, 3.
endure (to), v.	pătĭŏr, 3 dep.
enemy, sub.	hostĭs -ĭs, 3 m.; ĭnĭmīcus, 2 m.
enforce (to), v.	fĭrmo, 1.
English, adj.	Anglĭcus, 2 m.
Englishman, sub.	Anglus, 2 m.
enjoy (to), v.	frŭor, 3 dep.
enough, adv.	sătĭs.
enquire (to), v.	quaero, 3.
entangle (to), v.	impĕdĭo, 4.
enter (to), v.	ingrĕdĭor, 3 dep.; ĭnĕo, irr.
entertain (to), v.	excĭpĭo, 3.
entrance, sub.	ădĭtus -ūs, 4 m.
entreat (to), v.	ōro, 1.
entreaty, sub.	prĕces, 3 pl. f.
entrenchment, sub.	mūnĭtĭo -ōnĭs, 3 f
entrust (to), v.	crēdo, 3.
enumerate (to), v.	nŭmĕro, 1.
envoy, sub.	lēgātus, 2 m.
envy (to), v.	invĭdĕo, 2.
Epicurus, sub.	Ĕpĭcūrus, 2 m.
equal, adj.	pār.
Erostratus, sub.	Ĕrŏstrătus, 2 m.
escape, sub.	fŭga, 1 f.
escape (to), v. act.	effŭgĭo, 3; vīto, 1.
escape (to), v. neut.	ēvādo, 3.
especially, adv.	praecĭpŭē, imprīmĭs.
estate, sub.	praedĭum, 2 n.
Euphrates, sub.	Euphrātēs -ĭs, 3 m.
Europe, sub.	Eurōpa, 1 f.
European, adj.	Eurōpaeus.
Eurystheus, sub.	Eurystheus -ĕi, 2 m.
even, adv.	ĕtĭam.
evening, sub.	vēspĕră, 1 f.
event, sub.	ēventus -ūs, 4 m.
ever, adv.	nunquam.
every, adj.	omnĭs.

evident, adj.	mănĭfestus.
example, sub.	exemplum, 2 n.
exceed (to), v.	excēdo, 3.
excellent, adj.	ēgrĕgĭus.
except, prep.	praetĕr, acc.
excuse, sub.	causa, 1 f.
exhausted, adj.	confectus.
exile, sub.	exŭl -ŭlĭs, 3 m.
exile, sub. (= banishment)	exsĭlium, 2 n.
exiled, adj.	exsŭl, extorris.
expel (to), v.	expello, 3; pello, 3.
experienced, adj.	pĕrītus.
expose (to), v.	objĭcĭo, 3.
extensive, adj.	lātus.
extinguish (to), v.	exstinguo, 3.
extraordinary, adj.	exĭmius.
eye, sub.	ŏcŭlus, 2 m.

F.

fable, sub.	fābŭla, 1 f.
Fabricius, sub.	Fābrĭcĭus, 2 m.
face, sub.	făcĭēs -ēī, 5 f.
face (to), v.	oppōno, 3.
faggot, sub.	fascĭs -ĭs, 3 m.
fail (to), v.	dēfĭcĭo, 3; dēsum, irr.
fair, adj.	pulchĕr -chră -chrum.
faithful, adj.	fīdus; fĭdēlis.
fall (to), v.	cădo, 3.
fame, sub.	fāma, 1 f.
famine, sub.	fămēs -ĭs, 3 f.
famous, adj.	inclўtus, cĕlĕber.
far, adv.	prŏcŭl.
far (by),	lōngē.
far (too),	longĭŭs.
farmer, sub.	ăgrĭcŏla, 1 m.
farthing, sub.	ās, assĭs, 3 m.
fasten (to), v.	allĭgo, 1.
fat, adj.	pinguis.
fatal, adj.	fātālis.
father, sub.	pătĕr -rĭs, 3 m.
fatherland, sub.	pătrĭa, 1 f.
fatherly, adj.	păternus.
fatigue, sub.	lassĭtūdō -ĭnis, 3 f.
fault, sub.	culpa, 1 f.
favour (to), v.	făvĕo, 2.
fawn, sub.	cerva, 1 f.
fear (to), v.	tĭmĕo, 2; vĕrĕor, 2 dep.

fear (for), *(render by)*	në, with subj.
feeble, adj.	dēbĭlis.
feed (to), v.	pasco, 3.
feel (to), v.	sentĭo, 4.
feign (to), v.	sĭmŭlo, 1.
fell (to), v.	dēcīdo, 3.
ferryman, sub.	portĭtŏr -ōrĭs, 3 m.
fetch (to), v.	aufĕro, irr.
fetch (to water), v.	ăquor, 1 dep.
field, sub.	ăgĕr, ăgri, 2 m. ; arvum, 2 n.
fierce, adj.	vĭŏlentus.
fiercely, adv.	vĭŏlentĕr.
fight (to), v.	pugno, 1.
fight, sub.	pugna, 1 f.
fighter, sub.	pugnātŏr -ōrĭs, 3 m.
file, sub.	līma, 1 f.
fill (to), v.	implĕo, 2.
filled, adj.	plēnus.
finally, adv.	dēnĭquĕ.
find (to), v.	invĕnĭo, 4 ; rĕpĕrĭŏ, 4.
find (to) = perceive, v.	sentĭo, 4.
fine, adj.	lautus.
finger, sub.	dĭgĭtus, 2 m.
finish (to), v.	confĭcĭo, 3 ; pĕrăgo, 3.
fire, sub.	ignĭs -ĭs, 3 m.
fire = conflagration, sub.	incendĭum, 2 n.
fireside, sub.	fŏcus, 2 m.
firm, adj.	firmus.
firmly, adv.	constantĕr.
first,	prīmus.
first (before some one else),	prĭŏr, prĭŭs.
fish, sub.	piscĭs -ĭs, 3 m.
fisherman, sub.	piscātŏr -ōrĭs, 3 m.
fit, adj.	aptus.
five, num. indec.	quinquĕ.
flame, sub.	flamma, 1 f.
flay (to), v. Phr.	pellem dētrăho, 3.
flee (to), v.	fŭgĭo, 3.
fleece, sub.	vellŭs -ĕris, 3 n.
fleet, sub.	classis -ĭs, 3 f.
fling (to), v.	prōjĭcĭo, 3.
flock, sub.	grex, grĕgĭs, 3 m.
flood, sub.	dĭlŭvĭēs -ēī, 5 f.
flourish (to), v.	flŏrĕo, 2.
flow (to), v.	flŭo, 3.
flower, sub.	flōs, flōrĭs, 3 m.
fly, sub.	musca, 1 f.
fly (of a bird) to, v.	vŏlo, 1.
flying, adj.	fŭgax.
foe, sub.	hostĭs -ĭs, 3 m.
follow (to), v.	sĕquor, 3 dep.
folly, sub.	stultĭtĭa, 1 f.
food, sub.	cĭbŭs, 2 m.
fool, sub.	insĭpĭens -entĭs, 3 m.
foolish, adj.	stultus.
foot, sub.	pēs, pĕdĭs, 3 m.
foot-soldier, sub.	pĕdĕs -ĭtĭs, 3 m.
foot (infantry), sub.	pĕdĭtēs, 3 pl. m.
foot (of a hill), sub.	rādix -īcĭs, 3 f.
forbid (to), v.	vĕto, 1.
force, sub.	vīs, 3 f.
force (to), v.	cōgō, 3.
forces, sub.	cōpĭae, 1 pl. f.
foreigner, sub.	barbărus, 2 m.
foreseeing, adj.	prōvĭdus (with gen.).
forest, sub.	silva, 1 f.
foretell (to), v.	praedīco, 3.
forge (to), v.	fingo, 3 ; prōcūdo, 3.
forget (to), v.	ōblīviscor, 3 dep.
forgive (to), v.	ignosco, 3.
form (to), v. (a conspiracy)	ĭnĕo, irr.
former, adj.	prĭŏr.
formerly, adv.	antĕā.
forsake (to), v.	dēsĕro, 3.
fortify (to), v.	mūnĭo, 4.
fortunate, adj.	fēlix.
fortune, sub.	fortūna, 1 f.
fosse, sub.	fossa, 1 f.
foul (to), v.	turbo, 1.
found (to), v.	fundo, 1.
founder, sub.	condĭtŏr -ōrĭs, 3 m.
fountain, sub.	fons, fontĭs, 3 m.
four, num. indec.	quāttŭŏr.
four hundred, num. adj.	quădrĭngenti -ae -a.
fox, sub.	vulpēs -ĭs, 3 f.
franchise, sub.	cīvĭtās -ātĭs, 3 f.
free (to), v.	lībĕro, 1.
free, adj.	lībĕr.
freedom, sub.	lībertās -ātĭs, 3 f.
freeze (to), v.	gĕlo, 1.
French, adj.	Gallĭcus.
fresh, adj.	nŏvus.

friend, sub.	ămīcus, 2 m.
friendship, sub.	ămīcĭtĭa, 1 f.
frighten (to), v.	terrĕo, 2.
frisk (to), v.	salto, 1.
frog, sub.	rāna, 1 f.
frostbound, adj. Phr.	gĕlū constrictus.
fruit, sub.	pōma, 2 pl. n.
fulfil (to), v.	praesto, 1.
full, adj.	plēnus.
funeral pile, sub.	rŏgus, 2 m.
furnish (to), v.	praēbĕo, 2 ; praēsto, 1.
furniture, sub.	sŭpellex -ectĭlis, 3 f.
furrow, sub.	sulcus, 2 m.
further, adv.	ultĕrĭŭs.
future, sub.	fŭtūrum, 2 n.

G.

gain, sub.	lŭcrum, 2 n.
gain (to), v.	ădĭpiscor, 3 dep.
Gallic, adj.	Gallĭcus.
game, sub.	lūdus, 2 m.
Ganymedes, sub.	Gănȳmēdēs -ĭs, 3 m.
garland, sub.	cŏrōna, 1 f.
garment, sub.	vestĭs -ĭs, 3 f.
gate, sub.	porta, 1 f.
gather (to), v.	lĕgo, 3 ; collĭgo, 3.
Gaul, sub.	Gallus, 2 m.
Gaza, sub.	Gāza, 1 f.
gaze (to), v.	intŭĕor, 2.
general, sub.	dux, dŭcis, 3 m. ; lēgātus, 2 m.
genius, sub.	ingĕnĭum, 2 n.
German, adj.	Germānus.
get (to), v.	ădĭpiscor, 3 dep. ; pŏtĭor, 4 dep.
get (to), v.	trăho, 3 ; dūco, 3.
get possession of, (to), v.	pŏtĭor, 4 dep.
ghost, sub.	sĭmŭlācrum, 2 n.
gift, sub.	dōnum, 2 n. ; mū- nŭs -ĕrĭs, 3 n.
gird (to), v.	cingo, 3.
girl, sub.	pŭella, 1 f.
give (to), v.	do, 1 irr.
give away (to), v.	largĭor, 4 dep.
give back (to), v.	reddo, 3.
give birth (to), v.	părĭo, 3.
give up (to), v.	dēdo, 3.
gladly, adv.	lĭbentĕr.

gloomy, adj.	tĕtrĭcus.
glorious, adj.	praeclārus.
glory, sub.	laus -dĭs, 3 f. ; dĕcŭs -ŏrĭs, 3 n.; glōria, 1 f.
glutton, sub.	hellŭo -ōnis, 3 m.
go (to), v.	ĕo, irr. ; prŏfĭcis- cor, 3 dep.
go (to), v.	fĕrŏr, irr.
go abroad (to), v.	pĕrĕgrīnor, 1 dep.
go away (to), v.	ăbĕo, irr. ; dís- cēdo, 3.
go in (to), v.	ingrĕdĭor, 3 dep.
go on (to), v.	prŏcēdo, 3.
go out (to), v.	exĕo, irr.
go up (to), v. = to climb,	scando, 3.
goat, sub.	căpĕr, căpri, 2 m.
God, sub.	Dĕus, 2 m.
goddess, sub.	dĕa, 1 f.
gold, sub.	aurum, 2 n.
golden, adj.	aurĕus.
good, adj.	bŏnus.
good (to be), v.	prōsum, irr.
goods, sub.	bŏna, 2 pl. n.
goose, sub.	ansĕr -ĕrĭs, 3 m.
Gordian, adj.	Gordĭānus.
Gordium,	Gordĭum, 2 n.
govern (to), v.	prōsum, irr.
Gracchus, sub.	Gracchus, 2 m.
Granicus, sub.	Grănīcus, 2 m.
grant (to), v.	do, irr. ; concēdo, 3.
grape, sub.	ūva, 1 f.
grasp (to), v.	tĕnĕo, 2 ; prĕhen- do, 3.
grass, sub.	herba, 1 f.
grasshopper, sub.	cĭcāda, 1 f.
great, adj.	magnus.
greatest, adj.	summus.
greatly, adv.	vāldē, admŏdum.
Greece, sub.	Graecĭa, 1 f.
greedy, adj.	ăvĭdus.
Greek, sub. or adj.	Graecus.
greet (to), v.	sălūto, 1 ; excĭpĭo, 3.
grief, sub.	dŏlŏr -ōrĭs, 3 m.
grieve (to), v.	dŏlĕo, 2.
groan, sub.	gĕmĭtŭs -ūs, 4 m.
groom, sub.	ăgāsō -ōnĭs, 3 m.
ground, sub.	hŭmŭs, 2 f.
ground (on the), adv.	hŭmī.
grow up (to), v.	ădŏlcsco, 3

grudge (to),	invĭdĕo, 2.	Helen, sub. Helena,	} Hĕlĕna, 1 f.
guard, sub. guardian, sub.	} custōs -ōdĭs, 3 m.	Hellespont, sub.	Hellespontus, 2 m.
guess (to), v.	conjecto, 1.	help, sub.	auxĭlĭum, 2 n.
guide (to), v.	dūco, 3 ; rĕgo, 3.	help (to), v.	succurro, 3; jŭvo, 1.
		hen, sub.	gallīna, 1 f.
H.		Henricus, sub.	Henrīcus, 2 m.
		Hephaestion, sub.	Hĕphaestĭon -ōnis, 3 m.
hair, sub.	pĭlus, 2 m.		
Halicarnassus, sub.	Hălĭcarnassus, 2 m.	herald, sub.	praecō -ōnĭs, 3 m.
halt (to), v.	subsisto, 3.	herd, sub.	armentum, 2 n.
hand, sub.	mănŭs -ūs, 4 f.	herdsman, sub.	bŭbulcus, 2 m.
hand (to be at), v.	adsum, irr.	hereafter, adv.	postĕā.
handsome, adj.	pulchĕr -chră -chrum.	hero, sub.	vĭr, vĭrī, 2 m.
		heron, sub.	ardĕa, 1 f.
Hannibal, sub.	Hannĭbăl -bălĭs, 3 m.	hesitate (to), v.	dŭbĭto, 1.
		hidden, adj.	abdĭtus.
happen (to), v.	ēvĕnĭo, 4 ; accĭdo, 3.	hide (to), v.	cēlo, 1.
		hiding place, sub.	lătĕbrae, 1 pl. f.
happy, adj.	bĕātus.	high, adj.	altus.
harass (to), v.	lăcesso, 3.	highest, adj.	praestantissĭmus.
harbour, sub.	portŭs -ūs, 4 m.	hill, sub.	collĭs -ĭs, 3 m.
hard, adj.	dūrus.	hinder (to), v.	impĕdĭo, 4 ; prŏhĭbĕo, 2.
harden (to), v.	dūresco, 3.		
hardship, sub.	mălum, 2 n.	his,	sŭus.
hare, sub.	lĕpŭs -ŏrĭs, 3 m.	hit (to), v.	percŭtĭo, 3.
harp, sub.	cĭthăra, 1 f.	hither, adv.	hūc.
hart, sub.	cervus, 2 m.	hoe, sub.	sarcŭlum, 2 n.
harvest, sub.	messĭs -ĭs, 3 f.	hold (to), v.	tĕneo, 2.
hastiness, sub.	tĕmĕrĭtās -ātĭs, 3 f.	hold (to) a council, v.	hăbeo, 2.
hatch (to), v.	exclūdo, 3.		
hate (to), v.	ōdī, defect.	holy, adj.	săcĕr ; sanctus.
have (to), v.	hăbĕo, 2.	Homer, sub.	Hŏmērus, 2 m.
hawk, sub.	accĭpĭtĕr -trĭs, 3 m.	honest, adj.	prŏbus.
hay, sub.	faenum, 2 n.	honesty, sub.	prŏbĭtas -tātĭs, 3 f.
head, sub.	căpŭt -ĭtĭs, 3 n.	honey, sub.	mēl, mellĭs, 3 n.
headlong, adj.	praeceps.	honour, sub.	laus, laudĭs, 3 f. ; hŏnŏr -ōrĭs, 3 m.
heal (to), v.	mĕdĕor, 2 dep.		
health, sub.	vălētūdō -dĭnĭs, 3 f.	honour (to), v.	cŏlo, 3.
		honourable, adj.	hŏnestus.
heap, sub.	ăcervus, 2 m.	hook, sub.	hāmus, 2 m.
heap (to), v.	ingĕro, 3.	hope, sub.	spēs -ĕi, 5 f.
hear (to), v.	audĭo, 4.	hope (to), v.	spēro, 1.
heart, sub.	cŏr, cordĭs, 3 n. ; ănĭmus, 2 m.	hope for (to), v.	spēro, 1.
		Horatius, sub.	Hŏrātius, 2 m.
heat, sub.	călŏr -ōrĭs, 3 m.	horn, sub.	cornū, 4 n.
heather, sub.	ērīcă, 1 f.	horse, sub.	ĕquus, 2 m.
heavenly, adj.	caelestĭs.	horse (cavalry),	ĕquĭtes, 3 pl. m.
Hector, sub.	Hectŏr -ŏrĭs, 3 m.	hospitality, sub.	hospĭtĭum, 2 n.
height, (rendered by adj.)	summus.	host, sub.	exercĭtus -ūs, 4 m.
		hot, adj.	călĭdus ; fervens.
heir, sub.	hērēs -ēdĭs, 3 m.	hound, sub.	cătŭlus, 2 m.

hour, *sub.* — hōra, 1 f.
house, *sub.* — dŏmŭs, irr. f. (see Grammar, p. 8): aedes -ĭum, 3 pl. f.
hover (to), *v.* — vŏlĭto, 1.
how many, *adj.* — quŏt.
however, *adv.* — tămĕn.
howl (to), *v.* — clāmo, 1.
huge, *adj.* — ĭngens.
human, *adj.* — hūmānus.
hundred, *num. indec.* — centum.
hungry, *adj.* — ēsŭrĭens.
hungry (to be), *v.* — ēsŭrĭo, 4.
hunt (to), *v.* — vēnor, 1.
hunter, *sub.* — vēnātŏr -ōrĭs, 3 m.
hurt (to), *v.* — nŏcĕo, 2.
husband, *sub.* — mărītus, 2 m.
husbandman, *sub.* — cŏlōnŭs, 2 m.
hut, *sub.* — căsa, 1.
Hydaspes, *sub.* — Hȳdaspēs -ĭs, 3 m.
Hyphasis, *sub.* — Hȳphăsis -ĭs, 3 m.

I.

ice, *sub.* — glăcĭēs -ēī, 5 f.
Ida, *sub.* — Ida, 1 f.
idle, *adj.* — ignāvus, ĭners.
idle (to be), *v.* — cesso, 1.
Idomeneus, *sub.* — Ĭdŏmĕneus -ĕī, 3 m.
ignorant, *adj.* — indoctus.
ignorant of, *adj.* — ignāvus.
ignorant (to be), *v.* — ignōro, 1.
Iliad, *sub.* — Ilĭăs -ădĭs, 3 f.
ill, *sub.* — mălum, 2 n.
ill, *adj.* — aegĕr.
ill (to be), *v.* — aegrōto, 1.
illness, *sub.* — morbus, 2 m.
illustrious, *adj.* — inclȳtus.
Illyrian, *adj.* — Illȳrĭus.
imbibe (to), *v.* — bĭbo, 3.
imitate (to), *v.* — ĭmĭtor, 1 dep.
immediately, *adv.* — stătim.
imminent (to be), *v.* — immĭnĕo, 2.
immortal, *adj.* — immortālĭs, sempĭternus.
impair (to), *v.* — mĭnŭo, 3.
impetuous, *adj.* — ācĕr, ācrĭs, ācrĕ.
imprison (to), *v. Phr.* — in vincŭla conjĭcĭo, 3.

imprudent, *adj.* — incautus.
imprudently, *adv.* — incautē.
imprudence, *sub.* — audācĭa, 1 f.
in particular, *adv.* — praecĭpŭē.
incautiously, *adv.* — incautē.
incessantly, *adv.* — sempĕr.
include (to), *v.* — contĭneo, 2.
increase (to), *v. neut.* — cresco, 3.
increase (to), *v. act.* — augeo, 2.
indeed, *adv.* — quĭdem.
India, *sub.* — Indĭa, 1 f.
indicate (to), *v.* — indĭco, 1.
indignant (at), *part.* — indignātus (with acc.)
industry, *sub.* — dīlĭgentĭa, 1 f.
infancy, *sub.* — infantĭa, 1 f.
inferior, *comp. adj.* — infērĭŏr, mĭnŏr.
influence (to), *v.* — mŏvĕo, 2.
inhabit (to), *v.* — cŏlo, 3 ; incŏlo, 3.
inhabitant, *sub.* — cīvĭs -ĭs, 3 m.
inheritance, *sub.* — hērēdĭtās -ātĭs, 3 f.
injure (to), *v.* — laedo, 3 ; nŏcĕo, 2.
injury, *sub.* — injūrĭa, 1 f.
innocent, *adj.* — innŏcens.
inscribe (to), *v.* — inscrĭbo, 3.
instantly, *adv.* — stătim.
insult, *sub.* — contŭmēlĭa, 1 f.
insult (to), *v. Phr.* — contŭmēlĭas ălĭcui injĭcĭo, 3.
intend (to), *v.* — cōgĭto, 1.
intention, *sub.* — consĭlĭum, 2 n.
intentionally, *adv.* — consultō.
interest (to be to anyone's), *v. n.* — intĕrest.
invade (to), *v.* — aggrĕdior, 3 dep.
invent (to), *v.* — rĕpĕrio, 4.
invention, *sub.* — inventĭo -ōnĭs, 3 f.
inventor, *sub.* — auctŏr -ōrĭs, 3 m.
invincible, *adj.* — invictus.
Iphigenia, *sub.* — Ĭphĭgĕnĭa, 1 f.
iron, *sub.* — ferrum, 2 n.
island, *sub.* — } insŭla, 1 f.
isle, —
Issus, *sub.* — Issus, 2 m.
isthmus, *sub.* — isthmus, 2 m.
Italian, *adj.* — Ĭtălĭcus.

Italy, sub.	Ĭtālĭa, 1 f.
Ithaca, sub.	Ĭthăca, 1 f.
its, poss. pron.	sŭus.
ivy, sub.	hĕdĕra, 1 f.

J.

jackdaw, sub.	grācŭlus, 2 m.
jewel, sub.	gemma, 1 f.
Joanna, sub.	Jŏanna, 1 f.
join (to), v.	jungo, 3.
join battle (to), v.	committo, 3.
journey, sub.	ĭtĕr, ĭtĭnĕrĭs, 3 n.
joy, sub.	laetĭtĭa, 1 f.; gaudĭum, 2 n.
joyful, adj.	laetus.
judge, sub.	jūdex -ĭcĭs, 3 m.: arbĭtĕr -trī, 2 m.
jump (to), v.	sălĭo, 4.
jump out (to), v.	prōsĭlĭo, 4.
Juno, sub.	Jūnō -ōnĭs, 3 f.
Jupiter, sub.	Juppĭtĕr, Jŏvĭs, 3 m.
just, adv.	mŏdŏ ; nūpĕr.
just, adj.	justus.
justice, sub.	justĭtĭa, 1 f.

K.

keep (to), v.	servo, 1.
keep to (feed), v.	pasco, 3.
keep to (celebrate), v.	cĕlĕbro, 1.
keep (sign of the imperfect tense)	
keep off (to), v.	arceo, 2.
kid, sub.	haedus, 2 m.
kill (to), v.	occīdo, 3.
kind, sub.	gĕnŭs -ĕrĭs, 3 n.
kindle (to), v.	accendo, 3.
kindness, sub.	bĕnĕfĭcĭum, 2 n.
king, sub.	rex, rēgĭs, 3 m.
kingdom, sub.	regnum, 2 n.
kite, sub.	mīluus, 2 m.
knee, sub.	gĕnu, 4 n.
knife, sub.	cultĕr -tri, 2 m.
knight, sub.	ĕques -ĭtĭs, 3 m.
knot, sub.	nōdŭs, 2 m.
know (to), v.	scĭŏ, 4.
know (not to), v.	nescĭŏ, 4.
knowledge, sub.	doctrīna, 1 f.

L.

labour, sub.	lăbŏr -ōrĭs, 3 m.
lack (to), v.	ĕgĕo, 2.
ladder, sub.	scālāē -ārum, 1 pl.
laden, adj.	ŏnustus.
lady, sub.	dŏmĭnă, 1 f.
lair, sub.	cŭbīlĕ, 3 n.
Laius, sub.	Lāĭŭs, 2 m.
lake, sub.	lăcŭs -ūs, 4 m.
lamb, sub.	agnus, 2 m.
lament (to), v.	plōro, 1.
lamp, sub.	lūcerna, 1 f.
lance, sub.	cuspĭs -ĭdĭs, 3 f.
land (to), v. Phr.	nāvĕ ēgrĕdĭor, 3 dep.
language, sub.	lingua, 1 f.
large, adj.	magnus.
large (how),	quantus.
larger, comp.	mājŏr.
lark, sub.	ălauda, 1 f.
last (to), v.	dūro, 1.
last, adj.	ultĭmus; summus.
late, adj.	sērus.
late (too), adv.	sērō ; sērĭŭs.
Latin, adj.	Lătīnus.
laugh (to), v.	rīdĕŏ, 2.
laugh (at), v.	irrīdĕo, 2.
lay (to), v. / *lay down (to), v.*	pōnŏ, 3.
lay an egg (to), v.	părĭo, 3.
lay siege (to), v.	obsĭdĕo, 2.
law, sub.	lex, lēgĭs, 3 f.
lazy, adj.	ignāvus, ĭners.
lead (to), v.	dūco, 3 ; addūco, 3.
lead away (to), v.	abdūco, 3.
lead back (to), v.	rĕdūco, 3.
leader, sub.	dux, dŭcis, 3 m.
leaf, sub.	frons -dĭs, 3 f. ; fŏlĭum, 2 n.
leap (to), v.	sălĭo, 4 ; insĭlĭo, 4.
leap down (to), v.	dēsĭlĭo, 4.
leap out (to), v.	prōsĭlĭo, 4.
leap over (to), v.	transĭlĭo, 4.
leap up (to), v.	exsĭlĭo, 4.
learn (to), v.	disco, 3.
learned, adj.	doctus.
learning, sub.	doctrīna, 1 f.
leave (to), v.	rĕlinquo, 3.
leave (to depart), v.	excēdo, 3 ; ăbĕo, irr.

leave off (to), v. dēsĭno, 3.
leg, sub. crūs, crūrĭs, 3 n.
leisure, sub. ōtĭum, 2 n.
leisure (to have), văco, 1.
v.
Lentulus, sub. Lentŭlus, 2 m.
less, comp. adj. mĭnŏr.
let (to)=allow, v. sĭno, 3 ; permitto, 3.
let drop (to), v. dēmitto, 3.
letter, sub. ĕpistŏla, 1 f.
levy (to), v. conscrībo, 3.
liar, sub. mendax -ācĭs, 3 m.
libation, sub. lībāmĕn -ĭnĭs, 3 n.
liberal, adj. lībĕrālĭs.
Libya, sub. Lĭbўa, 1 f.
lie, sub. meudācium, 2 n.
lie (to), v. jăcĕo, 2.
lie down (to), v. dēcumbo, 3.
lieutenant, sub. lēgātus, 2 m.
life, sub. vīta, 1 f.
lift (to), v. tollo, irr.
light, sub. lux, lūcĭs, 3 f.
lightning, sub. fulgŭr -ŭrĭs, 3 n.
like, adj. sĭmĭlĭs.
limbs, sub. membra, 2 n. pl.
limit (to), v. Phr. mŏdum ădhĭbĕo, 2.
lingerer, sub. cunctātŏr -ōrĭs, 3 m.
lion, sub. lĕo -ōnĭs, 3 m.
listen (to), v. audĭo, 4.
little (a), adv. paulŭlum.
little (after a), adv. brĕvī.
live (to), v. vīvo, 3 ; ăgo, 3.
liver, sub. jĕcŭr, jĕcĭnŏrĭs, or jĕcŏrĭs, 3 n.
load, sub. ŏnŭs -ĕrĭs, 3.
load (to), v. ŏnĕro, 1.
lofty, adv. ēlātus.
long, adj. longus.
long, adv. (of time), dĭū.
longer, adv. non jam.
long (for a long while), dĭū.
look at (to), v. intŭeor, 2 dep. ; specto, 1.
look around (to), v. circumspĭcĭo, 3.
look down (to), v. despĭcĭo, 3.
lose (to), v. perdo, 3 ; āmitto, 3.

loud, adj. ingens.
love, sub. ămŏr -ōrĭs, 3 m.
love (to), v. ămo, 1.
lovely, adj. formōsus.
luck, sub. fortūna, 1 f.
lull (to, to sleep), v. sōpĭo, 4.
lurk (to), v. lăteo, 2.
Lycurgus, sub. Lўcurgus, 2 m.
Lycian, adj. Lўcĭus.
lying, sub. mendācĭa, 2 pl. n.
lyre, sub. lўra, 1 f.

M.

Macedonia, sub. Măcĕdŏnia, 1 f.
Macedonian, sub. Măcĕdō -ŏnis, 3 m.
Macedonian, adj. Măcĕdŏnius.
mad, adj. insānus ; dēmens.
mad (to be), v. fŭro, 3.
madness, sub. fŭror -ōris, 3 m.
magi, sub. măgi, 2 pl. m.
magician, sub. măgus, 2 m.
magistrate, sub. măgistrātus -ūs, 4 m.
maiden, sub. virgo -ĭnis, 3 f.
make (to), v. făcio, 3 ; creo, 1.
make for (to), v. pĕto, 3.
make (war) (to), v. infĕro, irr.
man, sub. hŏmo -ĭnis, 3 m. ; vir, 2 m.
manage (to), v. rĕgo, 3.
manfully, adv. Phr. prō vĭrīli parte.
mankind, sub. hŏmĭnes, 3 pl. m.
many times, Phr. multis partĭbus.
Marathon, sub. Mărăthōn -ōnis, 3 f.
Marcellus, sub. Marcellus, 2 m.
March, sub. Martius, 2 m.
march, sub. ĭtĕr, ĭtĭnĕris, 3 n.
march (to), v. prŏfĭciscor, 3 dep.
mark, sub. signum, 2 n. ; jūdĭcium, 2 n.
marry (to), v. nūbo, 3 ; dūco, 3.
marshal (to), v. instrŭo, 3.
Marsyas, sub. Marsўas, -āē, 1 m.
marvellous, adj. mīrus.
master (of a school), sub. măgister -trī, 2 m.
master (of a slave), sub. dŏmĭnus, 2 m.

matter, *sub.*	rēs, rĕi, 5 f.
mattock, *sub.*	lĭgō -ōnis, 3 m.
mean (*to*), *v.*	sĭgnĭfĭco, 1 ; vŏlo, irr.
meanwhile, *adv.*	intĕreā.
measure (*to*), *v.*	mētior, 4 dep.
meat, *sub.*	cărō, carnĭs, 3 f.
medicine, *sub.*	mĕdĭcīna, 1 f.
meditate (*to*), *v.*	mĕdĭtor, 1 dep.
meet (*to*), *v.*	occurro, 3.
meeting, *sub.*	conventus -ūs, 4 m.
melt (*to*), *v.*	lĭquesco, 3.
Memnon, *sub.*	Memnōn -ŏnĭs, 3 m.
memory, *sub.*	mĕmŏrĭă, 1 f.
Menelaus, *sub.*	Mĕnĕlāus, 2 m.
mention, *sub.*	mentĭō -ōnĭs, 3 f.
mention (*to*), *v.*	commĕmŏro, 1.
mercenary, *sub.*	mercēnārĭus, 2 m.
merchant, *sub.*	mercātŏr -ōrĭs, 3 m.
merciful, *adj.*	clēmens.
Mercurius, *sub.*	Mercŭrĭus, 2 m.
mercy, *sub.*	clēmentĭa, 1 f.
messenger, *sub.*	nuntĭus, 2 m.
Metaurus, *sub.*	Mĕtaurus, 2 m.
Metellus, *sub.*	Mĕtellus, 2 m.
Midas, *sub.*	Mĭdās -ae, 1 m.
middle, *sub.* (rendered by adj.)	mĕdĭus.
midnight, *sub.* Phr.	mĕdĭa nox.
midst, *sub.* (rendered by adj.)	mĕdĭus.
might, *sub.*	vīrēs, vīrium, 3 pl. f.
mile, *sub.*	mīllĕ passūs ; pl. mīllĭa passŭum
Miletus, *sub.*	Mīlētus, 2 f.
milk, *sub.*	lăc, lactĭs, 3 n.
million = a thousand thousand.	
mind, *sub.*	ănĭmus, 2 m. n. ; mens -tĭs, 3 f.
mind to = take care,	căveo, 2.
mine, *poss. adj.*	mĕus.
Minerva, *sub.*	Mĭnerva, 1 f.
miserable, *adj.*	mĭsĕr.
mistaken (*to be*), *v.*	erro, 1.
mistakes (*to make*), *v.*	pecco, 1.

Mithridates, *sub.*	Mĭthrĭdātēs -ĭs, 3 m.
mix (*to*), *v.*	misceo, 2.
moderation, *sub.*	tempĕrantĭa, 1 f.
money, *sub.*	pĕcūnĭa, 1 f.
monkey, *sub.*	sīmia, 1 f.
monster, *sub.*	monstrum, 2 n.
month, *sub.*	mensĭs -ĭs, 3 m.
moon, *sub.*	lūna, 1 f.
moreover, *adv.*	praetĕreā.
morning (*in the*), *adv.*	mānĕ.
mortal (*of a wound*), *adj.*	lētālĭs.
mother, *sub.*	mātĕr -rĭs, 3 f.
motion, *sub.*	mōtus -ūs, 4 m.
mount (*to*), *v.*	ascendo, 3.
mountain, *sub.*	mons -tĭs, 3 m.
mourning, *sub.*	complōrātĭo -ōnĭs, 3 f.
mouse, *sub.*	mūs, mūrĭs, 3 m.
mouth, *sub.*	ōs, ōrĭs, 3 n.
mouth (*of a cave*), *sub.*	ădĭtŭs -ūs, 4 m.
mouth (*of a river*), *sub.*	ostĭa, 2 pl. n.
move (*to*), *v. act.*	mŏvĕo, 2.
move (*to*), *v. neut.*	mŏvĕor, 2.
much, *adj.*	multus.
much, *adv.*	admŏdum.
murmur, *v.*	frĕmo, 3.
murmur, *sub.*	frĕmĭtus -ūs, 4 m.
Mycenae, *sub.*	Mȳcēnae, 1 pl.
Myrmidons, *sub.*	Myrmĭdŏnes, 3 pl. m.

N.

nail, *sub.*	clăvus, 2 m.
name, *sub.*	nōmĕn -ĭnĭs, 3 n.
name (*to*), *v.*	commĕmŏro, 1.
Naples, *sub.*	Nĕăpŏlĭs -ĭs, 3 f.
narrowly, *adv.*	vix.
nation, *sub.*	pŏpŭlus, 2 m. ; gēns -tĭs, 2 f.
natural, *adj.*	insĭtus.
near, *adv.*	prŏpĕ.
nearer, *comp. adv.*	prŏpĭŏr.
nearly, *adv.*	prŏpĕ ; fērē.
necessary, *adj.*	ĭdōnĕŭs.
necessity, *sub.*	nĕcēssĭtās -ātĭs, 3 f.
neck, *sub.*	collum, 2 n. ; cervix -īcĭs, 3 f.

need, sub.	ŏpus, n.
need (to), v.	indĭgĕo, 2.
needle, sub.	ăcŭs -ūs, 4 f.
neighbour, sub.	fīnĭtĭmus, 2 m.; vīcīnus, 2 m.
neighbouring, adj.	vīcīnus.
Neptunus, sub.	Neptūnus, 2 m.
Nereides,	Nērĕĭdĕs -um, 3 pl. f.
Nero, sub.	Nĕrō -ōnĭs, 3 m.
Nervii,	Nervĭi, 2 pl. m.
nest, sub.	nīdŭs, 2 m.
Nestor, sub.	Nēstŏr -ŏris, 3 m.
net, sub.	rētĕ -ĭs, 3 n.
never, adv.	nunquam.
new, adj.	nŏvus.
night, sub.	nox, noctĭs, 3 f.
nightingale, sub.	phĭlŏmēlă, 1 f.; lūscīnĭa, 1 f.
nine, num. indec.	nŏvem.
Niobe, sub.	Nĭŏbē -ēs or -āē, 1 f.
no, adj:	nullus.
no longer, adv. Phr.	non jam.
none, no one sub.	nēmō. (See List of Conjunctions.)
noble, adj.	ēgrĕgĭus.
noise, sub.	strĕpĭtŭs -ūs, 4 m.
not, adv.	nōn.
notary, sub.	scrība, 1 m.
nothing, sub.	nĭhĭl, indec.
notice (to), v.	ănĭmadverto, 3.
nowadays, adv.	hŏdĭē.
number, sub.	nŭmĕrus, 2.
nurse, sub.	nūtrix -īcĭs, 3 f.
nut, sub.	nux, nŭcis, 3 f.
nymph, sub.	nympha, 1 f.

O.

oak, sub.	quercŭs -ūs, 4 f.
oaken, adj.	quernus.
obey (to), v.	pārĕo, 2.
oblige (to), v.	cōgo, 3.
obliged, part.	cŏactus.
obsequies, sub.	exsĕquĭae, 1 pl. f.
obstinate, adj.	obstĭnātus.
obtain (to), v.	pŏtior, 4 dep.; ădĭpiscor, 3 dep.

occasion, sub.	tempŭs -ŏrĭs, 3 n.
offend, v.	laedo, 3.
offer (to), v.	reddo, 3; offĕro, irr.
office, sub.	mūnŭs -ĕrĭs, 3 n.
often, adv.	saepĕ.
often (so), adv.	tŏtĭēs.
oil, sub.	ŏlĕum, 2 n.
old, adj.	priscus, vĕtustus, vĕtus.
old man, sub.	sĕnex, sĕnĭs, 3 m.
older, adj. comp. Phr.	nātū mājŏr.
Olympic, adj.	Ŏlympĭcus.
Olympias,	Ŏlympĭăs, 1 f.
Olympus,	Ŏlympus, 2 m.
one, adj.	ūnus.
only, adv.	sōlum.
only, adj.	sōlus.
open (to), v.	ăpĕrĭo, 4; rĕcludo, 3.
opinion, sub.	sententĭa, 1 f.
opportunity, sub.	occāsĭo -ōnĭs, 3 f.
oppose (to), v.	oppōno, 3; objĭcĭo, 3.
oracle, sub.	ōrācŭlum, 2 n.
orator, sub.	ōrātŏr -ōrĭs, 3 m.
ordain (to), v.	dēcerno, 3.
order, sub.	ordō -dĭnĭs, 3 m.
order (to), v.	jŭbĕo, 2.
ornament, sub.	ornāmentum, 2 n.
other, adj.	ălĭus.
ought, v.	dēbĕo, 2; ŏportĕt, 2, impers.
ounce, sub.	uncĭa, 1 f.
our, poss. adj.	nostĕr.
out of doors, adv.	fŏrās.
outpost, sub.	stătĭō -ōnĭs, 1 f.
outside, adv.	extrā.
outstrip (to), v.	praeverto, 3.
overcome (to), v.	vinco, 3.
overtake (to), v.	consĕquor, 3 dep.
overthrow (to), v.	ēverto, 3.
overturn (to), v.	ēverto, 3.
overwhelm (to), v.	obruo, 3; prĕmo, 3.
owe (to), v.	dēbeo, 2.
owl, sub.	būbō -ōnĭs, 3 m.
own (with his, her, their, &c.)	sŭus.
ox, sub.	bōs, bŏvis, 3 m.
oyster, sub.	ostreum, 2 n.

P.

page, *sub.*	pāgĭna, 1 f.
pail, *sub.*	mulctra, 1 f.
pain, *sub.*	dŏlor -ōrĭs, 3 m.
paint (to), *v.*	pingo, 3.
painter, *sub.*	pictŏr -ōrĭs, 3 m.
palace, *sub.*	aula, 1 f.
Pan, *sub.*	Pān, Pānĭs, 3 m.
panic, *sub.*	păvŏr -ōrĭs, 3 m.
panic-stricken, *adj.*	perterrĭtus.
papyrus, *sub.*	păpȳrus, 2 m. & f.
parch (to), *v.*	sicco, 1.
pardon, *sub.*	vĕnĭa, 1 f.
pardon (to), *v.*	ignosco, 3.
parent, *s.*	părens -entĭs, 3 m.
Paris, *sub.*	Părĭs -ĭdĭs, 3 m.
Parmenio, *sub.*	Parmĕnĭō -ōnĭs, 3 m.
part, *sub.*	pars, partĭs, 3 f.
part (to), *v.*	dissĭdĕo, 2.
particular (in), *adv.*	praecĭpŭē.
pass, *sub.*	angustĭae, 1 pl. f.
pass (to), *v.*	ăbĕo, irr.
pass by (to), *v.*	praetĕrĕo, irr.
passage, *sub.*	transĭtŭs -ūs, 4 m.
pat (to), *v.*	permulcĕo, 2.
Patroclus, *sub.*	Pătrōclus, 2 m.
pay (to), *v.*	solvo, 3.
peace, *sub.*	pax, pācis, 3 f.
peacock, *sub.*	pāvō -ōnĭs, 3 m.
pearl, *sub.*	bāca, 1 f.
pebble, *sub.*	lăpillus, 3 m.
Peleus, *sub.*	Pēlēūs -ĕŭs or ĕī, 3 m.
Pella, *sub.*	Pella, 1 f.
Penelope, *sub.*	Pēnĕlŏpē -ĭs, 3 f.
people, *sub.*	gens -tĭs, 3 f.; pŏpŭlus, 2 m.
perceive (to), *v.*	sentĭo, 4.
Perdiccas, *sub.*	Perdiccas, 1 m.
perform (to), *v.*	pĕrăgo, 3; exsĕquor, 3 dep.
perfume, *sub.*	unguentum, 2 n.
Pericles, *sub.*	Pĕrĭclēs -ĭs, 3 m.
perish (to), *v.*	pĕrĕo, irr.
perpetual, *adj.*	perpĕtuus.
Persian, *sub.*	Persa, 1 m.
Persian, *adj.*	Persĭcus.
persuade (to), *v.*	suadĕo, 2; persuadĕo, 2.

Phaethon, *sub.*	Phăĕthōn -ontĭs, 3 m.
Philippus, *sub.*	Phĭlippus, 2 m.
Philonicus, *sub.*	Phĭlŏnīcus, 2 m.
philosopher, *sub.*	phĭlŏsŏphus, 2 m.; săpĭens -tis, 3 m.
philosophy, *sub.*	phĭlŏsŏphĭa, 1 f.
Phoebus, *sub.*	Phoebus, 2 m.
Phoenicia, *sub.*	Phoenĭcĭa, 1 f.
Phoenix, *sub.*	Phoenix -īcĭs, 3 m.
physician, *sub.*	mĕdĭcus, 2 m.
pick up (to), *v.*	tollo, irr.
picture, *sub. phr.*	tăbŭla picta.
piety, *sub.*	pĭĕtās -tātĭs, 3 f.
pig, *sub.*	porcus, 2 m.
pigeon, *sub.*	cŏlumba, 1 f.
pillow, *sub.*	pulvīnus, 2 m.
pirate, *sub.*	praedō -ōnĭs, 3 m.
pitcher, *sub.*	urcĕus, 2 m.
pity, *sub.*	mĭsĕrĭcordĭa, 1 f.
pity (to), *v.*	mĭsĕrĕt, imper.; mĭsĕrĕŏr, 2; mĭsĕror, 1.
place, *sub.*	lŏcus, 2 m.
place (to), *v.*	pōno, 3.
place at (to), *v.*	appōno, 3.
plague, *sub.*	pestĭs -ĭs, 3 f.
plain, *sub.*	campus, 2 m.
plan, *sub.*	consĭlĭum, 2 n.
plan (to), *v.*	mĕdĭtor, 1 dep.
Plato, *sub.*	Plăto -ōnis, 3 m.
play, *sub.*	lūdus, 2 m.
play (to), *v.*	lūdo, 3.
play (to) a part,	ăgo, 3.
play (to) a lyre,	căno, 3.
pleasant, *adj.*	jūcundus, grātus.
please (to), *v.*	plăcĕo, 2.
pleasure, *sub.*	vŏluptās -ātĭs, 3 f.
pledge, *sub.*	pignŭs -ŏrĭs, 3 n.
plentiful (to be), *v.*	ăbundo, 1.
plot (to), *v.*	mōlĭŏr, 4 dep.
plough, *sub.*	ărātrum, 2 n.
plough (to), *v.*	ăro, 1.
pluck (to), *v.*	carpo, 3.
plunder, *sub.*	praeda, 1 f.
plunder (to), *v.*	dīrĭpĭo, 3.
plunge (to), *v. Phr.*	mē immitto.
poem, *sub.*	carmĕn -ĭnĭs, 3 n.; pŏēma -ătĭs, 3 n.
poet, *sub.*	pŏēta, 1 m.; vātēs -ĭs, 3 m.

point out (to), v.	indĭco, 1.
poison, sub.	vĕnēnum, 2 n.
polished, adj.	nĭtĭdus.
politics, sub.	respūblĭca, 5 & 1.
pomp, sub.	appărātŭs -ūs, 4 m.
Pompey, sub.	Pompēĭus, 2 m.
pool, sub.	stagnum, 2 n.
poor, sub. or adj.	paupĕr -ĕrĭs, 3.
poplar, sub.	pōpŭlus, 2 f.
portend (to), v.	portendo, 3.
portion, sub.	pars -tĭs, 3 f.
Porus, sub.	Pŏrus, 2 m.
possess (to), v.	hăbĕo, 2.
possessions, sub.	bŏna, 2 pl. n.
possession (to get), v.	pŏtior, 4 dep.
post (to), v.	pōno, 3; collŏco, 1; lŏco, 1.
posterity, sub.	nĕpōtes, 3 pl. m.
Potidæa, sub.	Pŏtĭdaca, 1 f.
potion, sub.	pōtĭo -ōnĭs, 3 f.
pound, sub.	lībra, 1 f.; ās, ās-sĭs, 3 m.
pour (to), v.	fundo, 3.
power, sub.	pŏtestas -ātĭs, 3 f.
powerful, adj.	pŏtens.
praise, sub.	laus, laudĭs, 3 f.
praise (to), v.	laudo, 1.
pray (to), v.	ōro, 1; prĕcor, 1 dep.
prayers, sub.	prĕces, 3 pl. f.
precept, sub.	praeceptum, 2 n.
preceptor, sub.	praeceptŏr -ōrĭs, 3 m.
precious, adj.	prĕtĭōsus.
predict (to), v.	praedīco, 3.
prefect, sub.	praefectus, 2 m.
prefer (to), v.	antĕpōno, 3; mālo irr.
preferable, adj.	pŏtĭor.
prepare (to), v.	păro, 1.
present (to be), v.	adsum, irr.; intersum, irr.
present (to make a), v.	dōno, 1.
preserve (to), v.	servo, 1.
preside over, v.	praesum, irr.
pretend (to), v.	sĭmŭlo, 1.
prevail (to), v.	vinco, 3.
prevent (to), v.	impĕdĭo, 4; prŏhĭbĕo, 2.
prey, sub.	praeda, 1 f.
Priam, sub.	Prĭămus, 2 m.
price, sub.	prĕtĭum, 2 n.
priest, sub.	săcerdōs -ōtĭs, 3 m.
priestess, sub.	săcerdōs -ōtĭs, 3 f.
prince, sub.	jŭvĕnĭs -ĭs, 3 m.
prison, sub.	carcĕr -ĕrĭs, 3 m.
prisoner, sub.	captīvus, 2 m.
prize, sub.	praemĭum, 2 n.
procession, sub.	pompa, 1 f.
procure (to), v.	compăro, 1.
produce (to), v.	părĭo, 3.
profit (to), v.	prōsum, irr.
promise, v.	prōmitto, 3; pollĭcĕor, 2 dep.
promise, sub.	prōmissum, 2 n.
prophet, sub.	vātēs -ĭs, 3 m.
prophetic, adj.	fātĭdĭcus.
propitiate (to), v.	plāco, 1.
proposal, sub.	consĭlĭum, 2 n.
protect (to), v. Phr.	praesĭdĭo esse.
protect (to), v.	tŭĕŏr, 2 dep.
prove (to), v.	prŏbo, 1.
proverb, sub.	prōverbĭum, 2 n.
province, sub.	prōvincia, 1 f.; rĕgĭo -ōnis, 3 f.
provoke (to), v.	lăcesso, 3.
prudence, sub.	prūdentĭa, 1 f.
prudent, adj.	prūdens.
puff out (to), v.	sufflo, 1.
pumpkin, sub.	cŭcurbĭta, 1 f.
punish (to), v.	pūnĭo, 4.
punishment, sub.	poena, 1 f.
purpose, sub.	consĭlium, 2.
pursue (to), v.	sĕquor, 3 dep.
put away (to), v.	pōno, 3.
put into (to), v.	immitto, 3; dēmitto, 3.
put on (to), v.	indŭo, 3.
put on (a crown) (to), v.	impōno, 3.
put round (to), v.	circumdo, 1.
put to death (to), v.	interfĭcĭo, 3.
put under (to), v.	suppōno, 3.
put up to (of hounds), v.	excĭto, 1.
pyramid, sub.	pȳrămĭs -ĭdĭs, 3 f.

Q.

quake, v.	trĕmo, 3.
quarrel (to), v.	rixor, 1 dep.
quarrel, sub.	rixa, 1 f.; līs, lītĭs, 3 f.
quarry, sub.	lautŭmĭae, 1 pl.

queen, sub.	rēgīna, 1 f.		*rejoice (to), v.*	gaudeo, 2.
quell (to), v.	comprĭmo, 3.		*relate (to), v.*	narro, 1.
quench (to), v.	restinguo, 3.		*relying on, part.*	frētus.
question (it is a),	quaerĭtŭr, impers.		*remain (to), v.*	mănĕo, 2 ; restc, 1.
questioner, sub.	percontātor -ōrĭs, 3 m.		*remarkable, adj.*	ēgrĕgĭus.
questions (to ask)	percontor, 1 dep.		*remedy, sub.*	rĕmĕdĭum, 2 n.
quiet, adv.	prorsŭs, omnīnŏ.		*remember (to), v.*	mĕmĭnī, defect.
			renew (to), v.	rĕdintĕgro, 1.
			renounce (to), v.	rĕnuntĭo, 1.
R.			*renown, sub.*	dĕcŭs -ŏrĭs, 3 n. laus -dĭs, 3 f.
race, sub.	gens -tis, 3 f. ; gĕnŭs -ĕrĭs, 3 n.		*repeat (to), v.*	ĭtĕro, 1.
rage, sub.	fŭrŏr -ōrĭs, 3 m.		*repel (to), v.*	fŭgo, 1.
rain, sub.	plŭvĭa, 1 f.		*repent (to), v.*	paenĭtĕt, impers.
raise (to), v.	lĕvo, 1.		*reply (to), v.*	respondĕo, 2.
ram, sub.	ărĭĕs -ĕtĭs, 3 m.		*repose, sub.*	rĕquiēs -ētis, 3 f.
rampart, sub.	vallum, 2 n.; mū-nīmentum, 2 n.		*republic, sub.*	respūblĭca, 5 & 1.
rank (to), v.	hăbĕo, 2.		*request (to), v.*	rŏgo, 1 ; ōro, 1.
ransom (to), v.	rĕdĭmo, 3.		*reserve (to), v.*	rĕtĭneo, 2 ; rĕ-servo, 1.
rash, adj.	tĕmĕrārĭus.			
rashly, adv.	tĕmĕrĕ.		*resist (to), v.*	rĕsisto, 3 ; obsto, 1.
rashness, sub.	tĕmĕrĭtās -ātĭs, 3 f.		*resolve (to), v.*	constĭtŭo, 3 ; stătŭo, 3.
rat, sub.	mūs, mūrĭs, 3 m.		*rest, sub.*	quĭēs -ētĭs, 3 f.
rate (to),	objurgo, 1 ; in-crĕpo, 1.		*rest of (rendered by adj.)*	rĕlĭquus.
rather, adv.	pŏtius.		*resting on, adj.*	fultus.
ravage (to), v.	vasto, 1.		*restore (to), v.*	rĕddo, 3.
ray, sub.	rădius, 2 m.		*result, sub.*	ēventŭs -ūs, 4 m.
reach (to), v.	attingo, 3 ; per-vĕnĭo, 4 (with "ad").		*retire (to), v.*	concēdo, 3 ; dis-cēdo, 3 ; rĕcēdo, 3.
read (to), v.	lĕgo, 3 ; perlĕgo 3.		*retreat (to), v.*	rĕcēdo, 3.
ready, adj.	părātus.		*return (to), v.*	rĕdĕo, irr. ; rĕ-vertor, 3 dep.
really, adv.	rēvērā.		*returning, part.*	rĕdĭens.
reason, sub.	causa, 1 f.		*revelry, sub.*	convīvĭa, 2 pl. n.
rebuild (to), v.	rĕfĭcĭo, 3.		*revenge, sub.*	ultĭŏ -ōnĭs, 3 f.
receive (to), v.	excĭpĭo, 3.		*revive (to), v.*	rĕfĭcĭo, 3.
recognize (to), v.	cognosco, 3.		*revive, Phr.*	vīrēs ălĭcui rĕ-fĭcio, 3.
reconcile (to), v. Phr.	in grātĭam rĕ-dūco, 3.		*revolt (to), v.*	dēfĭcio, 3.
reconnoitre (to), v.	explōro, 1.		*reward, sub.*	praemĭum, 2 n.; mūnŭs -ĕrĭs, 3 n.
record (to), v.	narro, 1.			
recover (to), v.	rĕcĭpĭo, 3.			
red, adj.	rŭbĕr.			
reflect to (of light)	reddo, 3.		*Rhone, sub.*	Rhŏdănus, 2 m.
refresh (to), v.	rĕcrĕo, 1.		*rich, adj.*	dīvĕs.
refuse (to), v.	nōlo, irr.; nĕgo, 1.		*ridicule (to). v.*	irrīdĕo, 2.
regret (to), v.	dēsīdĕro, 1.		*right, sub.*	fās, indecl. n.
Regulus, sub.	Rēgŭlus, 2 m.		*rightly, adv.*	jūrĕ.
reign (to), v.	regno, 1.		*ring, sub.*	annŭlus, 2 m.
reject (to), v.	imprŏbo, 1.		*ring (to), v.*	sŏno, 1.

ripen (to), v. act.	cŏquo, 3.
ripen (to), v. neu.	mātūresco, 3.
rise (to), v.	surgo, 3.
rise to (of the sun), v.	ŏrĭor, 3 dep.
rise to (of the tide), v.	accēdo, 3.
rise (of the sun), sub. *rising,*	} ortŭs -ūs, 4 m.
rising, part.	ŏrĭens.
rival, sub.	aemŭlus, 2 m.
river, sub.	amnĭs -ĭs, 3 m.; flūmĕn -ĭnĭs, 3 n.
road, sub.	vĭa, 1 f.
roam (to), v.	văgor, 1 dep.
roar (to), v.	rŭdo, 3.
rob (to), v.	prīvo, 1.
robber, sub.	lătro -ōnis, 3 m.
robe, sub.	tŏga, 1 f.
rock, sub.	saxum, 2 n.; rū-pēs -ĭs, 3 f.
roll (to), v.	volvo, 3.
roll down (to), v.	dēvolvo, 3.
Roman, adj.	Rōmānus, (pl. Rōmāni may be used as a sub.)
Rome, sub.	Rōmă, 1 f.
Romulus, sub.	Rōmŭlus, 2 m.
rout (to), v.	fŭgo, 1.
rove (to), v.	văgor, 1 dep.
royal, adj.	rēgĭus.
Rubicon, sub.	Rŭbĭcō -ōnĭs, 3 m.
ruin (to), v.	perdo, 3.
rule (to), v.	impĕro, 1; rĕgo, 3
rumour, sub.	rūmŏr -ōrĭs, 3 m.
run (to), v.	curro, 3.
run to (of water)	flŭo, 3.
run away (to),	fŭgĭo, 3.
run short (to),	dēfĭcĭo, 3.
rush (to), v.	rŭo, 3.
rush upon (to), v.	irrŭo, 3.
rustling, sub.	sŏnĭtŭs -ūs, 4 m.

S.

sack (to), v.	expugno, 1.
sacred, adj.	săcĕr.
sacrifice, sub.	caedēs -ĭs, 3 f.
sacrifice (to), v.	macto, 1.
safe, adj.	incŏlŭmĭs; tūtus.
safety, sub.	sălūs -ūtĭs, 3 f.
Saguntum, sub.	Săguntum, 2 n.

sail, sub.	vēlum, 2 n.
sail (to), v.	nāvĭgo, 1.
sailor, sub.	nauta, 1 m.
Salamis, sub.	Sălămĭs -īnĭs, 3 f.
sally forth (to), v.	ēgrĕdĭor, 3 dep.
salute (to), v.	sălūto, 1.
same, pron.	īdem.
sand, sub.	ărēna, 1 f.
sane, adj.	sānus.
Sarpedon, sub.	Sarpēdōn -ŏnĭs, 3 m.
satyr, sub.	Sătўrus, 2 m.
sausage, sub.	hilla, 1 f.
save (to), v.	servo, 1.
say (to), v.	dīco, 3.
say not (to), v.	nĕgo, 1.
scale (to), v.	scando, 3.
Scamander, sub.	Scămandĕr -dri, 2 m.
scarce, adj.	rārus.
scarcity, sub.	paucĭtas -ātĭs, 3 f.; ĭnŏpĭa, 1 f.
schoolmaster, sub. Phr.	lūdī măgistĕr, 2.
scold (to), v.	objurgo, 1.
scourge (to), v.	verbĕro, 1.
scout, sub.	spĕcŭlātŏr -ōrĭs, 3 m.
scream (to), v.	strīdĕo, 2.
Scylla, sub.	Scylla, 1 f.
sea, sub.	mărĕ -ĭs, 3 n.; pĕlăgŭs, 2 n.
season, sub.	tēmpŭs -ŏrĭs, 3 n.
second (a second time),	ĭtĕrum.
sedition, sub.	sēdĭtĭō -ōnĭs, 3 f.
see (to), v.	vĭdĕo, 2.
seek (to), v.	pĕto, 3; quaero, 3.
seem (to), v.	vĭdĕor, 2.
seer, sub.	vātēs -ĭs, 3 m.
seize (to), v.	arrĭpĭo, 3.
sell (to), v.	vendo, 3.
senate, sub.	sĕnātŭs -ūs, 4 m.
senate-house, sub.	cūrĭa, 1 f.
senator, sub.	sĕnātŏr -ōrĭs, 3 m.
send (to), v.	mitto, 3.
send away (to), v.	dīmitto, 3.
send for (to), v.	arcesso, 3.
send forth (to), v.	ēmitto, 3.
send upon (to), v.	immitto, 3.
sense, sub.	sensŭs -ūs, 4 m.
senseless, adj. phr.	sensū cărens.
serious, adj.	grăvis.
Sertorius, sub.	Sertōrĭus, 2 m.

servant, sub.	puer, pŭĕrī, 2 m.; fămŭlus, 2 m.
serve (a campaign, to), v.	mĕrĕo, 2.
serve (to be of service to), v.	prōsum, irr.
sesterce, sub.	sestertĭus, 2 m.
set (of the sun, to), v.	cădo, 3.
set in order (to), v.	constĭtŭo, 3.
set on fire (to), v.	incendo, 3.
set out (to), v.	prŏfĭciscŏr, 3 dep.
set up (to), v.	ērĭgo, 3.
settle (to), v.	collŏco, 1.
seven, num. indec.	septem.
seventy, num. indec.	septŭāgintā.
several times, adv.	ălĭquŏtĭēs.
severely, adv.	grăvĭtĕr.
shadow, sub.	umbra, 1 f.
shame, sub.	pŭdŏr -ōrĭs, 3 m.
share, sub.	vōmĕr -ĕrĭs, 3 m.
share (to), v. phr.	partĭceps sum.
sharp, adj.	ăcūtus.
sharpen (to), v.	ăcŭo, 3.
sheep, sub.	ŏvĭs -ĭs, 3 f.
shell, sub.	concha, 1 f.
shew (to), v.	monstro, 1; ostendo, 3; prōdo, 3.
shew (to prove), v.	praesto, 1.
shield, sub.	scūtum, 2 n.
shine (to), v.	fulgĕo, 2.
ship, sub.	nāvĭs -ĭs, 3 f.
shoot (to), v.	ēmitto, 3.
short, adj.	brĕvĭs.
shout (to), v.	clāmo, 1.
shrewdness, sub.	astūtĭa, 1 f.
shut up (to), v.	claudo, 3; inclūdo, 3.
Sicilian, adj.	Sĭcŭlus.
side, sub.	lătŭs -ĕrĭs, 3 n.
siege, sub.	obsĭdio -ōnĭs, 3 f.
siege (to lay to), v.	obsĭdeo, 2.
sign, sub.	signum, 2 n.; indĭcĭum, 2 n.
silence, sub.	sĭlentium, 2 n.
silent, adj.	tăcĭtus.
silent (to be), v.	tăcĕo, 2.
silly, adj.	insulsus.
silver, sub.	argentum, 2 n.
silver, adj.	argentĕus.
sing (to), v.	căno, 3.
singular, adj.	ēgrĕgĭus.
sink (to), v.	sīdo, 3.
sip (to), v.	lībo, 1.
sister, sub.	sŏrōr -ōrĭs, 3 f.
Sisyphus, sub.	Sīsўphus, 2 m.
sit (to), v.	sĕdĕo, 2.
sit at meat (to), v.	accumbo, 3.
sit down (to), v.	consĭdĕo, 3.
skilful, adj.	pĕrītus.
skill, sub.	callĭdĭtās -ātĭs, 3 f.; ars -tĭs, 3 f.; peritia, 1 f.
slave, sub.	servus, 2 m.; serva, 1 f.
slavery, sub.	servĭtūs -ūtĭs, 3 f.
slay (to), v.	occīdo, 3; interfĭcĭo, 3.
sleep, sub.	somnus, 2 m.
sleep (to), v.	dormĭo, 4.
slight, adj.	lĕvis.
slippery, adj.	lŭbrĭcus.
slow, adj.	tardus.
small, adj.	parvus.
smarting, part.	ardens.
smith, sub.	făbĕr, 2 m.
smoke, sub.	fūmŭs, 2 m.
snail, sub.	cŏchlĕa, 1 f.
snake, sub.	anguĭs -ĭs, 3 m.
snatch up (to), v.	arrĭpĭo, 3.
snow, sub.	nix, nĭvĭs, 3 f.
so, adv.	tam, ădĕō; ĭtăquĕ.
so many,	tŏt.
so much,	tantum.
soap, sub.	sāpō -ōnis, 3 m.
Socrates, sub.	Sōcrătēs -ĭs, 3 m.
soft, adj.	mollis.
soften (to), v.	mollĭo, 4.
soil, sub.	sŏlum, 2 n.
solace, sub.	sōlātĭum, 2 n.
soldier, sub.	mīlĕs -ĭtĭs, 3 m.
Solon, sub.	Sŏlōn -ōnĭs, 3 m.
some, adj.	quīdam.
something, pron.	ălĭquĭd.
son, sub.	fīlius, 2 m.
song, sub.	carmĕn -ĭnĭs, 3 n.
soon, adv.	mox.
soothsayer, sub.	hăruspex -ĭcĭs, 3 m.
sorrow, sub.	luctŭs -ūs, 4 m.; dŏlŏr -ōrĭs, 3 m.
sound, sub.	sonus, 2 m.
sour, adj.	ăcerbus.
source, sub.	fons, fontĭs, 3 m.
south wind, sub.	Nŏtus, 2 m.
sovereign, sub.	dŏmĭnus, 2 m.

spare (to), *v.*	parco, 3.
sparrow, *sub.*	passĕr -erĭs, 3 m.
Sparta, *sub.*	Sparta, 1 f.
speak (to), *v.*	lŏquor, 3 dep.
specially, *adv.*	praecĭpŭē, imprī-mis.
spectator, *sub.*	spectātŏr -ōrĭs, 3 m.
speech, *sub.*	ōrātĭo -ōnĭs, 3 f.
spend time (to), *v.*	ăgo, 3.
spider, *sub.*	ărānĕa, 1 f.
spirits, *sub.*	ănĭmi, 2 pl. m.
spoils, *sub.*	spŏlĭa, 2 pl. n.
sport, *sub.*	lūdus, 2 m.
spouse, *sub.*	sponsa, 1 f.
spread (to), *v.*	pando, 3.
spring (*season*), *sub.*	vēr, vērĭs, 3 n.
spring (*of water*), *sub.*	fons, fontis, 3 m.
spur, *sub.*	calcăr -ārĭs, 3 n.
spy, *sub.*	spĕcŭlātŏr -ōrĭs, 3 m.
stag, *sub.*	cervus, 2 m.
Stagira, *sub.*	Stāgīra, 1 f.
stained, *part.*	adspersus.
stake, *sub.*	pălūs -ūdĭs, 3 f.
stand (to), *v.*	sto, 1.
stand by (to)	adsto, 1.
star, *sub.*	stella, 1 f.
start (to), *v.*	prŏfĭciscor, 3 dep.
state, *sub.*	respublĭca, 5 & 1 f.; cīvĭtās -ātĭs, 3 f.
statue, *sub.*	stătŭa, 1 f.
stay (to), *v.*	rĕmăneo, 2; măneo, 2; mŏrŏr, 1 dep.
steal (to), *v.*	surrĭpio, 3; fūror, 1.
step-mother, *sub.*	nŏverca, 1 f.
stick, *sub.*	virga, 1 f.
stick (to), *v.*	haereo, 2; ĭnhaereo, 2.
still (*nevertheless*)	nĭhĭlōmĭnus.
still (*even*),	ĕtĭam.
stir (to), *v.*	turbo, 1; mŏveo, 2.
stoic, *sub.*	Stōĭcus, 2 m.
stomach, *sub.*	ventĕr -trĭs, 3 m.
stone, *sub.*	lăpĭs -ĭdis, 3 m.; saxum, 2 n.
stone, *adj.*	saxĕus, lăpĭdĕus.
stoop (to), *v. Phr.*	mē dēmitto, 3.
stop (to), *v. n.*	măneo, 2.
stop (to), *v. act.*	impĕdio, 4 ; prŏhĭbeo, 2.
stop (to cease), *v.*	dēsĭno, 3.
store (to), *v.*	condo, 3.
storm, *sub.*	prŏcella, 1 f.
story, *sub.*	fābella, 1 f.
strange, *adj.*	mīrus.
straw, *sub.*	strāmĕn -ĭnĭs, 3 n.
straw, *adj.*	strāmĭnĕus.
strawberry, *sub.*	frāgum, 2 n.
stream, *sub.*	flŭvĭus, 2 m.; undă, 1 f.
street, *sub.*	vīcus, 2 m.
strength, *sub.*	vīrēs -ĭum, 3 pl. f.; rōbŭr -ŏrĭs, 3 n.
stretch out (to), *v.*	porrĭgo, 3.
strife, *sub.*	līs, lītĭs, 3 f.
strike (to), *v.*	fĕrĭo, 4.
strike a camp (to)	mŏveo, 2.
strike down (to)	dējĭcio, 3.
strip (to), *v.*	exuo, 3.
strive (to), *v.*	ēnītor, 3 dep.
strong, *adj.*	rōbūstus, fortis.
struggle (to), *v.*	cōnŏr, 1.
study (to), *v.*	stŭdĕo, 2.
stupid, *adj.*	stŏlĭdus.
subdue (to), *v.*	sŭbĭgo, 3.
subject, *sub.*	cīvĭs -ĭs, 3 m.
subjugate (to), *v.*	sŭbĭgo, 3.
submit (to), *v.*	pāreo, 2.
suburb, *sub.*	sŭburbĭum, 2 n.
succeed (to), *v.*	vinco, 3.
succour (to), *v.*	succurro, 3.
such, *adj.*	tālĭs ; ējusmŏdi.
sudden, *adj.*	sŭbĭtus.
suddenly, *adv.*	sŭbĭtō.
suffer (to), *v.*	pătior, 3 dep.
suitor, *sub.*	prŏcus, 2 m.
summer, *adj.*	aestīvus.
summer, *sub.*	aestās -ātĭs, 3 f.
summon (to), *v.*	arcesso, 3.
sun, *sub.*	sōl, sōlĭs, 3 m.
sunny, *adj.*	ăprīcus.
sunrise, *sub. Phr.*	sōlĭs ŏrtŭs -ūs, 4 m.
sunshine, *sub.*	sōl, sōlĭs, 3 m.
sup off (to), *v.*	cēno, 1.
superior, *adj.*	sŭpĕrĭor.
supper, *sub.*	cēna, 1 f.
supply (to), *v.*	praebeo, 2.
support, *sub.*	sustĭnĕo, 2.
suppose (to), *v.*	pŭto, 1 ; rĕor, 2.
surpass (to), *v.*	sŭpĕro, 1.

surpassing, adj. exĭmius.
surprised (to be), admīror, 1 dep.
v.
surrender (to), v. dēdo 3 ; (oneself),
phr., mē dēdo.
surround (to), v. cingo, 3.
Susa, sub. Sūsă, 2 pl. n.
suspicion, sub. suspīcĭo -ōnĭs, 3 f.
swallow, sub. hĭrundō -ĭnĭs, 3 f.
swallow (to), v. sorbeo, 2.
swan, sub. cȳgnus, 2 m.
swear (to), v. jūro, 1.
sweet, adj. dulcis.
swiftness, sub. cĕlĕrĭtās -tātĭs,
3 f.
swim (to), v. năto, 1.
Swiss, sub. Helvētĭi, 2 pl. m.
sword, sub. glădĭus, 2 m. ;
ensĭs -ĭs, 3 m.
Syracuse, sub. Sȳrācūsae -ārum,
1 pl. f.
Syria, sub. Sȳrĭa, 1 f.

T.

table, sub. mensa, 1 f.
tablets, sub. tăbellae, 1 pl. f.
tail, sub. cauda, 1 f.
tailor, sub. sartŏr -ōris, 3 m.
take (to), v. căpĭo, 3 ; sūmo, 3 ;
accĭpĭo, 3.
take (advice) (to), sĕquor, 3 dep.
v.
take away (to), v. aufĕro, irr. ; ădĭ-
mo, 3.
take care (to), v. cūro, 1 ; căveo, 2.
take off (to), v. exuo, 3.
take prisoner (to), căpio, 3.
v.
take by storm expugno, 1.
(to), v.
take up (arms) tollo, irr. ; sūmo,
(to), v. 3.
take up (to), v. suscĭpio, 3.
talent, sub. tălentum, 2 n.
talk together (to), collŏquor, 3 dep.
v.
teach (to), v. dŏceo, 2.
tear (to), v. lăcĕro, 1.
Telemachus, sub. Tēlĕmăchus, 2 m.
tell = say (to), v. dīco, 3.
tell = relate (to), narro, 1.
v.

tell = order (to), jŭbeo, 2.
v.
tell lies (to), v. mentior, 4.
temple, sub. aedes -is, 3 f. ;
templum, 2 n.
ten, num. indec. dĕcem.
tender, adj. tĕnĕr.
tent, sub. tentōrĭum, 2 n.
tenth, dĕcĭmus.
terrible, adj. dīrŭs ; grăvĭs.
territory, sub. rĕgĭo -ōnĭs, 3 f.
Teucer, sub. Teucĕr -crī, 2 m.
Thebes, sub. Thēbae, 1 pl. f.
Theban, sub. Thēbānus.
theft, sub. furtum, 2 n.
Themistocles, sub. Thĕmistōclēs -ĭs,
3 m.
then, adv. tum.
Thermopylae, Thermŏpȳlae, 1 f.
sub. pl.
thereupon, indĕ.
Thessalian, adj. Thessălus.
Thetis, sub. Thĕtĭs, ĭdŏs, 3 f.
thief, sub. fūr, fūrĭs, 3 m.
thin, adj. măcĕr, măcra,
măcrum.
thing, sub. rēs -rĕī, 5 f.
think (to), v. pŭto, 1 ; rĕor, 2
dep.
third (a third tertĭum.
time),
thirteen, num. trēdĕcim.
indec.
thirst, sub. sĭtĭs -ĭs, 3 f.
thirty, num. trīgintă.
indec.
thorny, adj. spīnōsus.
though. quamvīs, quam-
quam.
thousand, num. millĕ. (See List
of English Con-
junctions.)
thoroughly, adv. pĕnĭtŭs.
Thracian, sub. Thrācĭŭs.
threaten (to), v. mĭnŏr, 1.
three, num. trēs.
throat, sub. fauces, 3 pl. f. ;
guttŭr -ŭrĭs,
3 n.
throw (to), v. jăcĭo, 3 ; prōjĭcio,
3.
throw away (to), abjĭcio, 3.
v.
thunderbolt, sub. fulmĕn -ĭnĭs, 3 n.

thy (poss. pro.).	tŭus.
Tiber, sub.	Tĭbĕrĭs -ĭs, 3 m.
tide, sub.	aestŭs -ūs, 4 m.
tie (to), v.	allĭgo, 1.
tie together (to),	collĭgo, 1.
v.	
time, sub.	tempŭs -ŏrĭs, 3 n.
timid, adj.	tĭmĭdus.
tire (to), v.	lasso, 1.
tired, adj.	fessus.
tired (to be), v.	taedĕt, impers.
Tiresias, sub.	Tīrĕsĭās, 1 m.
to-day, adv.	hŏdĭē.
together, adv.	ūnā, sĭmŭl.
toil (to), v.	lăbōro, 1.
toil, sub.	lăbŏr -ōrĭs, 3 m.
tomb, sub.	sĕpulcrum, 2 n.
to-morrow, adv.	crās.
tongue, sub.	lingua, 1 f.
too much, adv.	nĭmĭs.
tooth, sub.	dens, dentis, 3 m.
top, sub. (render-	summus.
ed by adj.)	
torture (to), sub.	crŭcĭo, 1.
totally, adv.	pĕnĭtŭs.
town, sub.	urbs -bis, 3 f. ; op-pĭdum, 2 n.
train (to), v.	ēdŭco, 1.
traitor, sub.	prōdĭtŏr -ōrĭs, 3 m.
travel (to)	pĕrĕgrīnor, 1 dep.
abroad, v.	
traveller, sub.	vĭātŏr -ōrĭs, 3 m.
treachery, sub.	fraus -dis, 3 f. ; perfĭdĭa, 1 f.
treat (to), v.	tracto, 1 ; ūtor, 3 dep.
treasure, sub.	thēsaurus, 2 m.; gāza, 1 f.
tree, sub.	arbŏr -ŏrĭs, 3 f.
tremble (to), v.	trĕmō, 3.
trial, sub.	jūdĭcĭum, 2 n.
tribe, sub.	gens -tis, 3 f.
tribune, sub.	trĭbūnus, 2 m.
trick, sub.	dŏlŭs, 2 m.
trident, sub.	trĭdens -tis, 3 m.
tried, adj.	spectātus.
triumph, sub.	trĭumphus, 2 m.
triumphantly,	ŏvans.
adj.	
Trojan, adj.	Trōjānus, m.
troops, sub.	mīlĭtes, 3 pl. m. ; cōpĭae, 1 pl. f.
trouble (to), v.	vexo, 1.
Troy, sub.	Trōja, 1 f.

truce, sub.	indūtiae, 1 pl. f.
true, adj.	vērus.
trunk, sub.	truncus, 2 m.
trunk of an ele-	mănŭs -ūs, 4 f.
phant.	
trust (to), v.	confīdo, 3.
truth, sub.	vērum, 2 n.
try (to), v.	cōnor, 1 dep.; nītor, 3 dep. ; tento, 1 ; expĕrior, 4 dep.
try for (to), v.	pĕto, 3.
tumult, sub.	tŭmultus -ūs, 4 m.
turn (to), v.	converto, 3.
turn aside (to), v.	āverto, 3.
turn back (to), v.	rĕvertor, 3 dep.
turn round (to),	convertor, 3 dep.
v.	
Tusculum, sub.	Tuscŭlum, 2 n.
twelve, num.	dŭŏdĕcim.
indec.	
twentieth,	vīcēsĭmus.
two, num.	dŭŏ.
two days, sub.	bĭduum, 2 n.
tyrant, sub.	tўrannus, 2 m.
Tyre, sub.	Tўrus, 2 f.
Tyrian, adj.	Tўrĭus.

U.

ugly, adj.	informĭs.
Ulysses, sub.	Ŭlysses -is, 3 m.
unable (to be), v.	nōn possum, irr.
unbroken, adj.	indŏmĭtus.
uncertain, adj.	incertus.
undertake (to), v.	suscĭpio, 3.
understand (to),	intellĭgo, 3.
v.	
ungrateful, adj.	ingrātus.
unheard of	ĭnaudītus.
unhappy, adj.	infēlix.
united, adj.	concors.
universe, sub.	mundus, 2 m.
unlucky,	infaustus.
untie (to), v.	solvo, 3.
unusual, adj.	ĭnūsĭtātus.
unweave (to), v.	rĕtexo, 3.
unwilling, adj.	invītus.
unwillingly, adv.	invītē.
unworthy, adj.	indignus.
up, adv.	sursum.
upbraid (to), v.	incrĕpo, 1 ; culpo, 1.

urge (to), v.	urgeo, 2; stĭmŭlo, 1.
use, sub.	ūsŭs -ūs, 4 m.
use (to), v.	ūtor, 3 dep. ; ădhĭbeo, 2.
used (i.e. was accustomed), v.	sŏleo.
useful (to be), v.	prōsum, irr.
useful, adj.	ūtĭlĭs.
useless, adv.	ĭnūtĭlĭs.
utmost, adj.	summus.
utterly, adv.	pĕnĭtŭs.

V.

vain (in), v.	frustrā.
vainly, adv.	frustrā.
valiant, adj.	fortis.
valley, sub.	vallĭs -ĭs, 3 f.
valour, sub.	virtūs -ūtĭs, 3 f.
value (to), v.	făcĭo, 3.
vanish (to), v.	vānesco, 3.
vapour, sub.	nĕbŭla, 1 f.
vast, adj.	ingens.
vengeance, sub.	poena, 1 f.
vengeance (to take), v.	ulciscor, 3 dep.
Venus, sub.	Vĕnŭs -ĕrĭs, 3 f.
very, adv.	admŏdum.
vessel, sub.	nāvĭs -ĭs, 3 f.
veteran, sub.	vĕtĕrānus, 2 m.
victor, sub.	victŏr -ōris, 3 m.
victorious, adj.	victŏr.
victory, sub.	victōrĭa, 1 f.
village, sub.	vīcus, 2 m.
vine, sub.	vītĭs -ĭs, 3 f.
vinegar, sub.	ăcētum, 2 n.
violence, sub.	vīs, 3 f.
violet, sub.	vĭŏla, 1 f.
viper, sub.	vīpĕra, 1 f.
virtue, sub.	vīrtūs -ūtĭs, 3 f.
visit (to), sub.	vīso, 3 ; invīso, 3.
visitor, sub.	hospĕs -ĭtĭs, 3 m.
voice, sub.	vox, vōcĭs, 3 f.
vow, sub.	vōtum, 2 n.
vow (to), v.	pōllĭcĕor, 2 dep.
vulture, sub.	vūltŭr -ŭrĭs, 3 m.

W.

wage (war) (to) v.	gĕro, 3.
wage (war against) (to), v.	infĕro, irr.
wait (to), v.	mŏrŏr, 1 dep.
wait for (to), v.	expecto, 1.
wake (to), v.	expergiscor, 3 dep.
wakeful (to be) v.	vĭgĭlo, 1.
wakeful, adj.	vĭgĭl.
walk (to) v.	ambŭlo, 1.
wall, sub.	mūrus, 2 m. ; moenĭa, 3 pl. n.
wane (to) v.	dēcresco, 3.
want (to), v.	indĭgĕo, 2.
wanting (to be), v.	dēsum, irr.
war, sub.	bellum, 2 n.
warm, adj.	călĭdus.
warm (to) v.	călĕfăcĭo.
warmth, sub.	călŏr -ōrĭs, 3 m.
warn (to), v.	mŏnĕo, 2 m.
warrior, sub.	mīlĕs -ĭtĭs, 3 ; bellātŏr -ōrĭs, 3 m.; bellatrix -trīcĭs 3 f.
wary, adj.	cautus.
wasp, sub.	vespa, 1 f.
waste (to), v.	perdo, 3.
watch (to) v.	vĭgĭlo, 1.
watch (to) v.	specto, 1.
watchful.	vĭgĭl.
water, sub.	ăqua, 1 f.
water (fetch to), v.	ăquŏr, 1 dep.
wave, sub.	fluctus -ūs, 4 m.
wax, sub.	cēra, 1 f.
way, sub.	vĭa, 1 f.
weak, adj.	infirmus ; imbēcillus.
wealth, sub.	ŏpēs -um, 3 pl. f.; dīvĭtĭae, 1 pl. f.
weapon, sub.	tēlum, 2 n.
wear out (to), v.	confĭcĭo, 3.
weariness, sub.	lassĭtūdō -ĭnĭs, 3 f.
weather, sub.	tempestās -ātĭs, 3 f.
weave (to), v.	texo, 3.
web, sub.	tēla, 1 f.
weep (to) v.	flĕo, 2.
weight, sub.	pondŭs -ĕrĭs, 3 n.
well (to be),	văleo, 2 ; convălesco, 3.
well, adv.	bĕnĕ.
well, sub.	pŭtĕus, 2 m.
west, sub.	occĭdens -entĭs, 3 m.
what,	quĭs.
wheel, sub.	rŏta, 1 f.

when, pron.	quandō (interrogative); quum (relative).
whence.	undĕ.
whenever, adv.	quŏtĭes.
whetstone, sub.	cōs, cōtĭs, 3 f.
while (for a long),	dĭū.
whirlpool, sub.	gūrgĕs -ĭtĭs, 3 m.
whistle (to), v.	sībĭlo, 1.
white, adj.	candĭdus.
who, pro.	quĭs.
whole, adj.	tōtus; ūnĭversus; omnĭs.
why,	cūr.
wicked, adj.	nēquam, indec.
wide, adj.	lātus.
wife, sub.	uxŏr -ōrĭs, 3 f.
wild, adj.	fĕrŭs.
wild boar, sub.	ăpĕr, ăprī, 2 m.
wild beast, sub.	fĕra, 1 f.
wild goat, sub.	cāprĕŏlus, 2 m.
will, sub.	vŏluntās -ātĭs, 3 f. arbĭtrĭum, 2 n.
will, sub.	testāmentum, 2 n.
willingly, adv.	lĭbentĕr.
win (to), v. act.	rĕporto, 1.
win (to), v. neut.	vinco, 3.
wind, sub.	ventus, 2 m.
window, sub.	fĕnestra, 1 f.
wine, sub.	vīnum, 2 n.
wing, sub.	penna, 1 f.; āla, 1 f.
winter, sub.	hĭems -ĭs, 3 f.
wintry, adj.	hībernus.
wisdom, sub.	săpĭentĭa, 1 f.
wise, adj.	săpĭens.
wish (to), v.	vŏlŏ, irr.; cŭpĭo, 3.
wish, sub.	vōtum, 2.
withdraw (to), v. act.	abdūco, 3.
withdraw (to), v. neut.	discēdo, 3, absisto, 3.
withdraw (a curtain), v.	rĕdūco, 3.
wither (to), v.	marcesco, 3.
without (to do), v.	cărĕo, 2.
wolf, sub.	lŭpus, 2 m.
woman, sub.	mŭlĭĕr -ĕris, 3 f.
woman (old), sub.	ănŭs, 4 f.
wonder (to), v.	mīror, 1 dep.
wonderful, adj.	mīrus, ēgrĕgĭus.
wont (to be), v.	sŏlĕo, 2.
wood, sub.	silva, 1 f.
wooden, adj.	lignĕus.
woodcutter, sub.	frondātŏr -ōrĭs, 3 m.
woodman, sub.	lignātŏr -ōris, 3 m.
wool, sub.	lāna, 1 f.
woollen, adj.	lānĕus.
word, sub.	verbum, 2 n.
word = promise, sub.	fĭdēs -ĕī, 5 f.
work, sub.	ŏpŭs -ĕrĭs, 3 n.
work (to), v.	lăbŏro, 1.
world, sub. phr.	terrārum orbĭs, 3 m.
worm, sub.	vermĭs -ĭs, 3 m.
worn out, part.	confectus.
worship (to) v.	cŏlo, 3.
worsted (to be), v.	sŭpĕro, 1.
worthless, adj.	vīlĭs.
worthy, adj.	dignus.
wound (to), v.	vulnĕro, 1.
wounded, adj.	saucĭus.
wrath, sub.	īră, 1 f.
wrath (in), adj.	īrātus.
wrathful, adj.	īrātus.
wreck (to), v.	dēmergo, 3.
wretched, adj.	mĭsĕr.
write (to), v.	scrībo, 3.
wrong, sub.	injūrĭa, 1 f.
wrong (to), v.	laedo, 3.

X.

Xerxes, sub.	Xerxēs -ĭs, 3 m.

Y.

year, sub.	annus, 2 m.
yellow, adj.	flāvus.
yesterday, adv.	hĕrī.
yet, adv.	tămĕn.
yonder, pron. adj.	istĕ.
young, adj.	tĕnĕr.
younger, comp. adv.	jŭnĭŏr.
young man, sub.	ădŏlescens -tĭs, 3 m.
your,	tŭus, istĕ, vestĕr. (See list of English Conjunctions.)
youth, sub.	ădŏlescens -tĭs, 3 m.